The Byzantine Empire

The Middle Ages Ancient History of Europe

Children's Ancient History

BABY PROFESSOR

EDUCATION KIDS

Speedy Publishing LLC

40 E. Main St. #1156

Newark, DE 19711

www.speedypublishing.com

Copyright 2017

The Byzantine Empire, centered on the city in Turkey that was called Constantinople and is now called Istanbul, was one of the longest-lived empires in history.

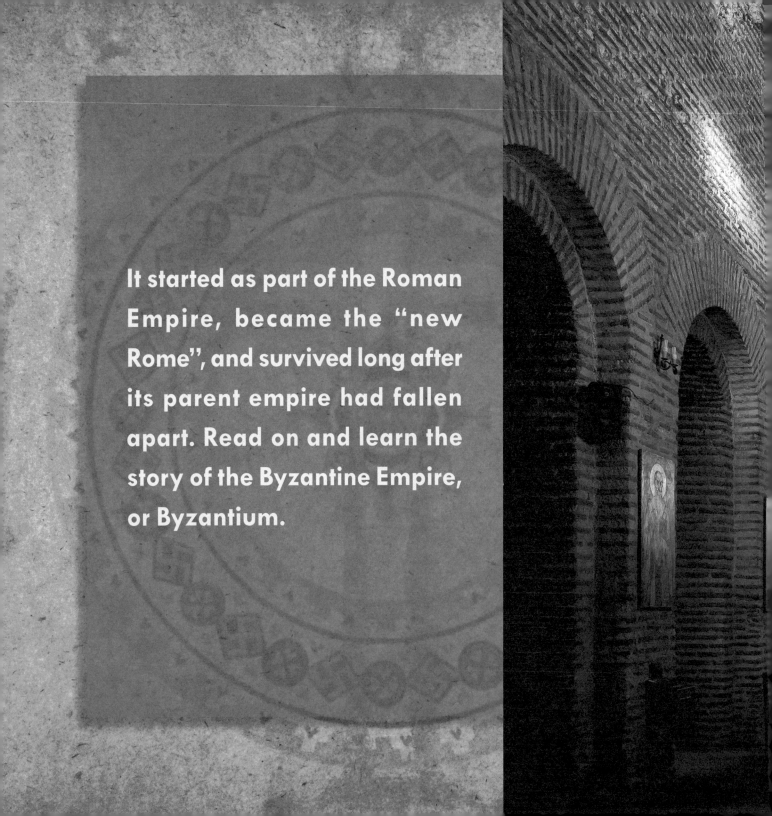

It started as part of the Roman Empire, became the "new Rome", and survived long after its parent empire had fallen apart. Read on and learn the story of the Byzantine Empire, or Byzantium.

BYZANTINE ARCHITECTURE

From Colony to Part of an Empire

The Roman world expanded from a small settlement in Italy to a republic that controlled much of what is now Italy and western Europe. As it continued to expand, it became an Empire and eventually controlled the lands all around the Mediterranean Sea, as far north as Scotland and as far east as Iran.

This expansion was not into empty lands. Rome conquered and absorbed ancient and complex civilizations, including Egypt, Gaul, and the Greek city-states.

ROMAN FORUM

Among the many cities added to the Roman Empire was Byzantium, a Greek colony on the shore of the Bosphorus channel that connects the Mediterranean with the Black Sea. Byzantium was small, but it had a great location both for trade and for defence in time of war. It had been on the border of the Greek and Persian worlds, although both sides of the Bosphorus were now rich parts of the Roman Empire.

TWO ROMAN EMPIRES

In time, the Roman Empire grew too big, and faced challenges from too many directions, for all the decisions to be made in Rome. In 330 C.E. the Emperor Constantine established Byzantium, which he renamed Constantinople after himself, as the eastern capital of the Empire.

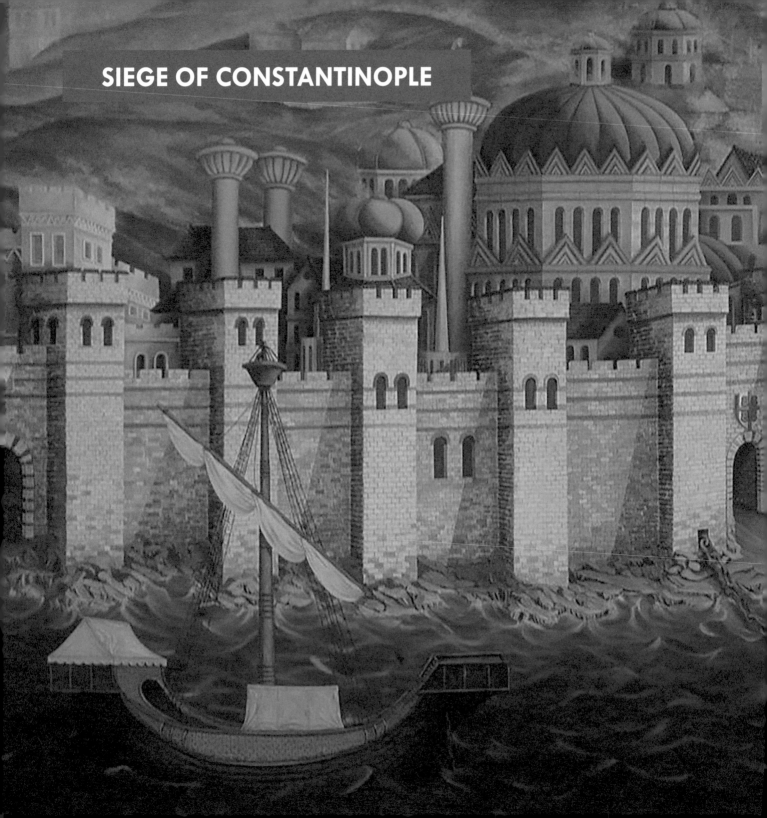

SIEGE OF CONSTANTINOPLE

In 364 Emperor Valentian I formally divided the Empire into eastern and western sections, with his brother Valens as Emperor of the East in Constantinople. The two sections were one when facing external enemies, but began to grow apart as their interests, challenges, and opportunities differed. The western Empire was now mainly on the defensive against waves of attacks by migrating peoples from northern and eastern Europe, while the eastern Empire was becoming the most powerful force in its part of the world.

In 476, Odoacer overthrew the last Roman Emperor and proclaimed himself King of Italy. This was the end of the Roman Empire in the west.

Learn more about the western empire in the Baby Professor book Everything You Need to Know about the Rise and Fall of the Roman Empire.

POWERFUL BYZANTIUM

Byzantium continued and even grew stronger. It had shorter supply lines to its frontiers, a shorter border to defend against the European migrations, and great resources from the riches of western Asia and the Middle East that it organized and deployed well.

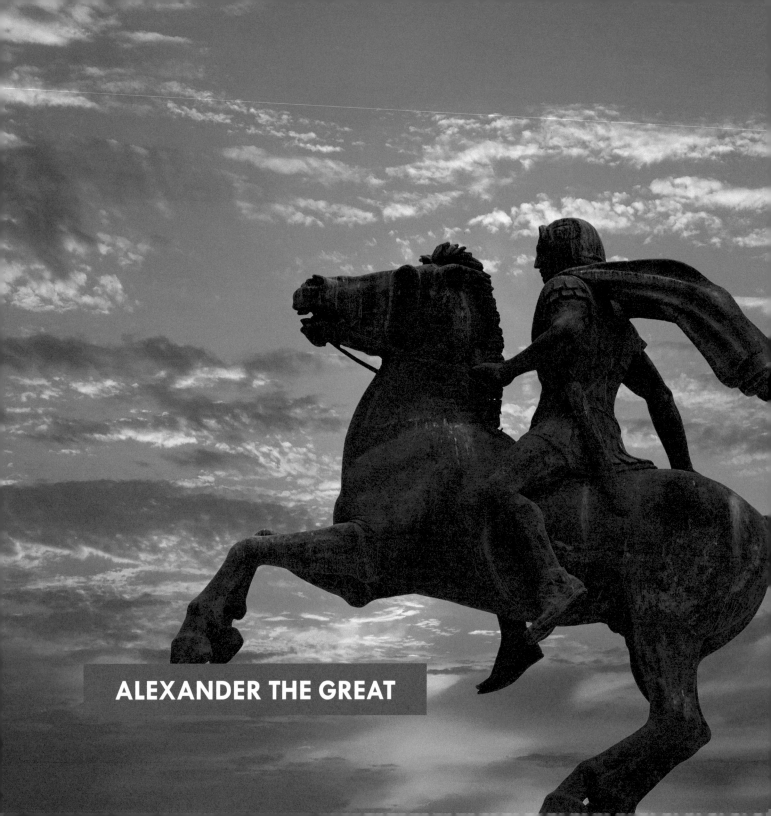

ALEXANDER THE GREAT

Although the Eastern Empire inherited Roman law and political structures, and Latin was its official language in its first centuries, it became more and more a culture of Greek traditions and language. Many of Byzantium's strongest emperors and military leaders came from Macedonia in Greece, and you could say they continued the traditions and success of the Macedonian Alexander the Great.

Justinian I became emperor in 527 and ruled until 565. His armies conquered much of North Africa and other parts of the former western empire. Justinian's court revised Roman law into the Byzantine legal and government system that would last for almost a thousand years and establish the basis of modern government.

JUSTINIAN 1

The Byzantine Empire was at the height of its power. However, it had built up huge debts to pay for its armies and other developments, and taxes rose sharply throughout the Empire. This slowed down the development of business in various regions, and even caused local revolts that the central government had to put down.

Byzantium tried to hold on to more territory than its armies could control and defend—the same problem the Roman Empire had faced. Attacks by Persians in the east and Slavs in the west combined with internal rebellions to strain and shrink the empire.

BYZANTINE ARCHITECTURE BASILICA

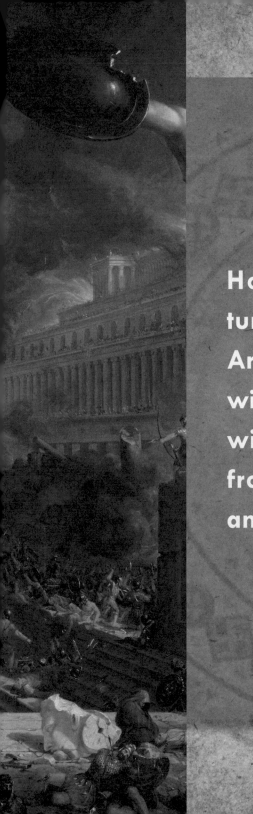

However, the biggest challenge turned out to be the rise of Islam in Arabia. The armies of Islam grappled with the armies of Byzantium across a wide front, gradually winning away from the Empire all of North Africa and much of the Middle East.

CRISIS OF POWER

In the 11th century Byzantium was under attack from both the Muslim armies and forces from the East. The Empire appealed to the western kingdoms for help, and under the Pope the West launched a series of Crusades that, over the next 200 years, tried to take back the "Holy Land" (where Israel, Lebanon, and Jordan now are) from the Muslims.

Some of these efforts succeeded for a while. But far too soon the leaders from the West started quarrelling with Byzantium over who should benefit from territory gained and victories won. In 1204 the Fourth Crusade turned from its plans to fight to gain the Holy Land, and attacked and captured Constantinople. Byzantium eventually recaptured the city, but it was much weakened by fighting with its allies at the same time as continuing to fight the Muslim forces and the Seljuk Turks pushing in from the east.

THE LONG FALL

From the middle of the 13th century, the effect of so many wars, against so many enemies, was cripplng the Byzantine Empire. It basically had no money to continue the services its people needed and also pay for its many armies.

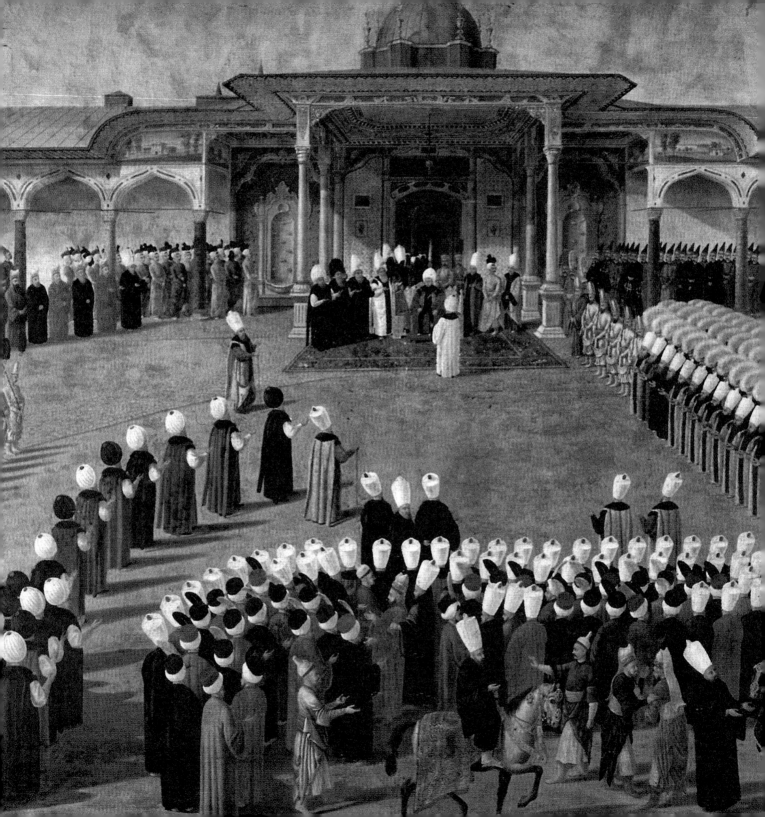

After a long struggle, Byzantium became a client kingdom, paying tribute to the Turkish Ottoman Empire. Periodially in the 14th century the situation got better, but the general trend was downward. Byzantium continued to lose territories and power, and to spend resources it could not afford on battles it could not win. Toward the end, the Byzantine Empire controlled very little territory outside of the city of Constantinople itself.

Finally, in the 1420s, the Ottoman Turks revoked all treaties with Byzantium and set out to destroy the Empire. And even then, it took 40 years before Constantinople finally fell!

LIFE IN BYZANTIUM

People in the west used to have a negative image of the Byzantine Empire. They saw it as corrupt and pleasure-seeking, with its rulers more interested in luxury than in ruling. This is very far from the truth.

For most of its thousand-year life, the Byzantine Empire had political and military leaders who were generally competent and energetic. If they had not been good at their jobs, the Empire would not have lasted a year, much less a thousand!

The central government was a strong patron of the arts, from painting and poetry to magnificant churches, towers, and other structures. Although taxes were high to pay for the constant wars, the government made sure business could function and goods could get from city to city. People in cities had access to education and many career opportunities, and there were many hospitals and doctors. Scholars studied and preserved the wisdom of Greek philosophers and scientists.

Things were tougher in rural areas, of course, and in areas near where armies were fighting. The goal for many was to get to a city for greater options, even if it meant joining the army and spending a career as a soldier.

RELIGOUS IMPACT

The Byzantine Empire was strongly Christian, but its understanding of God and how Christians should live developed in a slightly different way from in the Western Empire. Crises developed over whether it was right to display and pray to images of God and the saints, and over details as small as a single word in the Creed, the statement of what Christians believe. Eventually Christianity developed two major sections: in the West, Christians were part of the Holy Catholic Church under the Pope, the bishop of Rome. In the East, a series of patriarchs guided what became known as the Orthodox Church.

Over the centuries, people have fought and killed each other over this separation, from the Crusaders onward. Now the major parts of Christianity work in better cooperation and more in the spirit of the teachings of Christ.

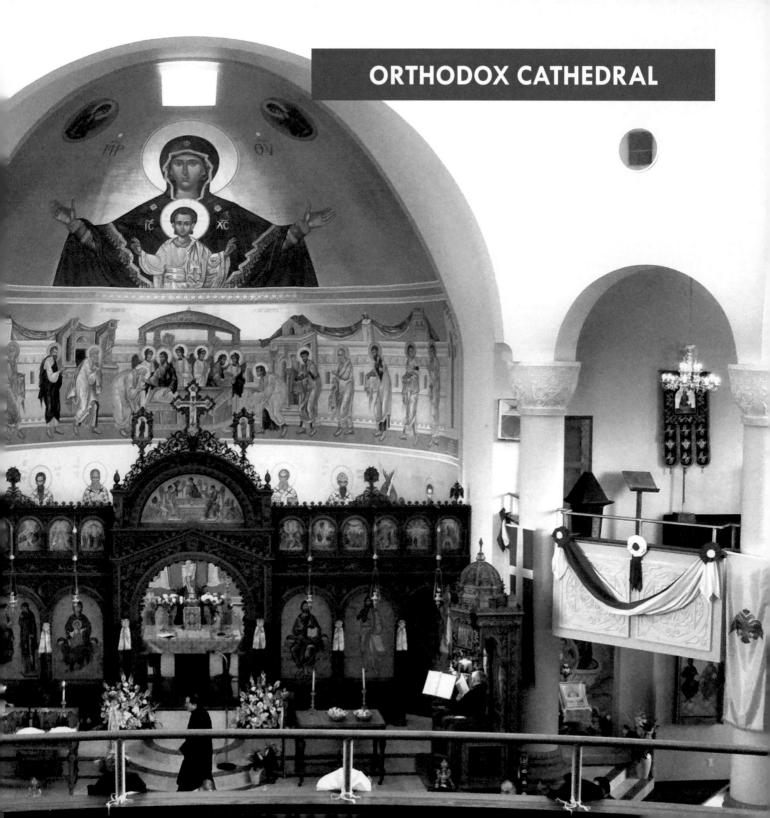

THE LEGACY OF THE EMPIRE

Even as the Byzantine Empire declined politically and as a miliary force, its cultural influence grew and spread. Byzantine scentists and artists influenced work and research both in Europe and in the Middle East. When Constantinople finally fell, many scholars and artists moved to western capitals and worked in European countries. They brought with them manuscripts from classical Greek times, and many writings from the early Christian era, that helped strengthen and speed up Europe's move out of the "dark ages".

The religious influence of the Eastern Orthodox Church continues among Christians in many countries, including Greece, Russia, Romania, Bulgaria, and Serbia.

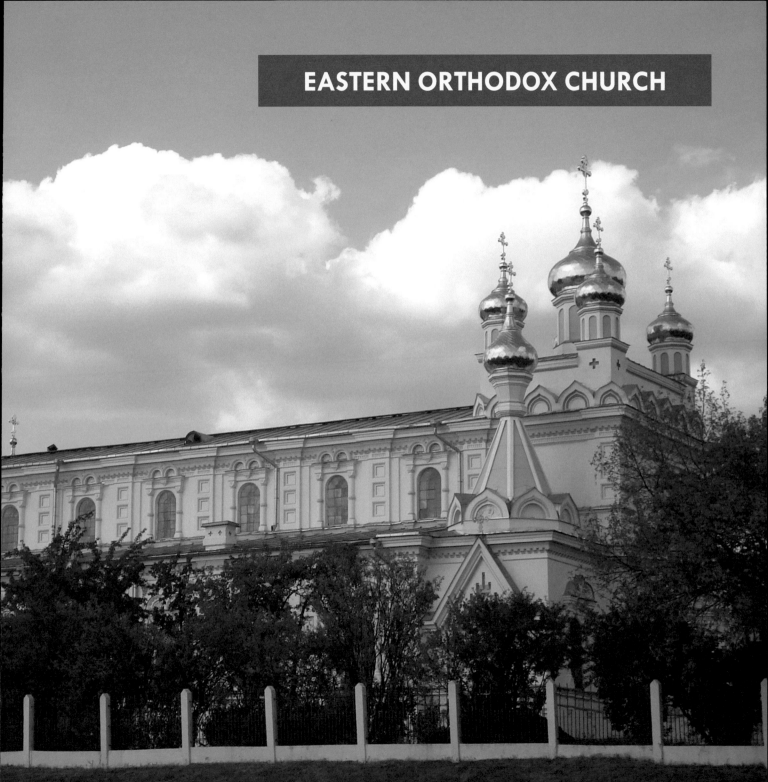

EASTERN ORTHODOX CHURCH

THE PAST SUPPORTS OUR PRESENT

The Byzantine Empire began about 1500 years ago and lasted for a thousand years. Only the Chinese empire had a longer continuous reign. The Byzantine Empire helped to form the world we live in now, both political structures and a sense of what makes effective government.

What other empires and kingdoms influenced how we live today?

Read further in Baby Professor books like Who Were the Barbarians? for some surprising answers.

MACEDONIAN ART (BYZANTINE)

Visit

BABY PROFESSOR
EDUCATION KIDS

www.BabyProfessorBooks.com

to download Free Baby Professor eBooks
and view our catalog of new and exciting
Children's Books

Made in United States
Troutdale, OR
07/12/2023

The only, truest question in love is:

"HAVE YOU YOU EATEN?"
—ELSA MORANTE

ITALOPUNK

145 RECIPES
TO SHOCK YOUR NONNA

VANJA VAN DER LEEDEN

T tra.publishing

CONTENTS

INTRODUCTION

ETRUSCAN PRINCESS An Italian book? But she's partly Indonesian, right? Sure, but before I dove into my mother's cuisine a few years back, I had a whole life in Italy. I always joke that I am the reincarnation of an Etruscan princess; I feel so at home in Italy. My love for this beautiful country came about through my father's love of buildings and travel. Seeing Italy through my dad's eyes as an architect gave me a deeper appreciation for this beautiful country. He showed us the cathedral of the architect Brunelleschi in Florence and explained how extraordinary it was that someone in the early fifteenth century managed to span such a huge diameter in a building. We wandered through the Colosseum and the ruins of Ostia Antica—a kind of Pompeii near Rome.

When I was a bit older, I took Latin in school, and we learned about Roman culture—those ancient buildings really came to life. My Latin teacher was also fluent in Italian, read Italian books, and made his own pasta. I made learning those three things my life goals.

EXPERIENCE AT THE BAR I began studying Italian language and literature when I was at university. After a year, I quit and went to Rome as an au pair. And then I realized that I could also practice those verb conjugations *al bar*. It was time to start living the language: standing in line for fish at the market, swimming with a whining child in a bloody hot pool, climbing the walls of the Roman Forum at night, at parties hosted by the Roman rowing club, or dipping cornetto in cappuccino (sometimes with Roberto, sometimes with Alberto). A few years later, I was living in Florence, where I met my ex, Lorenzo. His parents had one of those ochre yellow country houses with green shutters in the hills of Fiesole with all the trimmings—cypress trees, a swimming pool, an olive grove, and a wine cellar where the Chianti never ran out. Life was one big dinner party. Their Filipino chef, Agostino, played an important role in this, cooking Lorenzo's mother's recipes, but with more flair. Every day, Ago gave us a five-course lunch in their fancy dining room full of antiques.

CULINARY DOGMATISM I enjoyed the theater surrounding Italian food and felt at home among the food fanatics, but I was also disturbed because there was so much culinary dogmatism. The fact that garlic in pasta Amatriciana is sacrilege, for example, and spaghetti with Bolognese was a travesty. Bolognese should only be served with tagliatelle, the exact ribbon width established by the Bologna Chamber of Commerce. I was also tired of traditional dishes—yet another ribollita, another pappardelle with hare. Restaurant menus seemed like state menus. Unappreciative and spoiled? Of course, but if you live somewhere long enough, the rose-colored glasses come off.

When I moved back home, I ended up working in a restaurant kitchen. After years of cooking in a restaurant, I began to look at Italian cuisine from the perspective of the cook I had now become. I felt the need for new combinations. But whenever I tried to order something new and interesting at a modern Italian restaurant, things always went wrong. They mimicked French cuisine with scallops striped with lines of balsamic syrup. Couldn't they just reinvent their trattoria food?

OBSESSION WITH TRADITION Reinventing classic Italian recipes is easier said than done in a country so obsessed with tradition. Where does this obsession come from? Italian food historian Alberto Grandi wondered that, too. He had the audacity to question Italian kitchen traditions in his book *Denominazione di Origine Inventata* (2018). Not because he doesn't appreciate his country's cuisine, but because as a scientist he distinguishes myths from facts. According to the professor, many traditions are actually a matter of marketing. And, Italian emigrants have played a big role in the worldwide success of Italian cuisine. For example, Southern Italian pizza and pasta only became famous after they were introduced from America throughout Italy. Ironic? For sure! Especially because the conservative Italian cook treats the cuisine like a protected species. Don't touch it! While that cuisine actually owes its success to evolution and outside interference.

IDENTITY The fact that tempers run so high when it comes to Italian cuisine is partly due to a need for identity. Italy became a unitary state in 1861. The kitchen was the place to cook up patriotism, which is partly why, the most famous Italian cookbook, published in 1891 by Artusi, became such a success. But there was no Italian cuisine as we know it today back then. Southern Italian pasta recipes could be counted on the fingers of one hand, and tiramisu emerged only a century later. After World War II, the economic boom catapulted the country from an agrarian society straight into the ranks of the ten largest industrialized countries. In the early 1970s, that growth stopped, and in Italy, there was even a decline. Distrust of industrialization rose and Italians sought a foothold in the past with nonna's pasta. From a historical perspective and given their urge for identity, it is understandable that Italians guard their food culture. But tradition also gets in the way: it is both the strength and the weakness of Italian cuisine. On the one hand, it preserves a food culture, but rigidity also leads to stagnation. Recipes were once created by chance, using what was available. Why not adapt the recipes? Kitchens should live and grow, shouldn't they, like language, music, art, and architecture?

NEO-TRATTORIA Because I love Italy so much, I wish for a gentle revolution, so that young chefs can playfully let nonna's recipes live on. Call it an evolution of tradition—three-star chef and pioneer of the new Italian cuisine Massimo Bottura has been calling it that for twenty years. I am not a starred chef, and Italian cuisine is, after all, primarily a cucina popolare, a cuisine of the people. That's why I focus on the more casual trattoria. In recent years in Italy, following the bistronomy trend in Paris, the neo-trattoria has emerged—a place where chefs cook in a new way, with respect for tradition and with contemporary techniques. While doing research for this book, Remko Kraaijeveld, my husband and the photographer of the visual feast in this book, and I have been to a number of these neo-trattorias. We also visited a Sicilian gelato maker, a Neapolitan pastry chef, and even a Dutch chef in Naples, because good Italian cooking is not reserved only for Italians, just look at Agostino. What all these people have in common is that, like me, their ambition is to keep Italian cuisine alive and kicking.

INTUITIVE COOKING By exploring traditional dishes and playing with Italy's amazing ingredients, I figured out how to put my spin on them. What tastes good together? What would make this dish more exciting? Basically just like I did with *Indorock*, my book on the new Indonesian cuisine. I stick to certain basic rules as I crisscross the country and cook intuitively. My dishes are a journey on the plate: a mix of Italian traditions, my experiences in Italy, and my years as a restaurant chef.

I wish you a beautiful journey through this book.

POSTE

CHRPRN

SISIFO FELICE

a simple place for da

KITCHEN UTENSILS

If you take Italian cooking seriously and want to make all the delicious recipes in this book, the kitchen items below are nice to have around the house.

COOKING KNIVES What kind of knife you choose depends on your personal preference. Japanese knives are lighter but also get dull more quickly. German knives are heavier but can take a beating and stay sharp longer.

ICE CREAM MAKER Okay, this is an investment but you are going to have so much fun making your own gelato (see page 312).

KITCHEN THERMOMETER Useful for making syrup or for frying.

KITCHEN SCALE Ensures accurate measurements if you are using weight rather than cups.

MEASURING CUPS and **MEASURING SPOONS** Which I use throughout this book.

MANDOLIN Slices vegetables so thin that it gives them a very luxurious mouthfeel. Either metal or plastic is fine.

PASTA MACHINE For the fresh pastas in this book, a pasta machine is a godsend. A rolling pin, a knife, and a ravioli maker will also help you along the way.

PASTA WHEEL Useful for cutting pasta and pizza doughs.

PEELER Good for anything that needs to be peeled thinly, like asparagus, or for peeling pumpkin in a flash, plus it fits more comfortably in your hand than a knife.

POTATO RICER Looks like a giant garlic press. Especially useful for making gnocchi. You can also buy it on your vacation in Italy.

SAUTÉ PAN Every Italian household and restaurant has a lightweight frying pan with a high raised rim. They are available in all sizes, from 1 to 10 servings. Because the pan is so light, you can easily multitask, pulling the pan back and forth to mix pasta and sauce, (see also page 78 for more information on cooking pasta). I have an Agnelli's sauté pan; they can be purchased through Amazon.

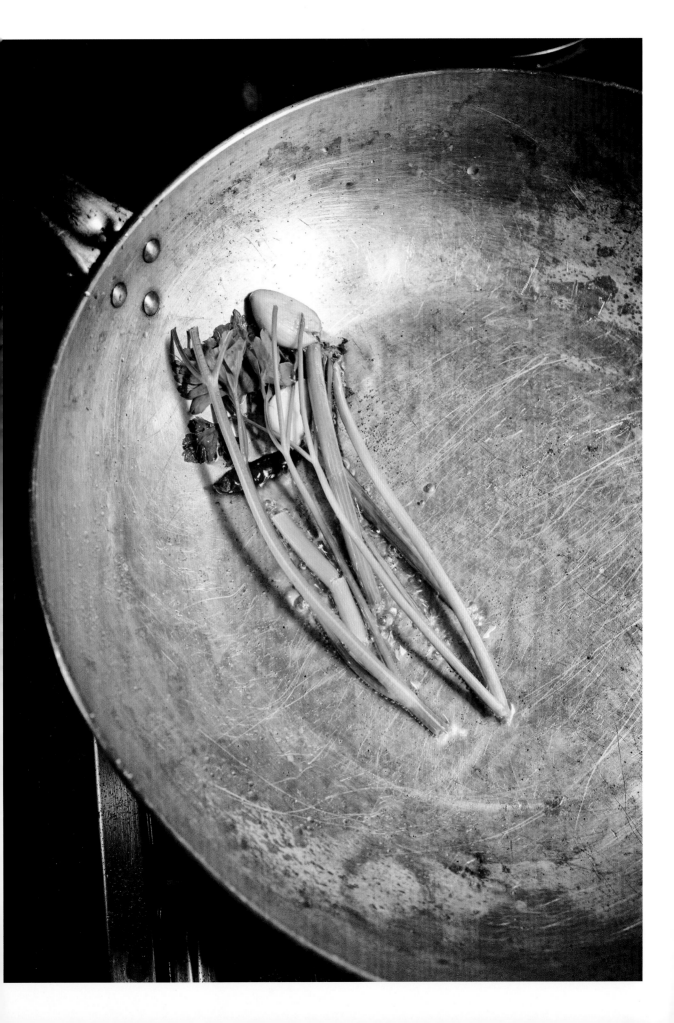

ABOUT THE RECIPES

Chef and icon of Italian nouvelle cuisine Fulvio Pierangelini's recipes are constantly changing, with the season, with new insights, with the cravings of its creator. Like him, I never follow my recipes exactly; I adjust them according to need and what's in the fridge. Think of a recipe as a guideline. If a spice is missing from the ingredients list, don't run back to the store. Replace it with something else; put your own spin on it. Follow your intuition!

FRUITS AND VEGETABLES Italian cuisine is predominantly a seasonal cuisine. You won't find pumpkin there in the summer or strawberries in the winter. I am a seasonal fanatic: if we get everything in the supermarket all year round, we lose track. If you go to an organic market or a good farmers' market, you get a better idea of the season. Seasonal, organic produce has more flavor, so you have to do less to make it tasty. When in doubt, look up "seasonal vegetables" to see what's available.

MEAT In all of my cookbooks, I deliberately include more vegetarian recipes than recipes with meat—with the exception of my satay book. There are so many delicious Italian meat dishes, yet I consciously choose not to include them all, for reasons such as animal welfare and the negative impact on the climate. I can enjoy a slice of porchetta immensely, precisely because I eat it only occasionally. I get the meat from a good butcher and pay more for it. I'm not saying you should do the same, maybe you already do, maybe you've been vegetarian for a long time, maybe you think it's all whining. Now you know where I stand on it, and this book reflects that philosophy.

FISH There is a lot of fish in Italian cuisine, especially in the coastal areas. But the fact is that the seas are becoming depleted of fish. You wouldn't know it when you see the huge pieces of tuna and swordfish in Sicilian markets, but they are an at risk fish species. That is why there are relatively few fish dishes in this book. For our health, it is recommended to eat fish once a week, so if you do eat fish, be sure to buy good-quality fish so you don't ingest too many microplastics. Also, with fish pay attention to the season, during certain months fish mate, and it is better not to eat them during those months.

EGGS I use the most animal-friendly, cage-free, organic eggs I can find.

SERVINGS All recipes are for 4 people unless otherwise indicated.

COSA MANCA OGGI?

CARNE	CAFFE'
SALAME	ZUCCHERO
PANCETTA	SALE
PROSCIUTTO	PATATE
PESCE	POMODORO
VINO	VERDURA
BIRRA	LATTE
FARINA	BURRO
PASTA	FORMAGGIO
RISO	LIMONE
PANE	SPEZIE
ACETO	UOVA

ESSENTIAL INGREDIENTS

Why is Italian cuisine so popular? There are several answers, but what always comes back is *la materia prima*, the raw materials. Italy is one of the most bountiful produce regions of the Mediterranean. And, while most produce is now also available worldwide, I only use the produce in my recipes if fresh varieties are widely accessible. For example, you won't find truffle in this book. I love it, but in many places in the world, it is impossible to get fresh, high-quality truffles. I have been spoiled by my years in Italy. Scrambled eggs with freshly shaved truffle at the market in Alba, complete truffle dinners in San Miniato, in Tuscany—conveniently paid for by my boyfriend's rich uncle—on the table were baskets with the nuggets of gold in them, heaven on Earth. But, in many other places, they taste like cardboard.

The recipes here are filled with readily available products when possible, but not everything is available at the supermarket. I get my vegetables, bread, cheese, meat, and fish from organic groceries or farmers' markets. But for some products, you have to make a little effort. I try to always give tips or alternative ingredients when something is tricky to find. There are many Italian online stores; ordering can be done from the comfort of your couch. In the next few pages I discuss the most common products in this book.

ANCHOVIES are extremely expensive at the moment, so I won't suggest getting them from Cantabria, Spain, although even Italians agree that the tastiest anchovies swim there. The tastiest anchovies are pickled in salt, but I also use anchovies in oil for convenience. To make them milder, you can put the fillets in water or milk for a while. Or take them out of the preserving oil they are packed in and put them in a nice olive oil.

BALSAMIC VINEGAR There are big differences between balsamic vinegars. Let's start with the "real" ones. There are two types: aceto balsamico di Modena IGP and aceto balsamico tradizionale DOP. The latter is made from mosto cotto, which is boiled down grape juice or must. The vinegar matures for twelve years in a series of wooden barrels and becomes naturally syrupy, sweet, and tart. A luxury product, it was reserved until recently for the noble circles of Modena and its surroundings. You don't use the tradizionale in salad, nor with caprese, mind you, but you would pair it with a piece of aged Parmesan, on a plate of tortellini in brodo, or over strawberries. "Regular" balsamic is made with one part must and one part wine vinegar and matures for sixty days to two years. As with olive oil, there is a lot of junk on the market. How do you recognize good balsamic? There are labels with leaves that indicate quality, but also look at the ingredients. Balsamic vinegar should consist only of mosto cotto and aceto di vino (wine vinegar). Good balsamic has a complex flavor, a viscosity a honey bee would envy, and is not too acidic. Supermarket balsamic is fine for dressing lettuce, but for a nice thick one, go to a specialty store.

BLACK GARLIC is fermented garlic with a drippy, fresh-sour taste. Not necessarily Italian, although this garlic is also made in Italy.

BOTTARGA or the dried roe of mullet or tuna, is used widely in Sardinia and Sicily and gives fishy oomph. I use it frequently in this book. You can grate it over dishes like spaghetti or creamy butter beans. It also comes in jars, already grated. I've also eaten it fresh on occasion. It's not cheap, but you don't need much of it, and it lasts forever. You can find bottarga at Italian specialty stores or online.

CAROB FLOUR is flour made from the beans of the carob tree; people who frequent health food stores (me!) know it. In Italy, the tree is called carrubo; the bean is called carruba and has a sweet, nutty taste. Carob flour is often used in gelato recipes. It makes gelato softer and reduces crystal formation.

CICORIA AND PUNTARELLE Cicoria (a type of chicory) also called catalogna chicory, is originally a southern Italian vegetable and related to endive and chicory. In Italy, it is on the menu everywhere when it's in season. Puntarelle are the shoots of what later becomes chicory. It is the lighter, inner part of the vegetable and is often eaten raw with anchovies. The darker leaves are stewed and sautéed with garlic and olive oil. Replace cicoria with endive if necessary and puntarelle with chicory if needed.

CIME DI RAPA, also called friarielli, rapini, broccoletti, or broccoli rabe, is a kind of wild broccoli from southern Italy with a slightly bitter taste. This vegetable is now grown in several places in Italy—its season depends on the location. If you have a difficult time finding it in your market, you can use broccoli florets or Bimi. In a pinch, you could also substitute it with spinach or chard.

COLATURA DI ALICI is translated as "leaking anchovy juice." Admittedly, leaking fish juice does not sound delicious. But colatura di alici is a true southern Italian delicacy. This sauce (sounds better when it's described as "sauce") is amber in color and chock-full of umami. For example, add a drop to spaghetti alle vongole or a fish risotto. You can find it at Italian specialty markets or online.

DRIED FAVA BEANS are usually puréed or used for soups. They can be eaten with or without their skins—the latter being pale yellow and easiest to process. Available at Italian, Turkish, and Moroccan stores.

NERO DI SEPPIA, or squid ink, is rich in flavor and is not just for the "gothic" look. It's delicious in pasta and risotto. Everything turns black, including your teeth, so don't use it on a first date! It's available at some fish stores, at Italian specialty stores, and online.

OLIVE OIL *L'oro verde* or green gold, as it's known! (As long as it hasn't been tampered with, that is.) The color can also be changed, so be careful when choosing olive oil. I use two types of olive oil: extra-virgin and mild olive oil. I use the latter mainly for cooking. A general high-quality olive oil will do the trick. Supermarket olive oil is often low quality or sometimes even spoiled if it has been on the shelf for too long.

Extra-virgin olive oil is cold pressed. It is said that you should not heat it, but they do in Italy. Some of the goodness may be lost, but the same is true when cooking broccoli for example. Furthermore, it depends on what you are preparing. I don't do long and high heat, but if, for example, I make a pappa al pomodoro on low heat, that's just right with extra virgin. For dressings, it is often advised to use extra-virgin olive oil but only do that if you are using high-quality olive oil. If you don't have access to high-quality olive oil (or don't want to spend the money, because it can be expensive) use half mild and half extra virgin for your dressing. Other than that, it depends on your taste.

I like grassy, but also peppery, Tuscan olive oil. When I lived in Florence, in November we always tasted the olio novello (new oil) with fettunta which is a crusty piece of bread for dipping. It was oily, fruity, and a bit spicy. Delicious, but such peppery oil certainly doesn't go with everything. So, look for varieties you like. When buying, check when the oil was made, because the older the oil the less tasty it will be. Do not store olive oil for too long. And, if possible, store it in a dark place and in a dark bottle or can. Light and heat makes it rancid.

PANE CARASAU is a crispy Sardinian flatbread. Delicious with cheese or just to nibble. Order online or find at specialized cheese stores and Italian delis.

PISTACHIO PASTE is a thick, creamy, brownish-green paste that you can find at Italian stores or online. It's delicious as a filling for cake or croissants. I fill maritozzi (Italian cream buns) with it.

SABA is boiled grape juice (mosto cotto) and a residual product of balsamic vinegar. It has a deep, fruity, caramel flavor. It's delicious with roasted fruit and creamy young cheeses. Order online, for example at gransardegna.com.

SCAMORZA is a pear-shaped cheese made from cow's milk from southern Italy that is often hung on a string. It is made the same way as mozzarella but is dried and aged. The taste is quite mild; the smoked variety, scamorza affumicata, is more pronounced in flavor and is my preference.

SHRIMP HEADS are not always available at your local grocery store, but they add so much flavor. If they're available (and you're not too squeamish), use them in the recipes that call for shrimp. First remove the heads from the bodies, then when the recipe calls for heating the oil in the skillet, add the shrimp heads. Sauté them in the oil for 2 to 3 minutes, then push down on the heads to release the juices. Continue with the recipe, adding ingredients and pushing down the heads to release more juice—just don't forget to remove the heads before serving.

STRACCHINO is a creamy, young soft cheese from northern Italy. It's delicious with a splash of olive oil on top. Available online or in Italian specialty stores.

TAGGIASCA olives are small, dark olives from Liguria with lots of flavor. If you can't fine Taggiasca olives, don't be tempted to buy canned black olives from the supermarket—they taste like rubber. Kalamata olives are a good alternative.

TALEGGIO is a creamy, nutty cheese made from red-skinned cow's milk from northern Italy. Most cheese stores carry it.

TOMINO is a soft cheese from Piedmont made from cow's, goat's, or sheep's milk. Tomino alla piastra can be baked on the grill, in a pan, or in the oven, which makes the inside run. So delicious! Available online or in specialty stores.

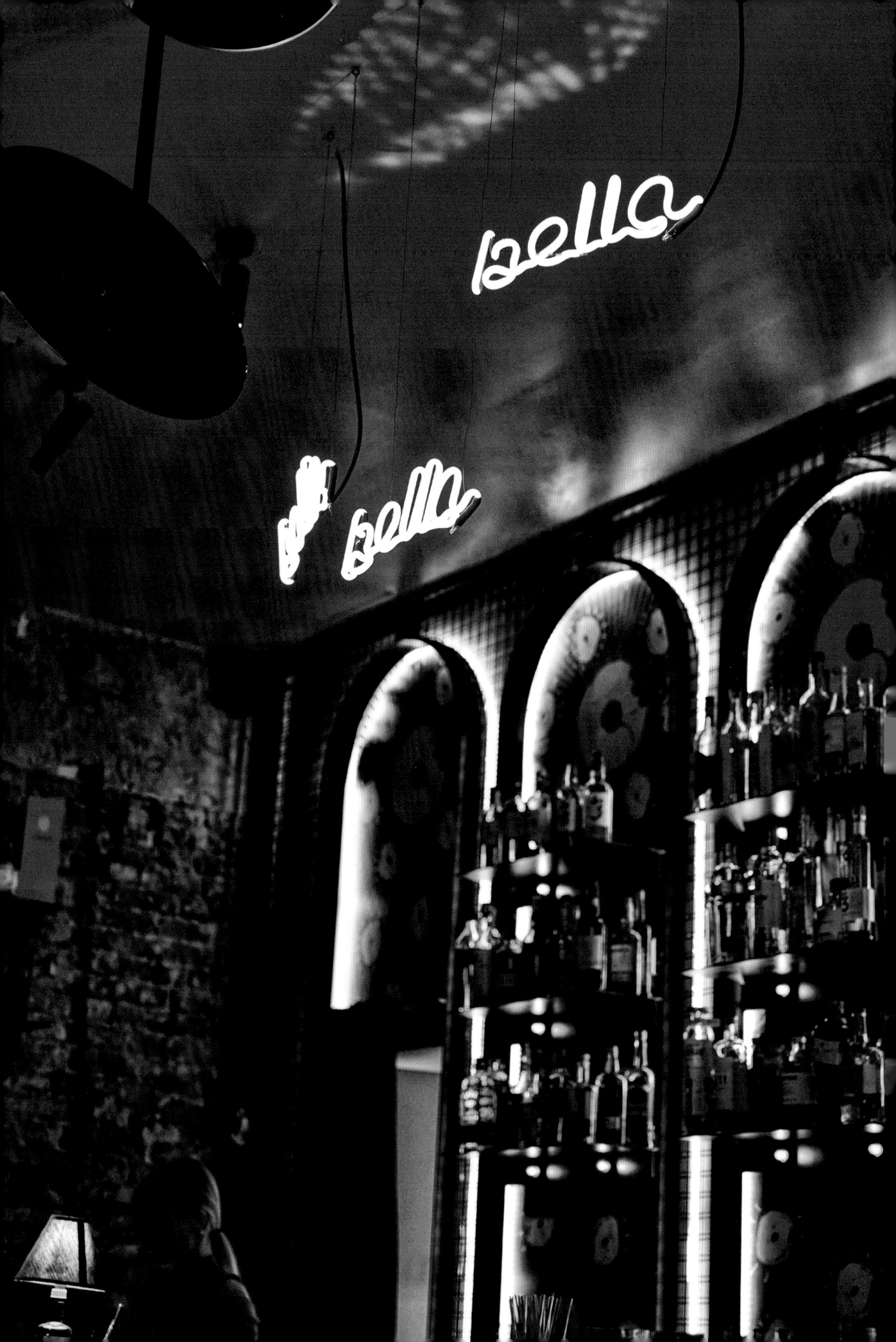
bella
bella

NATURAL WINE PROPHET
Lorenzo "Titto" Dzieduszycki

In my twenties, I lived in Florence for several years and because my boyfriend was part of the nobility's inner circle, we sometimes partied in the Torrigiani's castles, one of the oldest Florentine families whose garden walls are also the ancient city walls. We hung out in mansions with whole hills as driveways and splashed in private pools. They were crazy times, but I also experienced the Florentinian upper class as a snobbish and stifling environment. Titto (real name Lorenzo, but there are already so many of those) whom I also met at that time, felt the same way. He exchanged Florence for Barcelona, New York, and finally, London.

Titto is one of the most open-minded Italians I know. A natural wine visionary who, back in 2004, was trying to get his family, which has been in the wine business for generations, to switch to biodynamic practices. He has lived in London for fifteen years where he works as a graphic designer and restaurateur. London is bursting with Italians— more than 350,000 live there, almost as if all of Florence lived in London. Italian restaurants in London are currently cooking in an exciting and new way. In an international metropolis you naturally cook differently than in an Italian provincial town. So, we start our Italian trip, surprisingly, in London. Titto had a wine bar called Rubedo in East London. There would always be homemade pasta and focaccia, and they would make the salumi themselves. They used to cook with carefully selected products. "Expensive products mostly, haha. We didn't earn anything with it," Titto tells me. Although it was a popular neighbourhood restaurant, Titto decided to close the place last year.'

> ### 'In Italy it's either the traditional trattoria food or nineties French gourmet, with tiny food to eat on big plates."

Dishes like crudo of sea bass with rhubarb aguachile and agretti (monk's beard) or their cacio e pepe with crab made us go crazy. But, also the fresh carne battuta (kind of smashed tartare) with toasted breadcrumbs was great and much more exciting than what I tasted in Italy. Zeppole (kind of like doughnut holes) were served with grapefruit curd. It was playful and high quality cooking. Titto and I baptized this way of cooking "Italian on acid," referring to the abundant use of sour ingredients by the Brits.

Titto has worked with several chefs at Rubedo, ironically the ones who understood Rubedo's cuisine well were not Italian. Or maybe that's not surprising either: if you grow up with strict kitchen rules, it's more difficult to break them. When he eats out in Italy, it is usually at a traditional trattoria because modern usually disappoints him.

Fortunately in London, Italian food crackles off the plates at other restaurants too, such as at Manteca in Shoreditch, thanks to chefs who have indeed breathed new life into the trattoria. Italian London was inspiring as a reference for this book, but it would be silly to portray only emigrated Italian chefs. That wouldn't help Italy either.

Having traveled extensively through Italy over the past few years, I am happy to report that several chefs there are also very refreshing. That is why we went in search of Italian chefs who dare to break free from the conservative corner in the country itself, to take Italian cuisine into the future without compromising the soul of that fine folk cuisine. They shared their stories and knowledge and provided much inspiration for this book. Titto, you would appreciate them too.

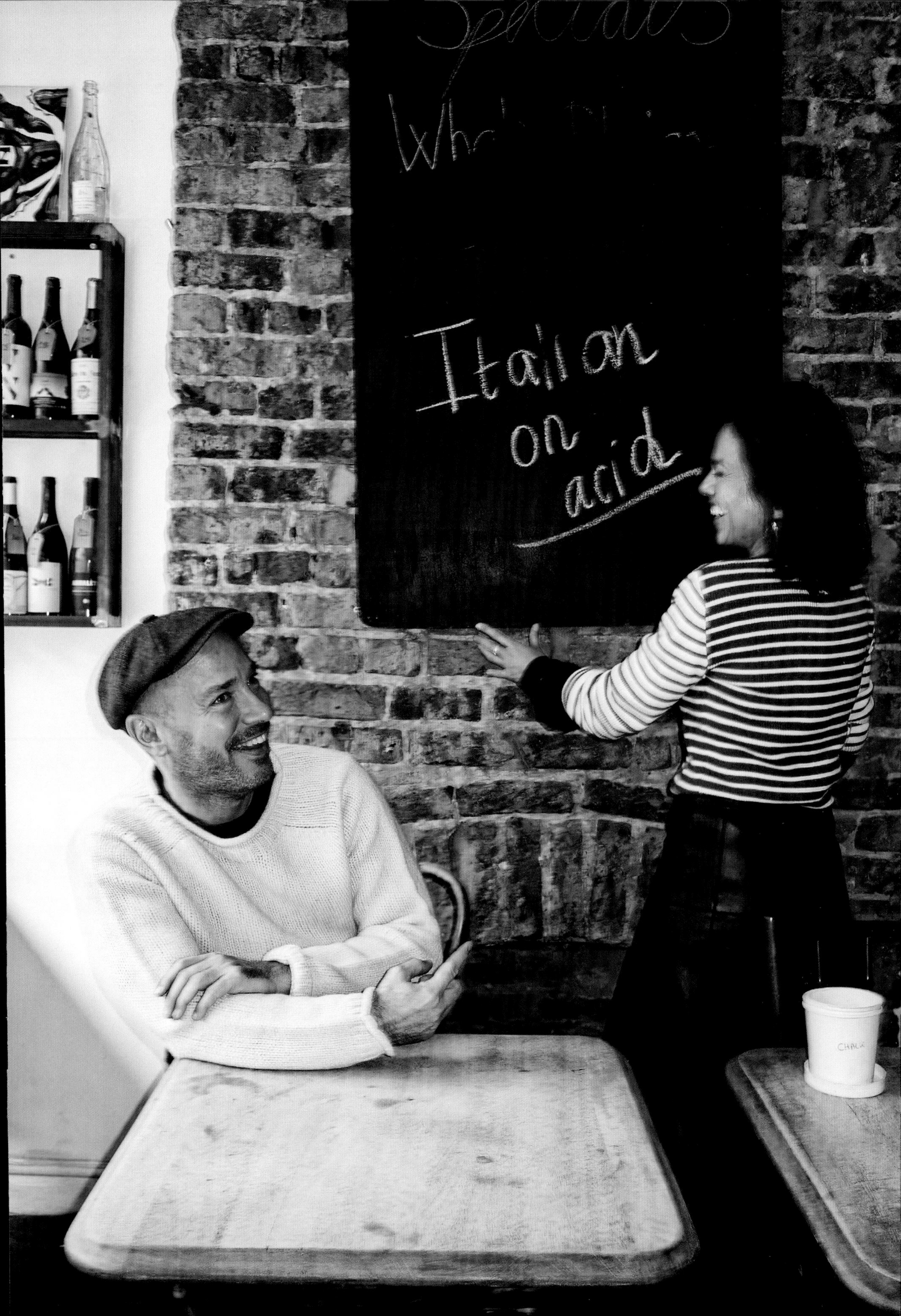
Italian
on
acid

ANTIPASTI
E FRITTI
APPETIZERS AND FRIED SNACKS

Panissa con pesto piccante

Chickpea flour fritti with spicy lime pesto

Preparation time:
30 minutes + 2 hours
to rest

Serves 4

___

INGREDIENTS

1 ¼ teaspoons sea salt
1 ½ tablespoons mild
   olive oil
2 ⅔ cups (250 g)
   chickpea flour
Sunflower or peanut oil,
   for frying
Spicy lime pesto
   (page 369)

Just off Genoa, there is a picturesque little bay called Boccadasse. There is a pebble beach surrounded by pastel-colored houses, a bar, a gelateria, and a friggitoria (a shop that sells fried foods). In short, everything you need in life and on vacation. After a day at the beach, we got all kinds of fritti at that friggitoria: from deep-fried ravioli to deep-fried calamari and panissa, which is kind of like polenta except made with chickpea flour that is cut and deep fried. It's a typical street snack of this region. Crispy on the outside, buttery soft and savory on the inside. The only thing that was conspicuous by its absence was sauce; Italians don't serve sauce with fritti.

But if you still want something fresh to dip your greasy snack into, I came up with a spicy lime pesto to go with the panissa. Don't let them hear it over there in Genoa though.

Pour 1 quart (945 ml) of water into a saucepan, add the salt and olive oil. Gradually add the chickpea flour through a sifter. Cook over low heat while stirring until a thick porridge forms. Keep stirring until all the liquid is absorbed by the flour and it loosens from the sides, about 10 minutes.

Grease a low baking dish and pour the batter into the prepared baking dish, smoothing with a spatula. Cover with plastic wrap and refrigerate for 2 hours to cool and set.

Meanwhile, make the spicy lime pesto.

Dump the chickpea "cake" onto a cutting board and cut it into thick strips that resemble thick-cut French fries.

Heat a generous amount of oil in a pan to 350°F (180°C). If you do not have a kitchen thermometer, throw a piece of chickpea cake into the oil; when the oil fizzes, it is hot enough. You can also use a deep fryer.

Fry the strips in portions for 3 to 4 minutes until golden brown. Remove from the oil with a slotted spoon and drain on paper towels while you fry the rest of the panissa.

Serve with the pesto.

Crostone con cachi e cren

Crostone with persimmon, gorgonzola, and horseradish with sweet and sour sauce

Preparation time:
35 minutes

Serves 4

___

INGREDIENTS

Sweet and sour mustard seeds
½ cup (100 g) yellow mustard seeds
½ cup (120 ml) mild vinegar (white wine, apple cider, or sherry vinegar)
2 tablespoons granulated sugar
½ teaspoon sea salt
Few bay leaves

Crostoni
1 ripe, firm persimmon, cut into thin slices
Juice from 1 lemon
½ bunch (5 ¼ oz/150 g) endive
Sea salt
2 tablespoons extra-virgin olive oil
4 to 6 tablespoons mild olive oil
4 thick slices stale bread
1 cup (100 g) Gorgonzola
1-inch piece fresh horseradish

Fuoriporta is a restaurant in Florence (see page 377 for the adress) where they serve crostone, which is a large piece of bread, toasted with big fat toppings—like crostini except bigger. Think fresh funghi porcini (porcini mushrooms) and cheese, fresh sausage and grilled vegetables, good-quality, simple ingredients. The crostoni are like meals, served in wicker baskets with checkered cloths inside. A bottle of wine completes the basic-but-perfect meal. I would jump for joy if someone was smart enough to open a crostoni restaurant near where I live now. It's also a very good, no-waste meal, because you can use slightly stale bread for the crostoni.

I first tried persimmon in my college days in Florence, which is why I will forever associate this fruit with Italy, even though it is originally from Asia. Horseradish is not widely used in Italy, but my Veronese friend, Barbara, told me that they eat it with bollito misto (roasted meat) and mustard, so I added it here.

To make the sweet and sour mustard seeds, place the seeds in a saucepan along with the vinegar, ½ cup (120 ml) of water, the sugar, salt, and bay leaves. Bring it to a boil, then turn the heat to low and simmer for 30 minutes until most of the liquid has evaporated, the seeds are soft, and you have a syrupy consistency. Ladle into a sterilized jar. It will last you weeks in the refrigerator, and is delicious with everything from cheese to roasted chicken and meat.

To make the Crostoni, drizzle the persimmon slices with a squeeze of lemon juice.

Divide the endive into bunches and sprinkle with a pinch of salt. Heat the extra-virgin olive oil in a large skillet and fry the endive bunches for a few minutes per side. Remove from the pan and season with more lemon juice.

Heat half of the mild olive oil in the frying pan and fry the sliced bread on both sides until crispy. Top with endive and persimmon slices. Crumble the gorgonzola on top, spoon the sweet and sour mustard seeds over the cheese, and finish with a generous amount of freshly grated horseradish.

Tomino con porri e bagnet verd

Fried cheese with soft leeks and salsa verde with leek greens

Preparation time:
25 minutes

Serves 4

INGREDIENTS

Salsa verde
4 young, thin leeks
Sea salt
1 large bunch (1 ounce/30 g)
   fresh parsley
1½ tablespoons white
   wine vinegar
1 tablespoon capers
4 anchovy fillets
½ cup (118 ml) mild
   olive oil

Fried cheese
Mild olive oil, for frying
3 ½ ounces (100 g) tomino
Few sliced radishes,
   to garnish

TIPS

If you can't find tomino,
you can substitute
camembert.

You can also serve the
tomino with grilled
vegetables, or on a salad
with lentils and squash.
The possibilities are
endless. Once tried,
you can't imagine life
without tomino.

Tomino alla piastra is a soft cheese that is baked on the grill or in a pan. In Piedmont, they serve tomino (from the grill or not) with bagnet verd (salsa verde). A simple but delicious dish. I serve it with soft leeks and use the green of the leeks for the bagnet verd. Looks like elevated cuisine but takes zero effort. Although, here comes the catch: tomino can be difficult to find so I have suggested an alternative if you need it. I try not to include difficult ingredients in this book, but this is such a fun and delicious cheese that I had to put it in. Help me make tomino mainstream! Please nag the buyer at your favorite cheese shop for it so it becomes a mainstay.

Remove the outer tough leaves from the leeks. Cut off the green stems of the leeks, rinse clean, and set aside. Halve the leeks lengthwise but leave the roots on for now and rinse off any dirt under running water.

Add water to a pot, sprinkle with salt and bring the water to a simmer. Add the white part and the green stems of the leeks to the pot. Cook for about 12 minutes until tender and soft. Remove from the cooking water, drain well, and then dry on a cloth. Now cut the roots off the leeks.

To make the salsa verde, put the green stems in a blender. Pick the leaves off the parsley stems and add along with the white wine vinegar, capers, and anchovy fillets. Season with a pinch of salt, add the oil, and blend until smooth. Taste to see if it is to your liking. It should be savory and fresh. Using a large ladle, rub the sauce through a fine sieve. This will give you a bright green, smooth sauce.

Pour the sauce onto plates. Drape a leek on each plate and set aside.

To make the fried cheese, grease a frying pan with a little oil and fry the cheeses until the crust is nicely browned; turn over and fry the other side as well. Remove the cheeses from the pan, cut in half, and divide between plates. Top with radish slices and serve.

Mozza in carrozza con chimichurri

Crispy mozzarella sandwich with chimichurri

Preparation time:
30 minutes + 30 minutes
of resting (optional)

Serves 4

Only in Naples can they come up with something as naughty (and delicious!) as mozzarella in carrozza: mozzarella sandwiched between sliced white bread and then deep-fried. It's crispy, it's savory, there's melty cheese. What more do you want? Contrast please. Come on in, spicy, sultry chimichurri!

INGREDIENTS

Chimichurri (page 371)
2 balls fresh mozzarella
  (not buffalo mozzarella,
  it's too wet!)
4 wide slices white bread
2 to 3 eggs (3 if you prefer
  double breaded)
Sea salt
⅓ cup (45 g)
  all-purpose flour
½ cup (70 g) dry
  breadcrumbs
Sunflower or peanut oil,
  for frying

TIPS

Add additional filling
to the mozzarella,
such as anchovies or
sun-dried tomatoes.

Instead of chimichurri,
you can add Spicy lime
pesto (page 369) or
Salsa verde (page 40).

For a super-deluxe version,
mix grated Parmesan into
the beaten eggs.

First, make the chimichurri and allow the flavors to infuse.

Slice the mozzarella and drain in a sieve then pat dry with a paper towel.

Cut the crusts off the bread slices (or leave them on if you would like it to be more rustic) and place four of them next to each other on a cutting board. Place slices of mozzarella on two of the slices of bread, and then close the sandwich by placing the two remaining pieces of bread on top. Press well so that the bread sticks to the mozzarella. Cut the sandwiches diagonally through the middle.

Next beat the eggs in a shallow bowl and add a pinch of salt. Add the flour to a second shallow bowl and the breadcrumbs to a third shallow bowl.

Dip the sandwiches first in flour, then in the beaten eggs using two forks. Allow the extra egg to slide off and then place the sandwiches in the breadcrumbs. (If you are going for double breadcrumbs, dip again in egg and breadcrumbs. Then set aside.)

Put the sandwiches in the refrigerator for 30 minutes so they become firm.

In a heavy-bottom pan, add the oil so it comes up the side of the pan about an inch (2.5 cm). Heat over medium-high heat until the oil starts to bubble. When the oil is bubbling, you can get started. Fry each sandwich for a few minutes per side until golden brown and drain on paper towels.

Serve with chimichurri and eat immediately. Mamma mia, che buona!

Caprese con mollica piccante

Caprese with roasted tomato and fennel-chili breadcrumbs

Preparation time:
1 hour roasting +
10 minutes

Serves 4

———

INGREDIENTS

1 pound (450 g) ripe cherry
  tomatoes, halved
Sea salt
5 garlic cloves, sliced
½ cup (120 ml) extra-virgin
  olive oil
Zest from ½ lemon

Fennel-chili breadcrumbs
1 thick slice stale bread
½ teaspoon fennel seeds
½ teaspoon chili flakes
2 tablespoons mild
  olive oil
2 rounds buffalo
  mozzarella
2 to 3 sprigs fresh basil

TIP
You can flavor the oil with
any fresh herbs you have
handy. Think oregano,
thyme, or sage.

I understood the enthusiasm about mozzarella only after I bit into a huge, dripping, fresh buffalo mozzarella ball from a mozzarella factory. I was nineteen and on my way to Caserta with my boyfriend at the time. I was used to rubbery white cheese, but that had nothing to do with this creamy buffalo mozzarella cloud. With mozzarella like this, I understood the magic of a caprese. It's salty and tangy, and mixes with the ripe tomatoes bursting out of their skins. Together they create a kind of dressing that ties the whole thing together. Once topped with fresh basil, the dish is comprised of the colors of the Italian flag, which is no coincidence! Caprese was invented in the 1920s when the Italians were feeling particularly patriotic. I pull some antics with the classic. I roast the tomatoes in lots of olive oil so the flavor of the tomatoes becomes more intense. I also sprinkle crusty breadcrumbs on top because, like the Italians, I know what to do with stale bread.

Preheat the oven to 325°F (160°C).

Place the tomatoes in a baking sheet lined with parchment paper and sprinkle them with a pinch of salt. Add the garlic and drizzle the extra-virgin olive oil on top. Zest half of the lemon over the top. Roast the tomatoes in the oven for 50 to 60 minutes, until they are lightly charred but still intact.

To make the Fennel-chili breadcrumbs, pulse the stale bread, fennel seeds, chili flakes, and mild olive oil in a food processor until rough crumbs form. Transfer the breadcrumbs to a dry skillet and toast them (stirring constantly so they don't burn) until they are brown and crispy.

Divide the buffalo mozzarella among four plates. Add a scoop of the roasted tomato mixture and drizzle on some of the tasty oil from the tray as well. Garnish with basil and finish with the spicy breadcrumbs.

"THE ITALIAN FLAVORS SPEAK FOR THEMSELVES. YOU DON'T HAVE TO MESS WITH THEM."

LONDON MEETS SICILY
Emilia Strazzanti

In curvaceous Scicli, a Baroque Sicilian town surrounded by hills and soaring monasteries, Emilia awaits us. We plan to make arancini in her cozy house that is built half in and half against the rocks. Despite her Italian-sounding name and Mediterranean appearance, Emilia greets us with a pure London accent. Her family moved to Britain after World War II, where Emilia grew up amid Sicilian delicacies and a garage full of homemade tomato sauce and wine. Her grandfather infused her with his passion for cooking and taught Emilia to bake at the age of five. By the time she was ten, she was making her first sugo (traditional Italian tomato sauce).

At school in London, the other kids didn't understand her Sicilian heritage and made fun of her. "Cooking became a way to escape reality," she remembers. She attended college and cooking school, and because Emilia is fiery and driven, she would work for free in exchange for knowledge. "I spent my twenty-first birthday in the kitchen," she says. She learned the pastry trade in Paris and worked in high-end establishments such as Alain Ducasse's Le Meurice.

Back in London, she worked for Burro e Salvia, a pastificio e trattoria (pasta factory), and cooked savory pies for none other than Elton John. When Emilia went back to Sicily on vacation, she found herself. She delved into the history of the island and got a deeper understanding of where her Arab features come from. "I just ran into it on the street; everyone here looks like me."

Traditional recipes tell stories, and for Emilia those stories feel like coming home. She decided to move to Sicily and teach cooking workshops there.

Arancini show the Arab influences on Sicilian cuisine. They resemble kubbeh or kibbeh, which are commonly eaten in the Middle East. I've eaten quite a few arancini by the time I get started with Emilia; I love those things.

But one arancino is not the other. There's a big difference between arancini fresh from the fryer or lying around all day sweating in a showcase. Emilia first talks about the rice, that was planted by the Arabs in Sicily. With the unification of Italy, rice cultivation was moved north, she explains. And then fiercely, "But this rice has nothing to do with risotto. Just so you know," referring to the rice she made the night before and left to set overnight. "I add salted butter to it, which adds flavor. And the solidified butter helps hold the rice together."

The ragù is also ready. It's a secret family recipe I am not allowed to know about. She grabs about a cup full of the golden rice, makes a pit in it and adds a heaping tablespoon of ragù into it. Then she starts kneading the rice around the ragù enclosing the filling. Emilia's hands begin to shine with grease. She shows me how she forms the rice into a closed ball. Then she shapes the top into a gentle cone.

A language note: in western Sicily, the fried rice ball is called arancina, in the east, arancino. In Sicily, they still argue about which is correct—male or female. Hopelessly old-fashioned, of course. Soon it will probably be arancinx. Because I don't know how you pronounce that and learned to make arancini, which is the plural form in the east, I stick with the masculine ending. The snack gets its name from its resemblance to an arancia (orange), but in the east, arancini often have a conical shape, resembling Mount Etna. Emilia briefly pulls open the just-fried arancino to show the inside. It's better than any I have eaten before. A perfect blend of nonna's recipe and Michelin techniques. If you're in the area, be sure to book a cooking class with Emilia (see page 380).

Tris di arancini

Filled rice balls

Preparation time:
2 hours + overnight
for cooling

Makes about 14 arancini

INGREDIENTS

Rice
½ cup (113 g) unsalted
  butter, separated
2 ½ cups (500 g)
  arborio rice
1½ teaspoons sea salt
1 pinch saffron threads
1 ¾ ounces (50 g) pecorino
  or Parmesan, grated

Arancini filling
(see page 50)

Pastella (batter)
1 ⅔ cups (210 g)
  all-purpose flour
1 cup (140 g) dry
  breadcrumbs
Sunflower or peanut
  oil, for frying

TIPS
If you make the arancini
ahead of time, warm them
up in the oven for a few
minutes before serving.

Instead of cooking
the rice in water, you
can substitute broth
(see page 163).

Even though the first thing
Emilia said to me while
cooking the rice was, "this
has nothing to do with
risotto," making arancini
with leftover risotto works
just fine.

You have to go to Sicily just for arancini. Rice balls with filling, just out of the fryer, are the most delicious. Golden yellow, crispy happiness! Arancini owe their origins to the Arabs, who ruled Sicily for centuries. They resemble Middle Eastern kubbeh or kibbeh, which I used to make with my Iraqi friend Sara. In Sicily, Emilia was my arancini teacher. Emilia is a Sicilian who grew up in London, where she worked as a chef (see page 47). Emilia combines her nonna's traditional recipe with her own insights. For example, she mixes butter into the rice, which once solidified, keeps it firm. I add grated cheese for the same reason. While forming the arancini, the butter melted in our warm hands and it sounded... buttery and sexy. Emilia makes her arancini with meat ragù, and I came up with three fillings of my own. Of course, you don't have to make all three. Choose for yourself. Two fillings will suffice. If you go for one filling, double the ingredients.

To make the rice, melt 2 tablespoons of the butter in a large, heavy skillet. Add the rice and toast it for 5 minutes, stirring constantly, like risotto, so it doesn't burn. Add 4 ¼ cups (1 L) of water along with the salt. Finely grind the saffron threads with a mortar and pestle, and add it to the rice. Cook for about 15 minutes, stirring frequently. This will loosen the starch. Remove the skillet from the heat when all the liquid has been absorbed.

Mix the remaining butter and the grated cheese into the rice and allow it to melt. Pour the rice into a shallow tray, cover with plastic wrap, poke holes in the plastic wrap to allow air to circulate, and refrigerate overnight.

Meanwhile, make two fillings or choose one and double the ingredients.

Take about 1 cup of the cold rice in your hand and press flat to create a sort of bowl. Spoon a generous tablespoon of filling into it and now begin to knead the rice around the filling with both hands until it's formed into a ball. Press firmly to close it up. The filling will peek out a little at the top, push it back in. Press and continue working it until the ball is closed at the top.

It takes some practice, so don't be discouraged if you don't succeed right away. When you get the hang of it, you can turn the round ball into a gentle cone shape, so it looks like Mount Etna, but they are just as tasty in a ball shape! Repeat with the rest of the rice.

To make the Pastella, pour 1 ¼ cups (300 ml) of water into a bowl, add the flour through a sifter and stir until it forms a smooth liquid. Sprinkle the breadcrumbs in a large deep dish. One by one, place the arancini in the batter and roll them thoroughly so that all sides get wet. Then place them in the breadcrumbs and sprinkle crumbs over the top and sides, until they are entirely covered. Repeat with the remaining arancini.

Heat a generous amount of sunflower or peanut oil in a pan, enough to completely cover the arancini. To check readiness, use a kitchen thermometer, bring the oil to 350°F (180°C); or throw in some crumbs, if they start to bubble, the oil is hot enough. Once the oil is ready, deep-fry the arancini for 5 to 6 minutes or until golden brown. Don't fry too many at once or the temperature of the oil will drop and they will absorb the oil and get soggy. Drain the cooked arancini on paper towels and eat while they are still hot.

Ripieno di arancini

Arancini Filling

Preparation time:
2 hours + overnight
for cooling

Makes about 14 arancini

INGREDIENTS

Alla Norma
1 large eggplant, diced
Sea salt
¼ cup (60 ml) mild olive oil
1 garlic clove, finely chopped
1½ tablespoons tomato paste
Pinch chili flakes (optional)
½ cup (100 g) canned diced tomatoes
1 ¾ ounces (50 g) ricotta salata (or
    another salty, hard cheese such as
    Parmesan or pecorino), grated
Half 8-ounce (225 g) mozzarella (not
    buffalo mozzarella, which is too wet),
    cut into small cubes
1 bunch (½ oz/15 g) fresh basil leaves,
    finely chopped

TIP
It's important that the filling
    is not too wet.

**Pistachio pesto, peas,
and scamorza**
¾ cup (90 g) frozen peas
½ cup (70 g) shelled pistachios
1 large bunch (¾ oz/20 g) fresh
    mint leaves
1 ounce (30 g) Parmesan, grated
3 tablespoons + 1 teaspoon (50 ml)
    extra-virgin olive oil
Sea salt and freshly ground
    black pepper
1 ¾ ounce (50 g) smoked scamorza
    (or another young, meltable
    cheese), diced

Shrimp ragù
3 tablespoons mild olive oil
1 garlic clove, crushed
1 bunch (½ oz/15 g) Italian parsley
2 tablespoons tomato paste
5 cherry tomatoes, quartered
½ tablespoon finely chopped
    preserved lemon
½ teaspoon chili flakes
7 ounces (200 g) large shrimp, peeled
    and deveined
Sea salt and freshly ground
    black pepper

Salt the eggplant cubes generously. Heat the olive oil over high heat in a large frying pan, add the eggplant, and brown on all sides.

Add the garlic and additional oil if necessary to cook the garlic. Add the tomato paste, chili flakes, and diced tomatoes, and simmer until most of the liquid has evaporated and the eggplant is soft and tender. Remove from the heat.

Stir both cheeses and basil into the eggplant mixture and fill the arancini (see page 48).

Cook the peas according to package instructions. Place the pistachios, mint leaves, Parmesan, and olive oil into a blender. Add salt and pepper to taste, and blend on low until it makes a pistachio pesto. Pour the pesto in a medium bowl, add the scamorza and peas, and mix to combine. Use the mixture to fill the arancini (see page 48).

Heat the olive oil in a skillet and add the garlic along with a few sprigs of the parsley, and stir to infuse the scent of the herbs into the oil. Add the tomato paste and mix. Add the cherry tomatoes, preserved lemon, and chili flakes. Continue to sauté until most of the liquid has evaporated. Remove the parsley.

Sprinkle the shrimp with salt, cut them into small pieces, and sauté until cooked through. Remove from the heat. Finely chop the remaining parsley and mix in. Use the mixture to fill the arancini (see page 48).

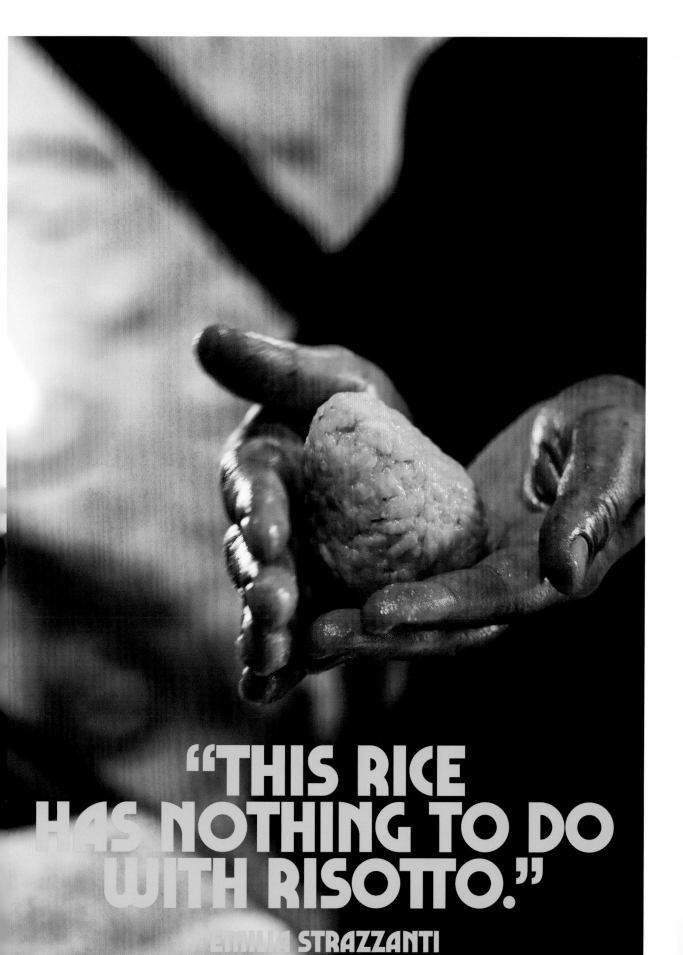

"THIS RICE HAS NOTHING TO DO WITH RISOTTO."
EMILIA STRAZZANTI

Farinata con lardo e spezie

Chickpea pancake with lardo or prosciutto and rosemary-fennel pepper

Preparation time:
10 minutes + 2 hours
(or longer) rest + 15
minutes of baking
per cake

Serves 8 (about 8 pieces
with a diameter of
8 ½ inches [21 ½ cm])

INGREDIENTS

Farinata
1 ¾ cups (250 g) chickpea
  or garbanzo bean flour
1 teaspoon sea salt
2 tablespoons extra-virgin
  olive oil + extra,
  for frying

Topping
1 tablespoon peppercorns
1 tablespoon fennel seeds
1 tablespoon fresh
  rosemary, finely
  chopped
5 ¼ ounces (150 g) lardo,
  prosciutto or coppa

TIPS
You can also add the
chopped rosemary
to the batter.

Sometimes I eat farinata
for lunch, with more
toppings (see page 56).

Farinata is a thin cake made of chickpeas from Liguria; crispy on the outside and creamy on the inside. It is baked in flat pans the size of wagon wheels in screaming hot ovens. In Italy, the farinata is sliced and served with lardo (cured back fat), but because that's often not widely available, you can use coppa or prosciutto. Either way, it melts with the heat. Heavenly. It's also incredibly delicious without meat products. Easy and cheap, it's a great snack. Eat farinata immediately. I do not recommend pre-baking and reheating.

Put the chickpea flour in a bowl. Add the salt and whisk in 2 cups + 2 tablespoons (500 ml) of lukewarm water until the batter is smooth. Stir in 2 tablespoons of the olive oil, cover with plastic wrap, and let rest at room temperature for at least 2 hours or overnight.

To make the topping, toast the peppercorns for about 5 minutes in a dry skillet and grind coarsely in a pepper grinder or with a mortar and pestle. Add the fennel seeds to the mortar and crush again. Combine the pepper, fennel seeds, and rosemary.

Preheat the oven to 450°F (230°C).

Stir the batter again just before you pour it. Pour a splash of olive oil into a cast iron skillet (I use a crepe pan), place in the oven and allow to become scalding hot. Remove the pan from the oven (use oven mitts!), pour a thin layer of batter (as if you were making a crepe) into the sizzling oil and immediately swirl the pan so that the batter runs to the edges. Work quickly and return to the oven. Bake for 15 to 20 minutes or until done. It is best when the cake is golden brown and crispy at the edges.

Cut or tear the farinata into pieces, top with lardo, prosciutto or coppa and sprinkle with the rosemary-fennel pepper. Eat immediately.

Repeat with the rest of the batter making sure you heat up the pan the same way before adding more batter. If you have multiple pans, you can bake multiple batches at a time.

Farinata con 'nduja di pomodoro

Chickpea pancake with tomato 'nduja, spinach, and egg

Preparation time:
20 minutes + 2 hours
(or longer) rest +
15 minutes of baking
per cake

Serves 4

INGREDIENTS

Farinata
(page 54)

Tomato 'nduja
2 ¾ cups (150 g)
 sun-dried tomatoes
½ cup (75 g) toasted
 almonds, coarsely
 chopped
3 tablespoons extra-virgin
 olive oil
1 teaspoon chili flakes
2 teaspoons pimentón
 (Spanish smoked
 paprika)
4 large eggs
2 garlic cloves, crushed
14 ounces (400 g)
 spinach, chopped
Sea salt
1 lemon wedge
Fresh dill to taste
 (optional)

Farinata is usually eaten as a happy hour snack. But this irresistible savory pancake made of chickpea flour can, of course, also serve perfectly well as a base for a meal. For example, if you top it with sautéd garlic, spinach, and tomato 'nduja, it's delicious for lunch or as part of an evening meal.

First, make the Farinata batter.

Bring a pot of water to a boil and prepare a bowl of ice water. Preheat the oven to 450°F (230°C).

To make the tomato 'nduja, place the sun-dried tomatoes, almonds, 3 tablespoons of the olive oil, the chili flakes, and pimentón in a blender and blend into paste.

Using a slotted spoon, carefully lower the eggs into the boiling water and cook for 6 minutes. After the eggs are cooked, scoop them from the boiling water into the ice water and set aside. Peel and halve them just before serving.

Pour a splash of olive oil into a cast iron skillet (I use a crepe pan), place in the oven and allow to become scalding hot. Remove the pan from the oven (use oven mitts!), pour a thin layer of farinata batter (as if you were making a crepe) into the sizzling oil and immediately swirl the pan so that the batter runs to the edges. Work quickly and return to the oven. Bake for 15 to 20 minutes or until its done. It is best when the cake is golden brown and crispy at the edges.

While the farinata is baking, heat another skillet and pour in the remaining 2 tablespoons of olive oil. Brown the garlic cloves in the oil. Add the spinach with a pinch of sea salt. Sauté until just wilted. Finish with a squeeze of lemon juice and remove from the heat.

Serve the farinata with the sautéed spinach, tomato 'nduja, and soft-boiled eggs. Finish with some fresh dill if you have any left over.

Crostini con baccalà mantecato
Crostini with salt cod and pickled radicchio

Preparation time:
40 minutes + 24 hours
soaking

Serves 4

___

INGREDIENTS

1 pound (450 g) salt cod
3 bay leaves
1 garlic clove, peeled
Juice from ½ lemon
½ cup (120 ml) mild olive
    oil + extra*
1 cup (240 ml) white
    wine vinegar
1 head radicchio
8 slices stale bread
3 sprigs Italian parsley,
    chopped
Freshly ground black
    pepper

*If the olive oil is slightly
bitter, then use a semi neutral
oil such as sunflower oil.*

TIPS
Baccalà left overs?
Make Beans with baccalà
and 'nduja croutons
(page 227).

It's important to desalt the
cod by soaking it in water.

Baccalà is typically Italian. Not. But once this fish from Scandinavia arrived in Italy, it became part of Italian cuisine. Not only in mountainous areas where there was no fresh fish, but even in coastal areas such as Venice and southern Italy. Together with olive oil, the fish becomes a kind of creamy salty whip, delicious paired with crispy toast and sweet and sour radicchio. This bite is inspired by Venetian crostini.

Soak the salt cod in water for 24 hours, changing the water 3 times while it's soaking. Rinse the cod well and place it in a pan with the bay leaves, garlic, and lemon juice. Cover the cod with water until just submerged. Bring to a boil and then simmer over low heat for 30 minutes or until the fish falls apart. Drain and remove the fish flesh.

If you have a food processor, use it. (Whisking by hand can be done, but you'll get a sore arm.) Place the fish in the food processor and, adding the olive oil in a thin stream; pulse the fish until you have a smooth but flaky consistency.

In a saucepan, combine the vinegar with ⅓ cup (80 ml) of water. Pick the leaves off the radicchio and cook them in the vinegar-water mixture for 5 minutes. Remove from the heat. Drain and cut into strips.

Next, brush stale slices of bread with some olive oil and toast in a hot skillet until crispy on both sides. Top with the radicchio and a chunk of salt cod. Finely chop the parsley, sprinkle it over the crostini, season with pepper, and serve.

Tortino alla parmigiana
Eggplant and tomato tart

Preparation time:
15 minutes + 45 minutes
of roasting + 30 minutes
baking

Serves 4

——

INGREDIENTS

1 large eggplant,
  thinly sliced
¼ teaspoon sea salt +
  extra for sprinkling
1 pound (450 g) cherry
  tomatoes, halved
¼ cup (50 g)
  granulated sugar
⅓ cup (75 g) unsalted
  butter, cut into
  small cubes
1 teaspoon chili flakes
1 tablespoon
  tomato paste
1 ¾ ounces (50 g)
  Parmesan, grated
7 ounces (200 g) fresh
  mozzarella, sliced and
  drained on paper towels
4 slices puff pastry, thawed

TIPS
This recipe uses four
4- to 5-inch (10- to 13-cm)
molds. If you don't have
those, 7- or 9-ounce (200
to 255-g) ramekins or 4- to
5-inch (10- to 13-cm) mini
cake or springform pans
would work here.

If you are new to making
caramel, add 1 tablespoon
of water to the sugar to
slow down the process.

You can also make a large
tarte tatin and cut it into
wedges. Simply bake the
cake for about 45 minutes.
And, it can be made
ahead of time by baking
the cake or tarts halfway
and then placing them in
the oven for another 15 to
20 minutes before serving.

Melanzane alla parmigiana is eggplant on steroids and is one of my absolute favorites. Salted eggplant is fried and then layered in a baking dish with tomato sauce, Parmesan cheese, and mozzarella. Umami, fat, and melted cheese—can't say no to that. The father of my former boyfriend, Alessandro (I mentioned him on page 45) had an abundant vegetable garden in his village in Campania. Everyone in the village may have thought we should get married, but I had other ideas. But one thing I did want to do was eat his mother's parmigiana with the vegetables from his father's garden. It was unparalleled in taste. Meaty and so full of flavor. By now there are plenty of good recipes for melanzane alla parmigiana around, so as an ode to the original I came up with a parmigiana tart. It has an unusual presentation and is fun as an appetizer.

Sprinkle the eggplant slices generously with salt; set a cutting board on top and place something heavy (such as a cast iron pan or a large mortar) on top. Let stand for at least 45 minutes. Then thoroughly pat the slices dry.

Preheat the oven to 400°F (200°C) and grease four 4- to 5-inch (10- to 13-cm) molds.

Sprinkle the tomatoes with salt. Place them cut side up in a large baking dish and roast in the oven for 45 minutes. Remove from the oven and let cool slightly.

Melt the sugar over very low heat in a thick-bottomed saucepan. The sugar will bubble and turn caramel-colored. Add the butter to the saucepan and melt. Add ¼ teaspoon of the salt and the chili flakes and stir in the tomato paste, then remove from the heat.

Divide the caramel among the four molds. Place the eggplant slices in them in a circle with the edges overlapping. Sprinkle each with 2 tablespoons of the grated Parmesan.

Divide the mozzarella among the molds. Place the cherry tomatoes cut side down in the molds.

Place a slice of puff pastry on each mold, tucking in at the sides. Slide into the oven and bake for 30 minutes.

Loosen the edges of the tart and carefully flip each over onto plates, then remove the mold, so the puff pastry becomes the bottom layer. Generously grate Parmesan on top and serve immediately.

Polpette di salsiccia all'ascolana
Sausage balls with olives

Preparation time:
30 minutes

Serves 4 (makes about
18 balls)

INGREDIENTS

2 sausages, remove
   and discard casings,
   then chop
¾ cup (115 g) large,
   green olives, chopped*
Freshly grated nutmeg
Zest of 1 lemon
Freshly ground
   black pepper
⅔ cup + 1 tablespoon
   (100 g) all-purpose flour
1 large egg
¾ cup (100 g) dry
   breadcrumbs
Sunflower or peanut oil,
   for frying
Lemon mayo
   (page 368; optional)

*Use large, bright green
sweet olives instead of the
pickled army green ones,
which are too salty.*

Olive ascolane are the tastiest appetizer and the best invention since the printing press. Only Italians overflowing with the love of food could come up with something as delicious as an olive stuffed with sausage meat, which is then also breaded and fried. How many days in Italy must have gone into stuffing all those olives? I like it, but I don't have the patience for it. That's why I came up with a faster version with sausage and olives that tastes exactly like olive ascolane. It's just faster to prepare. Win-win.

In a large bowl, add the sausage and olives and season with a generous amount of nutmeg, lemon zest, and freshly ground black pepper.

Form small olive-shaped balls from the mixture—they must be really small balls, or the inside won't cook through.

Sprinkle the flour onto a plate, whisk the egg in a shallow bowl, and add the breadcrumbs to a separate, shallow bowl. Roll the balls first in the flour, then in the egg, and finally through the breadcrumbs. (You can place on a baking sheet and place them in the refrigerator until you are ready to cook if you would like to prepare them ahead of time. Be sure to remove them from the fridge in time for them to come back up to room temperature before you fry them.)

Heat a generous amount of the oil in a large pan to 340°F (170°C). If you do not have a kitchen thermometer, throw a piece of olive into the oil; when the oil fizzes, it is hot enough. Deep-fry the balls in batches for 3 ½ to 4 minutes or until golden brown and cooked inside. If you have a deep fryer, you can use that, too. Set aside on a paper-towel lined plate.

They are delicious as is, but since I'm into dipping and double-dipping, I suggest serving them with Lemon mayo (page 368).

PRIMI
FIRST COURSE

Pappa al pomodoro con burrata

Tomato bread soup with burrata and spicy ginger oil

Preparation time:
45 minutes

Serves 4

INGREDIENTS

2 cups + 2 tablespoons (500 ml) vegetable broth (page 357 or store bought)
2 thick slices stale bread (I use sourdough)
4 garlic cloves
1 ¼ pounds (570 g) extremely ripe tomatoes (I use not-too-large vine tomatoes)
½ cup (120 ml) extra-virgin olive oil + 3 tablespoons + extra for drizzling
1 tablespoon tomato paste (optional)*
Few sprigs basil
Sea salt
1 ⅛-inch (3-cm) piece ginger, peeled and chopped
1 tablespoon Aleppo pepper
1 ½ teaspoons coriander seeds
½ bulb burrata, quartered

I like to use the tomato paste for extra flavor if the tomatoes aren't quite ripe enough.

TIP

Do like Diego and serve the pappa with fried eggplant slices. Salt these heavily in advance and pressurize them for at least 1 hour to squeeze out as much moisture as possible.

This Tuscan "frugal" bread soup was originally made with pane sciocco (literally, "fool's bread," the typical saltless Tuscan bread) and beautifully ripe tomatoes. Chef Diego Rossi of trattoria Trippa (see page 84) serves it with stracciatella (creamy burrata) and fried eggplant, which is incredibly delicious. My version has less bread and adds spicy oil with ginger. Diego would never do the latter, but what we do agree on is that you make the pappa with fresh tomatoes—never canned! And that it tastes best with sourdough bread, toasted and rubbed with garlic.

Bring a pot of water to a boil and heat the vegetable broth.

Toast the bread and rub it with a garlic clove. Break the bread into pieces, place them in a bowl, and pour the hot broth on top.

Cross the tomatoes with a sharp knife at the top and place them in boiling water for 30 seconds. Rinse them to cool then peel, halve, and remove the hard crown tips. Chop into coarse pieces.

Heat the olive oil in a large pan. (It will seem like a lot, but it's important to use it all). Crush the second of the garlic cloves and let it lightly brown in the oil. Then, remove the garlic if you don't want the flavor to be strong (or you can keep it in, if you love garlic!). Add the tomato paste, if using, the tomatoes, a sprig of basil, and a generous pinch of salt, and cook for 10 minutes.

Add the soaked bread and the broth and stir occasionally. Cook over low heat until all of the liquid is absorbed and it is a thick porridge, about 30 minutes. Remove from the heat and let rest for 10 minutes.

Finely chop the remaining 2 garlic cloves. Heat the remaining 3 tablespoons of olive oil in a saucepan and add the chopped garlic, ginger, and Aleppo pepper. Crush the coriander seeds in a mortar, and add it to the saucepan. Sauté until the garlic is browned and crisp and the herb flavors have infused into the oil. Remove from the heat.

Spoon the lukewarm pappa into bowls. Place a generous helping of Burrata on each, and drizzle the infused oil on top. Garnish with a few torn basil leaves.

Cacciucco di ceci

Tuscan soup with gremolata

Preparation time:
soaking overnight + cooking
for 1½ hours + 20 minutes
or 30 minutes if using
canned chickpeas.

Serves 4

INGREDIENTS

Tuscan soup
1 pound (450 g) dried
  chickpeas, rinsed and
  soaked overnight*
Few sprigs rosemary
1 tablespoon coarse sea salt
3 ½ tablespoons (50 ml)
  extra-virgin olive oil
1 red onion, finely chopped
3 garlic cloves, finely
  chopped + 1 garlic clove
1 tablespoon fennel seeds,
  crushed
8 anchovy fillets,** finely
  chopped
4 to 5 ripe tomatoes
  (10 ½ oz/300 g), sliced
Aged Parmesan cheese crust
  (optional)
14 ounces (400 g) colored
  chard or wild spinach,
  stems removed and
  coarsely chopped
4 thick slices stale bread

Gremolata
1 large bunch (1 oz/30 g)
  Italian parsley, chopped
1 teaspoon fennel seeds,
  crushed
1 garlic clove
Zest of ½ lemon
1 teaspoon lemon juice
Extra-virgin olive oil
Sea salt and freshly ground
  black pepper

*Forgot to soak the chickpeas?
Rinse the dry chickpeas, place
them in a pot with water, bring
them to a boil, and simmer.
Or use 1 ⅓ pounds (600 g) of
canned chickpeas—then you'll
be done really quickly!*

**To make this vegetarian,
replace the anchovies with
1 to 2 tablespoons of red
miso paste.*

This soup, like the better-known ribollita, is made creamy by puréeing some of the legumes with the cooking water. The traditional version calls for chard, but other vegetables such as spinach, kale, or cabbage also taste delicious. While not traditional, it's delicious to finish the soup with gremolata. Topped with a piece of toasted garlic bread, this is the ultimate soup to warm you up on a gray day.

To make the soup, put the soaked chickpeas in a pan with 6 ¼ cups (1 ½ L) of water and the coarse sea salt. Cook over low heat with a lid on the pan until they are soft but still firm, which will take a good 1 to 1½ hours.

Heat the olive oil in a large skillet and sauté the onion over medium-high heat until translucent and soft. Add the chopped garlic and sauté for a few more minutes. Add the fennel seeds and chopped anchovies. (The amount of anchovy sounds ridiculously high, but it won't taste fishy.)

Add the tomatoes then continue to sauté for another few minutes until the liquid has evaporated. Next, hold the pan at an angle and purée with a hand blender until smooth, or transfer to a blender and blend until smooth.

Using a slotted spoon, add a third of the cooked chickpeas into the pan with the tomato purée. Separately, using a blender, purée the rest of the chickpeas with 3 ⅓ cups (800 ml) of the cooking liquid and add to the tomato mixture. Add the chard (if using chard, add the stems first and cook them a few minutes longer than the leaves). If you have a leftover Parmesan rind, throw it in and cook it with the mixture to add complexity to the flavor. Simmer for another 15 minutes, adding additional liquid if the mixture becomes too thick. Season the soup with salt and freshly ground black pepper.

To make the Gremolata, place the parsley and fennel seeds in a bowl. Grate ¼ of a garlic clove on a sharp, fine grater over the bowl. Add the lemon zest along with the juice and a pinch of salt. Add 1 to 2 tablespoons of olive oil and mix together.

Brush the slices of bread with olive oil, grill them, and rub with the remaining garlic. Remove the Parmesan rind and serve the soup with a drizzle of olive oil and gremolata with toast on the side.

Passatina di ceci con gamberi

Creamy chickpea and shrimp soup with spicy tomato oil

Preparation time:
soaking overnight +
1½ hours (or 40 minutes
with canned chickpeas)

Serves 4

___

INGREDIENTS

¼ cup (60 ml) extra-virgin
   olive oil
2 garlic cloves, sliced
1 sprig rosemary
1 carrot, diced
2 celery stalks, sliced
12 ¼ ounces (350 g) dried
   chickpeas, soaked
   overnight and drained
6 ½ cups (1 ½ L) vegetable
   broth (page 357 or store
   bought)
Sea salt
12 large shrimp, peeled
   and deveined
Few sprigs Italian parsley,
   finely chopped

Spicy tomato oil
(optional; page 369)

TIP

For a quick version,
use two cans of canned
chickpeas, or to hurry
your soaking if you got a
late start, check out the
chickpea soaking tip
on page 68.

This creamy soup is a rip-off of chef Fulvio Pierangelini's passatina di ceci e gamberi, a 1980s dish that every Italian knows. Fulvio doesn't believe in recipes; he thinks it's pointless to solidify dishes in writing when they are constantly evolving. So, you can adapt this soup to the ingredients you have on hand. You can replace chickpeas with dried fava beans or white beans, and in place of shrimp you could use langoustines (or even crawfish). But shellfish or squid is also delicious. I like a kick so I finish my passatina with spicy tomato oil. That's extra tasty, but you can do without, too, if you prefer.

Heat a large saucepan and add 2 tablespoons of the olive oil, the garlic slices, and rosemary, and sauté until the garlic is a toasty brown. Add the carrot and celery and sauté the vegetables for a few minutes. Add the drained chickpeas, broth, and season with salt. Cook the chickpeas for 1 to 1 ½ hours or until soft. Remove the sprig of rosemary. Purée the mixture into a smooth, even creamy texture with a hand blender. Taste and season with salt if necessary.

Cut the shrimp in half lengthwise and sprinkle with a pinch of salt.

Heat the remaining 2 tablespoons of olive oil in a skillet and fry the shrimp briefly until just cooked through.

Divide the soup among four bowls. Place the shrimp on top, drizzle on the spicy tomato oil, if using, and garnish with the parsley.

ABOUT PASTA

"More than the Italian national anthem and the constitution of the republic, pasta is an indispensable part of the Italian nationality," writes food historian Alberto Grandi in his book *Denominazione di Origine Inventata*. He then goes on to show how Italian a plate of pasta with tomato sauce actually is. Not that Italian, actually with tomatoes from South America and pasta that came to Italy via the Middle East. But those are historical details. Interesting for perspective, but no matter how you look at it, today pasta is the symbol of Italy. From Sophia Loren to Prime Minister Giorgia Meloni, everyone has grown up with it. In this chapter, I tell you more about fresh pasta.

FARINA '00' (sometimes just called "00") flour is prescribed for fresh pasta, which sounds very specialized. The number refers to the degree of milling: the lower the number, the more milled, and the finer the flour. Flour with a number above Type 2 is whole-wheat flour.

SEMOLA DI GRANO DURO RIMACINATA Semola rimacinata is what we, in the US, refer to as "semolina." There are also non-fine groats, semola di grano duro, which is ideal for dusting your work surface when kneading or rolling out pasta sheets. The grit is larger and does not soak into the dough as quickly. So, it also affects the dough less. It's tricky, I know! They all sound similar, but there is a difference!

Often pasta is made with one part "00" flour and one part semolina di grano duro. The more semolina, the firmer the pasta. Semolina is high in protein, and it has a pale-yellow color.

To make pasta, therefore, you need: "00" flour, semolina, and the coarser semola di grano duro to dust the work surface and pasta sheets. The proportions vary for each pasta and depend on personal preference. You can also use all-purpose flour, but the dough will be less firm in structure and paler in color.

WITH OR WITHOUT EGG? You also need water or egg, or sometimes both. Traditionally egg is used in the north and water is used in the south, but nowadays you can also find pasta with egg in southern Italy. With large eggs, you sometimes need to add more flour to avoid sticky dough, and with small eggs, add just a pinch of water so the dough doesn't get too dry. In Italy, no one agrees on what the correct proportions are. In Emilia-Romagna, they use 1 whole egg to ⅔ cup + 1 tablespoon (100 g) of flour while in Lombardy they use a combination of whole eggs and egg yolks. The Piemontesi take the crown: their luxurious tajarin (tagliolini) uses as many as 30 egg yolks to 6 ¼ cups (¾ kg) of flour (in the north they often use regular flour and not semolina). Eggs make for beautifully pliable and resilient pasta. Sometimes a drop of oil is added to the dough, sometimes a pinch of salt. Neither is right or wrong; it depends on personal preference and the type of pasta you're making.

MAKING PASTA DOUGH This outline is very general because as you have just read, opinions and techniques differ. The specific ratios per recipe are mentioned on pages 360-365. Making pasta dough by hand is best, especially for a small quantity. It can also be done in a food processor, preferably using the plastic dough blades, which stress the dough less than metal blades.

Heap oo flour and semolina (if using) into a pile on a clean work surface and form a wide pit in the center with your fist. Sprinkle a pinch of salt in there, if desired, and then break the eggs into it, or add water if you are working with water. Also have a bowl of water ready to moisten your hands if the dough feels too stiff.

Break up the yolks with your fingertips or with a fork. Moving your fingers in a circular motion, combine the flour little by little until you have a coarse dough. Scrape it together with a dough scraper or your hands and form it into a ball. Knead for 10 minutes by pressing it away from you with the palms of your hands, folding it in half and repeating. Turn the dough each time so you work it evenly. Moisten your hands if it feels too dry. The dough should be firm and elastic but not sticky. If it springs back when you prick it with your finger, it's good. Otherwise, knead a little longer. Let the dough rest on the counter in plastic wrap for 30 minutes to 1 hour.

Dust your work surface with semola di grano duro. Divide the pasta dough into quarters, and work with one piece at a time. Cover the remaining dough with a cloth or plastic wrap to keep it from drying out. Flatten the piece of dough and pass it through a pasta machine, starting at the widest setting. Turn the handle with one hand and catch the pasta with your other hand. Fold in half and repeat. Move to the next position and pull the sheet through again. Repeat and move on to the next position, and so on. If the sheets get too long, cut them in half, so it is more workable. To make the dough elastic and shiny, you can repeat this process multiple times. Just fold the rolled-out pasta sheet again and start from scratch. The thickness of the pasta depends on the variety. The thicknesses are specified with the recipes.

ROLLING PIN If you don't have a pasta machine, you can roll out the dough with a rolling pin. Let the dough hang partially off the table, that way it stretches well. With a knife, you can cut tagliatelle or pappardelle from the pasta sheets or you can make stuffed pasta from them.

STUFFED PASTA Make sure the filling is not too wet, or the dough may tear. If it feels too wet, add extra Parmesan or breadcrumbs. Be sure to salt the filling generously because some of the flavor is lost during cooking. Do not dust the pasta with semola di grano duro if you are making filled pasta or the sheets will not stick together when you are ready to seal them.

COLORS Pasta can be colored! For example, add unsweetened cocoa powder, squid ink, tomato paste, beet juice, or well squeezed, chopped spinach until it forms the shade of color you would like.

STORING PASTA Dust a baking sheet with semola di grano duro, place the fresh pasta sheets on top and dust again with more semola. Place long pasta in piles, turning them occasionally to allow them to dry on all sides. Place ravioli side by side, never on top of each other.

Cover the pasta with a cloth. It is best not to store fresh uncooked pasta in the refrigerator; the dough may turn green. However, you can store fresh pasta in the freezer. This is especially handy for stuffed pasta. Stuffed pasta cannot be kept too long before cooking because the stuffing can go bad or make the dough wet, which can cause it to tear. So, freeze it if you don't plan to cook stuffed pasta right away. When you are ready to eat it, put the pasta directly into boiling water without defrosting it.

COOKING PASTA

If you want to depress an Italian, give him pasta scotta (overcooked pasta), cook it in unsalted water and then blob the sauce on top, serve pasta as a side dish, or—the worst—throw in a seasoning packet so you have a one-pot meal. Pasta in Italy is a primo (the first course), and that's how I serve it because I was thoroughly brainwashed in Italy. The quantities in this book are also based on that. I serve side dishes like vegetables or meat and fish separately. Maybe you already know how to cook pasta like an Italian, and you are not reading anything new here. Still, I'm going to give you a stern talking to just to be sure.

LA PASTA NON ASPETTA The pasta doesn't wait. Cook it just before serving and preferably serve in preheated shallow bowls.

PASTA MUST SWIM IN WATER AS SALTY AS THE SEA My nineteen-year-old ears heard the message loud and clear: *"Non c'hai messo il sale!"* ("You didn't add salt!"). For cooking pasta, I use a tablespoon, per 4 ¼ cups (1L) of boiling water. Not all that salt ends up in the pasta; it just adds flavor. Also, use a pot large enough so the pasta isn't crowded. I use 4 ¼ cups (1 L) of water per 3 ½ ounces (100 g) of pasta.

AL DENTE Fresh pasta is cooked before being dried so cooking times are quick. Thin, long pasta needs 2 to 3 minutes and stuffed pasta 4 to 5 minutes. With dried pasta, it depends on the type so it's best to cook for the shortest time noted on the package instructions. Then check the doneness by tasting and your preference. What I find al dente, you may find al chiodo (hard as nails). But err on the side of cooking a little too al dente, because pasta will continue to cook once in the sauce.

PREVENT STICKY PASTA When you add the pasta to the boiling water, stir a few times to prevent it from sticking to the bottom or to itself. Stop stirring when the water boils again. Do not add oil to the water. The oil floats on the water and stays there. It is a waste and doesn't help with sticking. What does help against sticking is mixing the cooked pasta directly into the sauce as soon as it's done.

SPADELLARE E MANTECARE Make sure you have the warm sauce on standby when you put the pasta in the boiling water. Never rinse cooked pasta with cold water, you'll rinse away the starch, and the sauce will roll right off the pasta. Instead, immediately transfer the pasta from the boiling water to the sauce. Preferably into a lightweight skillet (see page 20). For long pasta, use tongs; and for delicate stuffed pasta, scoop it from the cooking water with a slotted spoon. Then start spadellare, which is mixing the pasta with the sauce. This way the pasta will take on the flavor of the sauce. Then, depending on the recipe, the 'mantecare' follows, adding something fatty like butter or cheese and stir vigorously. Do this off the heat and mix until you have a creamy consistency. If it's dryer than you would like, ladle in some of the water the pasta was just cooked in to create a saucy consistency.

NOT TOO MUCH SAUCE The pasta should swim in the boiling water, but not in the sauce! The amount of sauce should be just enough to stick to your pasta.

COOKING WATER Always keep the water you just used to cook the pasta handy because you can add a ladleful into the sauce if things are too dry. Pasta cooking liquid is flavorful, because it's salty as the sea and rich in starch, which binds the sauce into a creamy consistency.

METAL BOWLS Pasta stays hot longer in a metal bowl, which is useful if you're cooking several batches, as is often the case when making stuffed pasta for a crowd. I have stacks of metal bowls and they are ideal for mixing large amounts of pasta and sauce. By making circular motions with the bowl, the pasta mixes by itself and does not break down.

FORK OR SPOON Unless it's in broth, pasta should be eaten with a fork. Never cut long pasta with a knife, duh. Instead, wind it around your fork using your spoon. Start with a few strands and twist it into a manageable roll.

WHICH PASTA GOES WITH WHICH SAUCE There are more than 300 different types of pasta. The most popular are spaghetti, penne, fusilli, and rigatoni. There are certain rules for combining sauce and pasta, some are more vague than others. Here's a rule of thumb: pasta with a lot of texture such as whole-wheat pasta, pappardelle, or bucatini goes well with hearty sauces such as ragù or spicy tomato sauce. Delicate pasta such as capellini goes well with light sauces and seafood. Pasta with a rough or ridged surface holds sauce better than smooth types. And orecchiette are good for sauces that are not very saucy, because all sorts of things remain in the shells.

"IF YOU WANT TO DEPRESS AN ITALIAN, GIVE HIM PASTA SCOTTA, OVERCOOKED PASTA."

OFFAL ACTIVIST
Diego Rossi

Milan. I once spent three months in this city of fashion dolls and pirla (Milanese for "jerks," not literally translated) with stand-up polo collars. You couldn't find a decent brioche there; you could forget about good pizza. How different it is now. After 2015, the year of Expo Milano, the world exhibition whose theme was food, the city experienced a renaissance. Milan transformed from a productive-but-boring metropolis into a bountiful food emporium.

Verona-born Diego Rossi is a passionate chef with an old soul and foresight. He opened trattoria Trippa the same year as the Expo, when the reinvention of the trattoria had just begun. Diego made his neo-trattoria into a place where he cooks stellar food in a setting without fancy fuss. Trippa has become one of Milan's most sought-after spots. Besides trippa fritta (fried tripe with lots of pepper), we eat roasted carrots with bacon, stuffed pasta with broccoli, and lasagna made of cabbage. There is a lot of meat, but also a lot of vegetables on the menu. Although Diego has named his joint Trippa, which means "tripe," he hardly eats meat himself. He is, however, an ardent fan of il quinto quarto or "the fifth quarter" which means that you use all parts of the animal. But with Diego, it goes further. He is a kind of offal fanatic who need only look at the texture of meat to understand what kind of preparation it requires.

When we visit Diego, his place is packed. The place is bubbling like champagne; there are creatives, sophisticated older people, and squeaky-clean young people. "When, as a kid, the day I was allowed to make coffee in the moka (percolator), my love of cooking began," he tells us. "For the first time, I felt I was doing something independently." Diego's mother was a teacher, his father drove a truck, and so fourteen-year-old Diego often had to whip up something at home by himself. That sparked his curiosity.

He honed his skills in the fine dining scene in the Dolomites and Piedmont. "But I wasn't free. I was not allowed to work with certain ingredients, a lot was thrown away and the dishes were mainly about the chef." A trattoria focuses on the real thing: the preparation by the nonnas and how and why it was created.

Diego makes traditional food sparkle again with modern techniques. Think cibreo, a Tuscan dish with chicken guts, or his famous bulbous vitello tonnato, a dish made of veal and fish. At Trippa, Diego is free. Free to open only during dinner, free to decide what ingredients he works with, though he won't use soy sauce. "But I've imposed that on myself." How important is tradition in such a modern trattoria? For Diego, "Tradition means history. To understand where we come from, we have to know that history, that's the only way you can face the future." In the past, terroir and season dictated what you used and that became tradition. "In Piedmont people combined anchovies with artichoke hearts because that was available; in Rome they used chicory instead. Now many vegetables can be found everywhere. To make new traditions today is difficult," the chef philosophizes. "Maybe we need a new word."

Diego hopes that in the future Italian cuisine will take its cue from nature, because right now we are eating wrong, he believes. "One of the success factors of Italian cuisine is the Mediterranean climate; our products are of unprecedented quality." That climate is now changing at an alarming rate, so we need to eat differently. Above all, we should eat more vegetables, he believes, and much less meat. But if we do eat meat, it should be of high quality and at a higher price. "And using the whole animal."

"ITALIAN CUISINE HAS HEARTY FLAVORS. WE USE A LOT OF SALT AND FAT IN EVERYTHING. IT IS A CUISINE ON STEROIDS!"

Triangoli con sauerkraut

Triangle pasta with sauerkraut, creamy Parmesan, and crumbled pancetta

Preparation time:
1½ hours

Serves 4

INGREDIENTS

Pasta dough with egg
(page 360)

10 ½ ounces (300 g)
   russet potatoes
Sea salt and freshly
   ground black pepper
3 tablespoons
   unsalted butter
¾ cup (175 g) sauerkraut,
   drained
3 bay leaves
4 juniper berries
5 ¼ ounces (150 g)
   pancetta, cubed
1 tablespoon caraway
   seeds, toasted
3 ½ ounces (100 g)
   Parmesan, grated

I ate this pasta at the mega-popular Trippa in Milan, Chef Diego Rossi (see page 84) stuffed them with broccoli, a creamy cheese sauce, and lots of pepper. Diego plans to live in the mountains in northern Italy at some point. I immediately envisioned a romantic wooden mountain hut, and on the menu this ravioli filled with tangy cabbage, creamy cheese sauce, and crispy pancetta. I described the recipe idea to him, somewhat embarrassed because of the sauerkraut. But he was very enthusiastic. "Buoni coi crauti!" (Very good with Sauerkraut!)

Make the pasta dough and let it rest for 30 minutes.

Boil the potatoes in their skins until tender, let cool, and pass through a masher or press through a fine sieve. Season with plenty of salt.

Melt the butter in a saucepan and add the sauerkraut and bay leaves. Finely crush the juniper berries and add them as well. Simmer on low for 10 minutes. Remove the bay leaf and mix the sauerkraut into the mashed potatoes.

To make the triangle pasta, cut squares about 4-by-4 inches (10-by-10 cm) from the pasta sheets. In the center of each square, place a spoonful of the potato-sauerkraut filling. Wet the edges of the pasta with water and fold the square into a triangle. Squeeze out the air and press the edges well. Store on a floured cloth or on a floured baking sheet. Continue until you have used all of the pasta squares. Never make stuffed pasta too far in advance; the moisture in the filling can cause the pasta to tear.

Wipe out the saucepan. Fry the pancetta until crispy then let cool on a paper towel-lined plate. Bring a large, salted pot of water to a boil.

In another saucepan, heat the cream (it must not boil!) and add the Parmesan. Stir so that the cheese melts evenly and then keep it warm over low heat.

Cook the triangles in the generously salted boiling water until they rise to the top. Remove them from the pan with a slotted spoon, shake off the cooking water, and set them onto plates. Cover the triangles with the cheese sauce, sprinkle with caraway seeds, crispy pancetta, and plenty of freshly ground black pepper.

Tortelloni di zucca e noci

Tortelloni with butternut squash, walnut, and black garlic butter

Preparation time:
2 hours

Serves 4 (makes about 26 pieces)

INGREDIENTS

Pasta dough with egg
(page 360)

1 large butternut squash
(about 2 ¼ lbs/1 kg)
Sea salt and freshly
ground pepper
3 tablespoons mild
olive oil
Freshly grated nutmeg
6 walnuts, shelled
6 sprigs sage
1 ¾ ounces (50 g)
Parmesan, grated +
extra
1 bulb black garlic
1 tablespoon balsamic
vinegar
3 tablespoons extra-virgin
olive oil
½ teaspoon chili powder
3 tablespoons unsalted
butter

I have no patience for making tortellini. There is too much folding. But, give me tortelloni—the larger version of the pasta—and I'm in. You have to set aside a Sunday afternoon for that too, but it's worth it. In northern Italy, pasta stuffed with butternut squash is a typical autumn classic. I came up with a variant made with black garlic, which has a pleasant flavor along with a hint of acidity because of the fermentation. And it tastes excellent with sweet butternut squash filling.

Make the pasta dough and let it rest for 30 minutes.

Preheat the oven to 400°F (200°C).

Peel the butternut squash, remove the seeds and threads, and dice the flesh. Spread on a baking sheet lined with parchment paper, sprinkle with salt, drizzle with the mild olive oil, and roast in the oven until you see brown spots here and there, approximately 45 minutes. Remove from the oven, and using a blender, purée until smooth. Season to taste with nutmeg. Roast the walnuts in the oven for 8 minutes, turning them halfway through. Remove from the oven and coarsely chop. Finely chop the leaves of 4 sage sprigs and mix in a small bowl with the walnuts and Parmesan.

Roll out the pasta dough into thin sheets as described on page 74. Cut out squares approximately 4-by-4 inches (10-by-10 cm). Bring a large salted pot of water to a boil.

Spoon 1 to 2 tablespoons of butternut squash filling into the center of each square and fold into a triangle. Press the edges well so that it's sealed tightly, moistening them with some water if necessary. Fold the edges along the filling and glue the ends together under the tortelloni.

Repeat with the remaining dough. Place the tortelloni on a work surface dusted with semola. Do not leave them for more than 20 minutes before cooking.

Mix the black garlic cloves with the balsamic vinegar, extra-virgin olive oil, and the chili powder in a blender. It will not be very smooth, which is not a problem. In a large frying pan, melt the butter and add the black garlic mixture with the remaining sage leaves.

Meanwhile, cook the tortelloni until tender in heavily salted water. Remove them from the pan with a slotted spoon when they float to the surface and place them into the skillet with the black garlic butter. Gently stir the tortelloni in the garlic-butter and spoon into deep plates. Sprinkle with more Parmesan.

Culurgiones con patate e porri

Pasta stuffed with potato, leek, and chili butter

Preparation time:
1½ hours

Serves 4 (makes about
30 pieces)

INGREDIENTS

**Pasta dough for
culurgiones**
(page 361)

1 ¼ pounds (570 g)
   russet potatoes
1½ tablespoons extra-virgin
   olive oil
1 garlic clove, crushed
½ cup (113 g) unsalted
   butter
3 leeks, greens removed
   and whites cut into rings
Sea salt and freshly ground
   black pepper
1 ¾ ounces (50 g) pecorino
   + more for topping,
   grated
6 sprigs fresh mint leaves,
   finely chopped
2 tablespoons olive oil
4 teaspoons
   Aleppo pepper
1 tablespoon dried
   mint leaves

TIPS
The older the potatoes,
the drier and the better
for stuffing.

Save discarded leek greens
for soup.

For more tips, see also
"About Pasta" on page 73.

Traditionally, culurgiones
are served with tomato
sauce or sage and butter.
Experiment with the sauce,
even with the filling. For
example, add seafood
or saffron to the mashed
potatoes.

Culurgiones can be described as Sardinian pasta pillows, filled
with potato, pecorino, and mint. I serve them with smoky Aleppo
pepper butter, like Turkish stuffed pasta. They are beautiful with
their chiusura a spiga (grain motif closure) but can be intimidating
to make. You really have to practice. My first one looked like crap,
but after some swearing, it improved. "Non mi rompere i culurgiones!"
I shouted, thinking of the famous Italian phrase "*Non mi rompere
i coglioni,*"which roughly translates as "Don't break my balls!"
The saying comes in handy with pushy types. It also helps
with culurgiones. Try it!

Make the pasta dough, and let it rest for at least 30 minutes.

Boil the potatoes in their skins thoroughly and let cool slightly.

Heat the olive oil in a saucepan, brown the garlic, remove from heat,
and allow the flavor of garlic to infuse the oil.

Melt ¼ cup (55 g) of the butter in a large saucepan. Sauté the leek rings
with a pinch of salt until soft and sweet, then purée the leeks with a
hand mixer until smooth.

Peel the potatoes and press them through a potato ricer or a fine sieve.
In a large bowl, mix the potatoes with the leeks and pecorino. Remove the
garlic from the oil and pour the oil into the potato mixture. Add the fresh
mint leaves. Mix everything together, taste and then add salt and pepper
if you want to.

Roll out the pasta dough into sheets and cut out rounds as described
on page 361.

Place 1 tablespoon of filling in the center of each round, press well, and
fold up the sides. Then, starting at the bottom, pinch the dough closed
between thumb and forefinger and push inward toward the filling. Press
the rest of the sides in the same way until the whole pillow is closed and
you have a nice grain pattern. If some stuffing comes out, it's no big deal.

It may not go well at first, but you'll soon get better at it. If it really doesn't
work out, you can always switch the plan to making ravioli, which is easier.
If you go that route, fold the rounds in half and glue them shut with some
water. Or if it's a complete disaster, just throw everything against the wall.

If things have gone well, place the culurgiones on a floured tea towel
(see page 74 for storage tips). Bring a large salted pot of water to a boil.
Cook them, a few at a time, in boiling salted water until tender.

Meanwhile, melt the remaining ¼ cup (55 g) of butter with the mild olive
oil in a large pan and add the Aleppo pepper and dried mint.

When the culurgiones come bobbing to the surface, use a slotted spoon to
scoop them into the pan with the chili-mint butter. Make sure all sides are
coated with butter, and serve. Add additional grated pecorino cheese,
if desired.

Pappardelle al ragù di cinghiale

Rye pappardelle with wild boar ragù

Preparation time:
marinate overnight +
30 minutes + 2 ½ hours
of stewing (or don't
marinate and then stew
a little longer)

Serves 6

___

INGREDIENTS

Rye pappardelle
(page 364 or store bought)

2 carrots
2 celery stalks
4 garlic cloves
2 ¼ pounds (1 kg)
   boar stew meat,
   cut into 2-by-2-inch
   (5-by-5-cm) cubes
1 branch sage
1 sprig rosemary
6 bay leaves
2 tablespoons
   juniper berries
2 tablespoons black
   peppercorns
1 bottle red wine
¼ cup (60 ml) mild olive oil
   + extra for searing
1 onion, chopped
2 tablespoons
   tomato paste
One 14.5 ounce (411g)
can peeled tomatoes
1 tablespoon sea salt
Grated Parmesan,
   for topping

Gianni, the father of my Florentine ex, Lorenzo, was a hunter. I once went with him on the hunt. I walked through a dew-shrouded landscape at the crack of dawn, following the men in fancy felt hunting suits. Whereas I wore an oversized bomber jacket against the cold with Lorenzo's borrowed 501 jeans. When the hunt was over, we ate idiotically delicious food at the gamekeeper's house. If babbo Gianni shot a boar, the Filipino house cook, Agostino, would make pappardelle with it. When I proudly told my girlfriends about it back home, they looked at me with slight disgust. Boar? Yuck. But they were wrong; it is a delicious and flavorful stewing meat and it doesn't taste too gamey. My children like it, anyway. Because of the hearty sauce, I pair it with pappardelle made with rye flour. You could also make whole-wheat pappardelle, or with part buckwheat flour. It's all delicious.

Make the pasta dough and allow it to rest for at least 30 minutes.

Roughly chop 1 carrot and 1 celery stalk, crush 2 garlic cloves, and add to a large bowl with the meat. Add the sage, rosemary, 3 bay leaves, 1 tablespoon juniper berries, 1 tablespoon black peppercorns, and enough wine for the meat to be submerged. Cover and let marinate for 1 night (preferably) or at least a few hours.

Pour out the wine and discard the herbs and spices.

Grate the remaining carrot on a fine grater and slice the remaining celery stalk. Pour the olive oil into a large saucepan and add the onion, carrot, and celery. Mix in the tomato paste and simmer until the vegetables are soft. Chop the remaining cloves of garlic, add to the pan and sautee with the vegetables.

Meanwhile, pat the meat dry and then add it to a large, heavy saucepan with a lid or a Dutch oven, drizzle with a small amount of oil and sear the meat over high heat. Deglaze with a splash of red wine. Add the tomatoes and some water (if the meat and vegetables are not fully submerged). Season with salt. Crush the remaining black peppercorns and juniper berries in a mortar and add along with the remaining bay leaves. Simmer over low heat for 2 to 2 ½ hours with the lid halfway on the pan.

Cook the pappardelle to al dente in the salted boiling water. Mix through the ragù and serve with grated Parmesan.

Fazzoletti con verdure e pesto

Fazzoletti with asparagus, peas, and bread pesto

Preparation time:
1 hour + 15 minutes

Serves 4

___

INGREDIENTS

Pasta dough with egg
(page 360 or store bought)

Bread pesto
1 thick slice stale bread
3 ½ ounces (100 g)
   basil leaves
5 tablespoons ice water
½ garlic clove
⅔ cup (160 ml) not-too-
   spicy extra-virgin olive
   oil + extra
3 ½ ounces (100 g)
   Parmesan cheese,
   grated
2 tablespoons lemon juice
Sea salt and freshly
   ground black pepper
1 pound (450 g) of green
   asparagus
7 ounces (200 g) peas

TIP

Instead of using only
basil, you can also add
other herbs to your
pesto. Think tarragon,
dill, and marjoram.
Or a combination.
Pesto is great for using
leftover herbs.

Fazzoletto means handkerchief, and that's where these 4-by-4-inch (10-by-10-cm) square pasta sheets get their name. I am not too precise with those squares and just cut pieces of dough into squarish rectangles. So, my handkerchiefs are somewhere between fazzoletti and maltagliati (literally "badly cut.") I use fazzoletti dough to make flat pasta sheets but it is also used to hold pasta fillings, like a surprise package. The bread pesto with it is an invention of Chef Massimo Bottura. He came up with it for a project on food waste. Bread is one of the most discarded ingredients in restaurant kitchens, and since Italian cuisine is keen on wasting as little as possible, and real Italian pine nuts are now screamingly scarce and expensive, Bottura came up with bread pesto.

First, make the pasta dough.

Cut the pasta sheets into squares about 3-by-3 inches (7 ½-by-7 ½ cm). If you make the pasta ahead of time, you can lightly dust the sheets with semola di grano duro and store them in a sealable refrigerator box.

Bring a large pot of water to a boil and salt it.

Grind the stale bread in a food processor. Remove and set aside half of the ground bread for the crispy crumb topping.

Next, add the basil and, while the food processor is on, add the ice water, garlic, oil, Parmesan, and lemon juice. Turn off the food processor and taste the pesto, then season with pepper.

Meanwhile, cut off and discard the woody lower part of the asparagus stems and then cut the soft, green part of the stems into thin, round slices. Leave the tops intact. Add the peas and asparagus to the boiling water and cook for 3 minutes (so they are still firm). Remove them from the boiling water with a slotted spoon and transfer to a large bowl.

Using the same boiling water, cook the pasta sheets in batches to al dente (it will only take a few minutes for each batch). Stir well while the pasta is cooking so the sheets don't stick. Scoop them out of the boiling water with a slotted spoon and place them into the bowl with the vegetables. Add the pesto and swirl the bowl to mix the pasta with the sauce. Add some pasta cooking water to loosen it, if needed.

Next, in a skillet over medium heat, add the reserved breadcrumbs and a drizzle of oil. Stir constantly until they are toasty brown.

Spoon the fazzoletti onto plates and sprinkle with the toasted breadcrumbs.

CLEMENTE X P M
ANNVENTE
ORATORII CONGREGATIO
PVBLICAE COMMODITATI
ET FACILIORI
AD ECCLESIAM ACCESSV
VIAM APERVIT STRAVITQVE
AN IVBILEI M DC LXXV

Carbonara blasfema
Blasphemous carbonara

Preparation time:
25 minutes

Serves 4

INGREDIENTS

- 5 ¼ ounces (150 g) guanciale (pork cheek bacon) or pancetta or bacon, cut into small cubes
- 12 ounces (340 g) spaghetti
- 4 egg yolks
- 1 whole egg
- 5 ¼ ounces (150 g) grated cheese (I use half Parmesan and half pecorino)
- 1 teaspoon black peppercorns
- 1 shot (30 ml) vodka (optional)

TIPS

Don't eat meat? Then make carbonara with one of the many plant-based bacon substitutes, or replace the bacon with fried capers.

If you would like to add vegetables, I suggest chicory, Brussel sprouts, or chard.

The Roman classic spaghetti alla carbonara is the most popular pasta dish of all. It is the pasta that conservative Italians are very theatrical and purist about while many hardly seem to know the history of the dish. For example, carbonara with cream would be blasphemy now, whereas the original actually contained cream, according to food professor Alberto Grandi. He explains that this pasta originated with the arrival of Americans in Italy after World War II. They brought bacon and egg powder with them, which was transformed into carbonara by the locals. I don't use cream, but mostly because I think it's cool that combining eggs, cheese, and starchy pasta water makes one of the riches sauces on earth. But I'm not going to be a purist if you want to add cream. I use 'guanciale' (pork cheek bacon) but if you prefer, you can use bacon or pancetta. My carbonara is pretty close to the original. I often add bitter vegetables, which taste great with the rich sauce. And sometimes, if I'm in a naughty mood, I pour in a shot of vodka.

Fill a pot with salted water and bring to a boil.

Fry the pork cheek bacon, pancetta or bacon until it is between chewy and slightly crispy, remove it from the pan, and place it on a paper towel. Leave the rendered fat in the pan; it will mix with your sauce later.

Add the pasta to the boiling water and stir often so the pasta does not stick together.

Meanwhile, in a bowl, mix the egg yolks with the egg and grated cheese. Add a tablespoon of pasta cooking water to the mixture and combine well. Set aside.

Grind the peppercorns in a mortar or pepper grinder.

Cook the pasta to al dente. It will be cooked more in the following step. Scoop the pasta out of the water with a slotted spoon or kitchen tongs and transfer it to the skillet with the bacon, pork cheek, or pancetta fat. Add a tablespoon of pasta water to the skillet.

Cook the pasta, water, and bacon grease over medium heat until the liquid has evaporated almost completely. Remove from the heat. Now you have a nice, starchy base that will pair deliciously with the sauce.

Next, add the egg and cheese mixture into the pan. Mix it well so it forms a creamy consistency. Pour in a shot of vodka, if using, and mix it in well. Finish with lots of black pepper.

Cacio e pepe con fave e menta

Cheesy pasta with fava beans and mint

Preparation time:
45 minutes

Serves 4

INGREDIENTS

3 pounds (1.5 kg)
   fava beans,
   in the pods
7 ounces (200 g)
   cheese (3 oz [80 g]
   pecorino and
   4 oz [120 g]
   Parmesan), grated
Coarse sea salt
12 ounces (340 g)
   long pasta
   (tonnarelli or
   thick spaghetti)
1 tablespoon black
   peppercorns
Few sprigs
   mint leaves

Cacio e pepe is a Roman classic. The preparation shows how simple yet ingenious Italian cuisine is. Starchy pasta water + melted grated cheese = creamy sauce. You do have to be careful so you don't end up with a melted cheese ball. If you get everything ready ahead of time and follow the instructions below, you'll be fine.

Traditionally you use pecorino but you can also mix in part Parmesan, which makes the flavor more refined. Adding the fava beans is a variation from the classic recipe and is reminiscent of the other well-known classic: fave con pecorino. At trattoria Sora Lella in Rome, they include mint with the cacio e pepe. Mannaggia (damn!), that's a genius addition to those hearty, peppery flavors!

Start by double podding the fava beans, which is a bit of a chore. You can also do this ahead of time, or use child labor if you have a cooperative kid on hand. Remove the beans from their pods. Blanch them, rinse in cold water and then remove from their individual shells: slice them open with your thumb nail and gently squeeze so they will pop out of their jackets. Very little ones don't need to be removed from their individual shells.

Mix the grated cheeses in a bowl. Bring another pot of water to a boil and salt it. Because you need a lot of starch in the pasta water to use for the creamy sauce, put less water in the pot than usual. I also salt it less because of the salty cheese. Say 1 tablespoon of coarse sea salt to 2 ½ quarts (2.4 L) of water. Cook the pasta al dente because it will cook more in the skillet later.

Meanwhile, toast the peppercorns over medium-high heat in a large skillet. Stop when the aroma is released, approximately 5 minutes, and then set the skillet aside. This is where the pasta will go later.

Allow the peppercorns to cool, transfer them to a mortar or pepper grinder, and grind coarsely. Return the pepper to the skillet and pour a tablespoon of pasta cooking liquid over the pepper.

Using tongs or a slotted spoon, transfer the pasta from the water, and place it in the skillet.

Over medium heat, use a spatula to stir the pasta, pepper, and pasta water mixture together vigorously. Then add a bit more pasta water and stir vigorously again. Continue the process until the pasta has fully cooked. Remove the pasta pan from the heat.

Next, mix in pasta water ½ tablespoon at a time into the melted cheese, until the sauce becomes creamy (be sure to add the water slowly and mix well, otherwise there is a chance that the cheese will get stringy!). Continue to stir the mixture until it becomes a kind of thick cheese paste. Add to the pasta and mix well. Pour in a little more pasta cooking liquid and then stir again. Repeat adding water and stirring until you have a smooth consistency that coats the pasta. You'll add more pasta cooking liquid than you think because the pasta soaks it up. When you stir the whole thing, it should make a wet sound. Mix in the fava beans at the last minute. Sprinkle with chopped mint and eat immediately.

Vignarola con fregola

Spring stew with fregola, fava beans, peas, and artichoke

Preparation time:
1 hour + 15 minutes

Serves 4

___

INGREDIENTS

2 ½ ounces (75 g) dried
  seaweed (kombu)*
2 ¼ pounds (1 kg) fava
  beans, in the pods
5¼ ounces (150 g) fresh
  shelled peas
6 small artichokes
1½ lemons
Sea salt and freshly ground
  black pepper
5 tablespoons extra-virgin
  olive oil
1 onion, chopped
8 ¾ ounces (250 g) fregola
  or pearl couscous
5 sprigs fresh thyme leaves
1 garlic clove
Freshly ground nutmeg
Few sprigs mint leaves

*You can substitute vegetable
broth for the kombu broth if
you prefer. Kombu is easy and
the seaweed has a lot of flavor,
but it can be difficult to find.*

TIP
Cleaning artichokes is not
a fun job, but they are a
thousand times tastier than
from a jar. If you do use
artichokes from a jar, pick
good quality ones,
I won't be mad.

If you visit Rome in the spring, you can go on a kind of artichoke pub crawl. This delicious thistle is on the menu everywhere. In the former Jewish ghetto, you can eat the best *carciofi alla giudia* (fried artichokes) and the tastiest *alla romana* (stewed artichokes with thyme). Definitely go to Piperno restaurant for vignarola con fregola with fava beans and peas. My version is a soup with toasted fregola, which is similar to pearl couscous. It used to be a vegetarian farmer's dish, later people added guanciale (pork cheek bacon). So with this vegan version, we are actually closer to the original. If you want to stick with the vegan version, fry the artichokes crispy and skip the bacon!

Soak the dried seaweed in a pot with 2 ½ quarts (2 ⅓ L) of cold water for 30 minutes then bring it to a boil and simmer on low heat for 15 minutes. Remove the seaweed.

Remove the beans from their pods. Blanch them, rinse in cold water and then remove from their individual shells: slice them open with your nail and gently squeeze so they will pop out of their jackets. Very little ones don't need to be removed from their individual shells.

To clean the artichokes, squeeze the juice from half of a lemon into a large bowl of water. Next, remove the outer leaves from the artichokes until the remaining leaves are soft yellow in color. Cut the tips off the leaves. (I find kitchen shears work best to do this.) Then, trim the stem and peel off the hard outer part of the stem with a vegetable peeler. Keep the lemon handy and dab it on the artichokes to prevent discoloration. Next, cut each artichoke in half and remove the choke with a paring knife. Place the cleaned artichokes in the lemon water to prevent discoloration. Salt them generously and boil the artichokes in water for 15 minutes until al dente. Remove them from the water and set aside.

Heat 2 tablespoons of the olive oil in a large skillet and sauté the onion until it's translucent. Remove the leaves from the thyme stems and add to the skillet. Add the fregola and pour a few ladles full of the seaweed stock on top. Cook for 25 minutes.

Meanwhile, heat the remaining olive oil in a separate skillet. Fry the artichokes with a pinch of salt on both sides over high heat until golden brown. Finely chop the garlic and add it to the artichokes and continue to sauté until the garlic is golden brown and crispy. Season the artichokes with freshly ground nutmeg.

Add the fava beans and peas to the fregola and add enough seaweed stock to make soup. Taste and season with a squeeze of lemon juice and possibly some salt and pepper. Spoon into shallow bowls, place a few artichokes in each and top with lemon zest. Finely chop the mint leaves and any leftover green herbs and sprinkle over the dish.

Mezze maniche con ragù di cipolle

Pasta with onion ragù and parsley breadcrumbs

Preparation time:
1 hour

Serves 4

INGREDIENTS

Onion ragù

2 ¼ pounds (1 kg) onions
½ cup (100 g) butter
1 teaspoon sea salt
2 tablespoon
   Worcestershire sauce
1 tablespoon tomato
   paste
10 sprigs thyme leaves
1 tablespoon shiro miso
   paste (optional)
½ cup (100 ml) white wine

Parsley breadcrumbs

4 ¼ ounces (120 g) white
   bread, crusts removed
¾ ounce (20 g) Italian
   parsley, finely chopped
1 tablespoon mild olive oil
10 ounces (300 g) pasta
Parmesan, grated

10 ounces (300 g) pasta
   of your choice
Parmesan, grated

I improvised this pasta recipe when I had a mountain of onions that needed to be used up.

It reminds me most of pasta Genovese, which has beef as well as onion. Genovese is divine, but this vegetarian pasta is just as good, especially if you add a tablespoon of miso, which gives the dish an incredibly rich taste.

To make the onion ragù, melt the butter in a large cast iron pan. Next add the onion rings and fry them on low heat, stirring occasionally, until translucent. Add the salt and continue stirring until the onions caramelize. Only stir occasionally, otherwise the onions do not fry well. Take your time with this, at least 30 minutes.

When the onions start changing color, add the Worcestershire sauce and tomato paste, and again, continue sautéing until the onions are even darker. Add the thyme leaves.

When the onions are really dark in color, add the miso paste, if using, and deglaze with the wine. Turn down the heat and reduce the liquid.

To make the parsley breadcrumbs, grind the bread into crumbs in a food processor. Combine the breadcrumbs with the parsley and olive oil and grind until smooth and the crumbs are green. Fry it in a dry frying pan until dry and crispy.

Bring a large pot of salted water to a boil.

Cook the pasta in the boiling, salted water until al dente. Reserve some of the cooking water when you strain the pasta then return the pasta to the pot. Add the onion mixture and stir everything together until the pasta is coated. If needed, add a dash of pasta water to loosen the sauce. Sprinkle with the parsley breadcrumbs and Parmesan cheese.

SCUGNIZZA NAPOLETANA
Michelle Bogers

When I first went to Naples from Rome as an au pair, I was immediately sold. Rome is like an open-air museum compared to Naples. Beautiful, but almost boring compared to this swirling city at the foot of Mount Vesuvius. Neapolitans don't talk, they shout. Testosterone surges there through the streets like a souped-up motorino (Vespa). Maradona and Jesus compete for street altars; you stumble over the bookstores, churches, and pastry shops. The city was founded by the ancient Greeks and was once the capital of the powerful kingdom of the Two Sicilies. Naples brims with history, but also with big breasts and cheap lip fillers. It's shabby chic.

Moluccan-Nigerian Michelle Bogers thrives in this cheerful chaos. She's not showy like her fellow city dwellers, but she is just as streetwise. That's why I call her scugnizza, a Neapolitan term, translated to something like "street urchin." She settled here six years ago and now has a baby daughter with her Neapolitan-Greek boyfriend and bartender, Mattia. Michelle studied art history and Italian, but soon decided the kitchen was more fun. She's worked in several restaurants in Naples, and she teaches cooking workshops.

She knows Neapolitan cuisine like the back of her hand and cooks better than Mattia's mother. (Hopefully she won't see this comment!) Mattia notes: "'Michelle has a very good culinary intuition." How sacred is tradition to her? "It is culture and preservation of that culture. But progress is also important. Traditions of today are innovations of the past. And not everything is as ancient as we think." By thoroughly researching recipes and diving into local ingredients, Michelle honors local kitchen mores. It's important to keep sentiments and flavors alive. "You cook a recipe better when you understand where it comes from." That's the strength of the Neapolitans. "They know exactly what to do with their products."

In her kitchen, we make scialatielli, a type of pasta from Amalfi often served with seafood. Michelle shows me how she makes the dough. She uses only durum wheat semolina. Scialatielli are nice and thick, stiff and creamy with the addition of milk and pecorino cheese. She folds the rolled-out dough loosely to show the right thickness. Then she rolls a few sheets on her chitarra, an instrument used specifically for this purpose. "You can just order it on Amazon." I know the device from the Marches, where they use it to make spaghetti alla chitarra, a kind of square spaghetti. Or you can cut it with a knife, so it's easier to make at home.

The garlic and parsley stalks go into the skillet with oil. Michelle lets them soak for a long time so that the smell not only permeates the entire apartment, but also curls up the street. She cooks the clams individually and works meticulously, giving everything attention and time. She scoops a deep orange clam from its shell. "Those are the tastiest." Then she fries the shrimp heads with tomatoes into a bisque-like base. She looks for a strainer for her clam broth. I hand one to her. "No, the very fine one," she says, "otherwise grit will come with it."

She scoops the cooked pasta into the seafood liquid and simmers it until the sauce is syrupy and intense. Only then does she toss in the clams.

The scialatielli are perfectly al dente and have a deep seafood flavor. As far as I'm concerned, she could start her own trattoria now. "I'm going to. And Mattia will make the cocktails." Whether that restaurant will be in Naples or somewhere else in the world, she doesn't know yet.

"TRADITIONS OF TODAY ARE INNOVATIONS OF THE PAST, AND NOT EVERYTHING IS AS ANCIENT AS WE THINK."

Scialatielli allo scoglio

Scialatielli with lime leaf and seafood

Preparation time:
1½ to 2 hours

Serves 4

___

INGREDIENTS

Scialatielli
(page 362 or store bought)

2 ¼ pounds (1 kg) mussels
2 ¼ pounds (1 kg) clams
10 large shrimp, shelled
   and deveined
1 pound (450 g) squid
   meat (optional),
   cleaned and cut into
   ½-inch pieces
¼ cup (60 ml) extra-virgin
   olive oil
2 garlic cloves, crushed
Few sprigs Italian parsley,
   stems and leaves
   separated
½ cup (120 ml) white wine
6 Roma or cherry
   tomatoes, halved

TIP
Michelle and I both like
to save the shrimp heads
and cook them with the
tomatoes. They add so
much flavor!

When I made the Amalfi pasta, scialatielli, with cream and pecorino cheese with Michelle Bogers (see page 114), I picked up fresh squid, clams, mussels, and shrimp at La Pignasecca, Naples's oldest market. If possible, you should get fresh fish too, because the better the fish, the better the dish. The squid is optional, but you really need the clams and shrimp for the sughetto, the divine seafood sauce. I saw a wild lime on Michelle's Neapolitan balcony, so I added some of the juice into the pasta dough. Amalfi meets Indonesia!

First, make the Scialatielli.

Clean the clams and the mussels well.

Rinse the squid, if you're using them, and pat them dry.

Add a drizzle of olive oil to a large skillet. Add the garlic and parsley stems and sauté until the garlic is light brown. "Or," as Michelle says, "until the whole house smells like it." Add the mussels, turn the heat on high, and deglaze the skillet with the wine. Cover the pan and cook for 3 minutes.

Add the clams and cover the pan again until the shells open. Move the opened mussels and clams into a large bowl and reserve the cooking liquid in another bowl.

Pour another drizzle of olive oil into the pan. Over high heat, fry the squid rings for 3 minutes. Place the squid in the bowl with the mussels and clams.

Drizzle more olive oil into the pan and cook the tomatoes until they release some of their juice and deflate a bit. Pour the shell liquid into the skillet through a fine sieve and simmer until reduced by half. (If you cooked the shrimp heads with the tomatoes, remove the shrimp heads, press them so they release their delicious flavor and then discard them.)

Bring a pot of salted water to a boil.

Cook the scialatielli in the salted, boiling water for 4 to 5 minutes, or until al dente.

Add the shrimp to the tomatoes and cook them briefly. Add the squid, mussels, and clams back to the skillet. (If the skillet is too full, you can remove the meat from the shells and discard the shells. If you do, take the shrimp off the heat first so they don't overcook). Add the scialatielli to the skillet. Stir everything well so that the pasta is coated in the seafood sauce. Finely chop the parsley leaves and sprinkle over the top.

Puttanesca integrale

Whole-wheat puttanesca

Preparation time:
25 minutes

Serves 4

INGREDIENTS

Whole-wheat pasta
(page 363 or store bought)

6 tablespoons (90 ml)
    extra-virgin olive oil
10 anchovy fillets, finely
    chopped
½ cup (60 g) pickled
    capers, drained and
    finely chopped
2 garlic cloves, crushed
1 ½ teaspoons chili flakes
¾ cup + 1 tablespoon
    (125 g) Taggiasca olives,
    chopped
1 pound 5 ounces (600 g)
    crushed tomatoes
Few sprigs fresh oregano
Zest from ½ lemon
3 to 4 tablespoons heavy
    whipping cream
Sea salt
Handful fresh Italian
    parsley leaves, chopped

Puttanesca is the world-famous pasta from Naples. According to Neapolitan folklore, the recipe originated from the red light district. They say it was made by a prostitute, or that the customers were fed it to regain their strength after an exhausting visit to a lady of the night. Others say perhaps the name was simply made up because the pasta turns "whorish red" because of the tomatoes. I will leave it as a mystery. In Lazio they add anchovies to the puttanesca; I love it. With its hearty flavors, this sauce is perfect for whole-wheat pasta, which benefits from the counterbalance. I finely chop the anchovies and capers so they can melt together in the olive oil. I also coarsely chop the olives, which is tastier and more subtle than having to eat them whole. Finally, I finish the sauce with a drizzle of cream, which makes it rich and complex.

First, make the whole-wheat pasta.

Pour the olive oil into a large pan and add the anchovies, capers, garlic, and chili flakes (if you want it less spicy, use less or omit chili flakes completely). Put on low heat and let the anchovies melt. Then add the olives.

Add the crushed tomatoes. Season with the oregano leaves and lemon zest, then simmer for 10 minutes. Add the cream.

Meanwhile, put on a large pot of water and generously salt it. Cook the pasta al dente and transfer the pasta to the pan with the sauce. Mix everything together well.

Serve in shallow bowls with the parsley leaves sprinkled over the top.

Pasta con ceci, bietola e 'nduja

Broken lasagna with chickpeas, chard, and 'nduja

Preparation time:
20 minutes

Serves 4

INGREDIENTS

3 tablespoons extra-virgin olive oil
2 garlic cloves, crushed
1 sprig rosemary, needles finely chopped
1 teaspoon fennel seeds, crushed
5 cherry tomatoes, coarsely chopped
1 can (15 oz/425 g) chickpeas, drained
5 ¾ ounces (160 g) lasagna noodles
1 teaspoon sea salt
1 ½ to 2 tablespoons 'nduja or finely chopped chorizo
10 ounces (300 g) chard, leaves removed and chopped
1 squeeze of lemon juice

TIP

Instead of chard, you can use spinach or broccoli. Cook spinach only very briefly until just wilted. If you use broccoli, cut into small florets and add a little more water to cook them until tender.

Pasta e ceci is a fantastic "poor man's dish" from southern Italy that shows that you can create something extraordinary with minimal ingredients. It was originally made with dried chickpeas, pasta water, and pasta. Since we have less time and more money these days, I make a quick cheat version using canned chickpeas. I mash some of the chickpeas, though, which helps make a thick, creamy sauce.

The chard and 'nduja are my own additions and are perfect for pasta e ceci!

Heat the olive oil in a large skillet and add the garlic, rosemary, and fennel seeds until the garlic is lightly browned.

Add the tomatoes to the skillet and sauté until the liquid has been reduced. Remove the garlic and rosemary if you don't want too strong a flavor. I leave them in because I like it to be robust!

Add the chickpeas to the skillet along with 2 cups (475 ml) of water. Break the lasagna into coarse pieces and add them to the skillet. Stir in the salt and 'nduja.

Add the chard stems to the skillet and cook for a few minutes, then add the leaves. Reduce the heat to low and continue to cook uncovered until pasta is al dente.

Remove 3 tablespoons of chickpeas from the pan with a slotted spoon and purée until smooth with a hand blender. Add the purée back into the skillet, season with a squeeze of lemon juice, and turn off the heat. The pasta will still soak up some of the cooking liquid, so don't worry if it looks too wet, it will thicken. Ladle the pasta into shallow bowls and serve immediately.

Fregola con conchiglie e pomodorini

Toasted fregola with cockles and tomatoes

Preparation time:
30 minutes soaking +
25 minutes

Serves 4

___

INGREDIENTS

1 tablespoon coarse
sea salt
2 ¼ pounds (1 kg) cockles
or clams
1 tablespoon tomato
paste
¼ cup (60 ml) extra-virgin
olive oil + extra for
serving
8 ¾ ounces (250 g) fregola
or pearl couscous
2 garlic cloves, crushed
14 ounces (400 g) cherry
tomatoes, halved
½ cup (120 ml) dry
white wine
½ bunch (¼ oz/7 g)
tarragon, finely chopped
½ bunch (¼ oz/7 g) dill,
finely chopped
Handful samphire
(also known as sea
beans; optional),
washed well

In Sardinia, during our honeymoon, Remko and I stayed at Agriturismo Bonzai, a rural affair where a pack of dogs, a Korean woman, and her stocky Sardinian husband caused merry chaos. She had been the first Korean on the island, she told me over a huge plate of fregola with cockles; a documentary had even been made about them. That plate was so enormous, I couldn't finish it. She didn't accept any excuses, so I kept eating. That evening I lay in bed with a painfully full belly, while Remko was invited to feast on a Sardinian maggot cheese with the men. I was very glad to have an excuse not to eat wiggly cheese. Since then I know that a modest proportion is fregola is enough. If you can't find fregola, pearl couscous is a good substitute.

Dissolve the salt in 1 cup (240 ml) of warm water. Place the cockles in a large bowl with cold water and add the salty water. Soak them for 30 minutes. The salt causes the cockles to open up and washes out any residual sand. Cockles are real sand diggers, so don't skip this step. Strain the soaking liquid through a cloth and save it. Rinse the cockles thoroughly.

Heat a skillet and sauté the tomato paste in 1 tablespoon of the olive oil. Add the fregola and the cockles' soaking liquid until the fregola is just submerged. Cook for 15 to 20 minutes until al dente. Add extra fresh water (no more soaking water, or it will be too salty) if it gets too dry while cooking.

Add the garlic and 3 tablespoons of the olive oil to a separate skillet and sauté over medium heat until the garlic is light brown. Increase the heat, and add the cherry tomatoes and cockles. Deglaze with the wine, reduce the liquid, and cover the pan. After 5 minutes, check to make sure the cockles are open. If not, cover and cook for another minute. Discard any that have remained closed.

Sprinkle the herbs over the cockles. Stir everything well and then remove from the heat. Remove half the cockles from the shells and then add them back into the skillet and stir.

Ladle into shallow bowls, top with the samphire, if using, drizzle olive oil on top, and serve immediately.

Orecchiette cime di rapa e polpo

Orecchiette with broccoli rabe, octopus, and spicy breadcrumbs

Preparation time:
30 minutes

Serves 4

INGREDIENTS

Spicy breadcrumbs
1 stale piece of bread
1 teaspoon chili flakes
4 tablespoons extra-virgin
   olive oil + extra for
   serving

1 pound (450 g) broccoli
   rabe (see page 26)
10 ½ ounces (300 g)
   orecchiette
7 ounces (200 g) octopus
   tentacles (precooked),
   cut into small pieces
2 garlic cloves, finely
   chopped
Zest from 1 lemon

TIP
Still want the classic?
Then replace the octopus
with 8 good-quality
anchovy fillets. Melt these
along with the chopped
garlic and a pinch of chili
flakes. Add the pasta and
the cooked vegetables
and mix everything well.
Finish with the lemon
zest and serve with
breadcrumbs.

Cime di rapa literally means "tops of turnips," but don't let that fool you because this recipe calls for broccoli rabe, which is a distant cousin of broccoli, but with more flavor and bitterness. The little bit of bitterness gives depth of flavor. Always combine bitter with hearty flavors, so you get an interesting dish that leaves you wanting more. The classic recipe, orecchiette with cime di rapa, peperoncino e acciughe, is from Puglia—once a poor southern region but now the new Ibiza. It's one of my favorite dishes, but that recipe is already out there, so I came up with a variation using fried octopus instead of anchovies. The principle is otherwise the same: you combine the bitter vegetables with fishy heartiness and finish it off with fried breadcrumbs (called pangrattato, mollica, or bricciole, depending on where in Italy you are).

Bring a pot of salted water to a boil.

To make the spicy breadcrumbs, finely grind the stale piece of bread with the chili flakes in a food processor. Heat 1 tablespoon of the olive oil in a large frying pan, add the breadcrumbs, and fry until crispy. Remove from the pan and wipe clean.

Cut the florets loose from the broccoli rabe and set aside. Cut the stems into very small pieces and add to the florets. Finely chop the leaves as well, and keep aside.

Add the orecchiette to the salted, boiling water, and after 3 minutes add the florets and stems of the broccoli rabe. Cook for 5 minutes, then add the chopped leaves. Cook for another 3 minutes or so until the pasta is al dente.

Meanwhile, reheat the skillet, add 3 tablespoons of the olive oil and fry the octopus on high heat until nice and crispy. Add the garlic, turn down the heat, and cook until it is light brown. Using a slotted spoon, spoon the broccoli rabe and the orecchiette with some of the cooking liquid attached into the pan with the octopus.

Grate the lemon zest over it and mix into the pasta. Finish with a drizzle of olive oil and a sprinkle of breadcrumbs.

Calamarata con crema di tonno

Calamarata pasta with spicy tuna and orange

Preparation time:
25 minutes

Serves 4

INGREDIENTS

Sea salt and freshly
   ground black pepper
Two (5 oz/142 g) cans
   tuna in olive oil
Zest from 1 large orange
5 tablespoons orange
   juice
7 tablespoons extra-virgin
   olive oil
12 ounces (400 g) cherry
   tomatoes, halved
2 teaspoons chili flakes
   (or less if you don't
   like it spicy)
10 ½ ounces (350 g) pasta
   (calamarata, mezzi
   paccheri, or paccheri,
   for example)
⅓ cup (40 g) shelled
   pistachios, chopped
Leaves of a few sprigs
   of mint, chopped

TIP

Use the leftovers as a
sauce with a piece of meat
or fish, on a sandwich,
or as a salad dressing.
For a vegan variant,
you can use vegan tuna
instead of regular.

This delicious calamarata pasta is named for the calamari-like tube shape. And, although I have ambivalent feelings about pasta with tuna (I can't help but think of dry pasta salad with tufts of tuna), Chiara from the Sicilian restaurant Bottega di Chiara in Amsterdam opened my mind. She gave me a jar of creamy sauce with orange and tuna from Sicily. Delicious! When it ran out, I recreated something similar to serve with pasta. I'm converted!

Bring a large pot of salted water to a boil.

Put the tuna and their oil in a blender. Add the orange zest, orange juice, and an additional 4 tablespoons of olive oil. Purée until smooth then season with a pinch of salt.

Heat a skillet and add the remaining 3 tablespoons of olive oil. Sear the cherry tomatoes along with the chili flakes on high heat until the juice is released but they still retain their shape.

Add the pasta to the boiling, salted water and cook until al dente.

Using a slotted spoon, transfer the cooked pasta into the pan with the cherry tomatoes. Add the tuna purée until the pasta is nicely coated but not drowned. Add some pasta cooking water and mix until it becomes a creamy sauce. Divide the pasta among four shallow bowls, top with the pistachios and mint, and serve immediately because the sauce dries up quickly.

Mafaldine alla norma con feta-ricotta

Mafaldine alla norma with orange, feta, and ricotta

Preparation time:
30 minutes + 30 minutes

Serves 4

_____

INGREDIENTS

2 large eggplants
   (or 3 smaller ones), diced
2 teaspoons sea salt +
   extra
1 pound 10 ounces (750 g)
   ripe tomatoes
¼ cup (60 ml) mild olive oil
2 garlic cloves, peeled and
   crushed
2 tablespoons tomato
   paste (omit if you have
   really ripe tomatoes)
Pinch of granulated sugar
½ orange
1 teaspoon chili flakes
1 cup (240 g) ricotta*
1 cup (240 g) sheep feta*
2 ⅓ ounces (300 g)
   mafaldine (any short
   pasta will do)
3 tablespoons toasted
   sesame seeds (optional)
2 sprigs basil

*Quantities are generous;
I use leftovers of this "feta
ricotta" in a fresh fennel and
orange salad or with lentils
the next day.*

TIPS

Since this is a summer
dish, I try to find whole,
ripe farmers' market
tomatoes. I usually choose
nice medium-sized vine
varieties. If there are no
ripe garden tomatoes to
be found, you can also
use good-quality canned
tomatoes.

Instead of ricotta salata
or my "feta ricotta" you
can also use pecorino
or Parmesan.

Sweet, ripe tomatoes, juicy eggplant, and Sicilian basil you can smell a mile away. In my mind, I had made one big mythical Mediterranean feast out of pasta alla Norma and then tasted it in Catania, where the recipe originated. Maybe I had dreamed about it for so long that the reality came up short. Or maybe I just had bad luck. In any case, I was disappointed, so I tweaked it with a nod to Sicily's Arab past. Orange peel here, sesame seed there. The original comes with ricotta salata, a hard cheese that is hard to get in some places. So, I replaced it with fresh ricotta, whipped up with feta. Like ricotta salata, but different.

Sprinkle the eggplant with the salt and let stand in a colander with a bowl underneath for at least half an hour. Not to extract the supposedly bitter juices but to flavor the eggplant. With this amount of salt, you don't need to rinse the eggplants.

Preheat the oven to 400°F (200°C) and bring a pot of salted water to a boil.

Score the tomatoes and submerge them in boiling water for 30 seconds. Remove them from the boiling water, rinse them in cold water, and then peel the tomatoes. Remove the tops and coarsely chop the tomatoes.

Heat 1 tablespoon of the olive oil in a large skillet and sauté the garlic until light brown. Add the tomato paste and continue to sauté for 1 minute. Add the chopped tomatoes with a pinch of salt and a pinch of sugar and sauté for an additional 5 minutes.

Using a peeler, peel the zest (not the white pith) from half of the orange and add it along with the chili flakes to the tomato mixture. Simmer on medium-high heat until the liquid has evaporated. Remove the garlic.

Place the eggplant cubes in a bowl and drizzle the remaining 3 tablespoons of olive oil over it and mix well. Place the eggplant on a baking sheet lined with parchment paper and bake for 20 to 25 minutes or until tender. Season with a squeeze of orange juice and add to the tomato sauce.

Next, blend the ricotta and feta in a blender until creamy. Transfer to a bowl and store in the refrigerator; you won't use all of it.

Cook the pasta al dente, transfer the pasta to the skillet with the tomato and eggplant sauce, and mix everything together. Ladle into plates, add spoonsful of feta ricotta, sprinkle with sesame seeds, if using, and garnish with a generous amount of basil.

Spaghettini con cavolfiore Siciliano
Sicilian-style spaghettini with cauliflower

Preparation time:
45 minutes

Serves 4

INGREDIENTS

1 medium cauliflower
3 tablespoons
    vegetable oil
1 thick slice stale bread
10 anchovy fillets,
    chopped
2 garlic cloves
6 tablespoons extra-virgin
    olive oil
Zest and juice from
    1 orange
⅓ cup (50 g) yellow raisins,
    soaked for 10 minutes
    in orange juice
Coarse sea salt
10 ounces (300 g)
    spaghettini
½ bunch (¼ oz/7 g) Italian
    parsley, finely chopped
8 ¾ ounces (250 g) burrata
2 teaspoons chili flakes

This cauliflower is dressed up with luscious flavors—anchovy, raisins, garlic, orange, and breadcrumbs—a typical combination in Sicily. I pair it with burrata, which, I admit, is everywhere these days, but I will never get sick of it.

Preheat the oven to 400°F (200°C). Bring a large pot of salted water to a boil.

Cut the cauliflower into small florets, drizzle with 2 tablespoons of the vegetable oil, and roast in the oven for 35 minutes until al dente and there are brown spots here and there.

Meanwhile, grind the bread into crumbs with the remaining tablespoon of vegetable oil in a food processor and sauté in a skillet until golden brown and crispy.

Place the anchovies in a saucepan. Grate the garlic over the pan and add the extra-virgin olive oil. Allow the anchovies to melt over very low heat. Finely chop the soaked raisins and add them, along with the soaking liquid and orange rind, to the saucepan. Remove from the heat.

Cook the spaghettini in the salted, boiling water to al dente.

Meanwhile, remove the cooked cauliflower from the oven, and add it to the saucepan with the anchovies and raisins.

Using tongs, transfer the spaghettini to the sauce and mix well. Add the parsley and mix again. Spoon the pasta into a large platter, top with the burrata, sprinkle with breadcrumbs and chili flakes, and serve immediately.

"THE TRADITIONAL SICILIAN CUISINE IS LIKE A LIGHTHOUSE FOR MY RESTAURANT. IT HELPS ME UNDERSTAND WHERE I AM AND WHERE I WANT TO GO."

SICILIAN NEPTUNE
Joseph Micieli

I met Joseph Micieli through other Sicilians. That's the way it works there. A friend of a friend is your friend, they say in Sicily. The first time I was introduced to a Sicilian via the Sicilian network was in '97 in Palermo. I was there with my Canadian friend Sue after a year of au-pairing in Rome. She wanted to see the mosaics of the Monreale monastery; I wanted to eat caldo-freddo, a kind of gelato sundae from San Vito Lo Capo. Some Roman friends suggested I talk to their friend, Angelo, and gave me his phone number. Palermo was still a bit sketchy back then. We didn't go out after eight at night! We met Angelo and after one cup of coffee, he gave us the key to his cottage in Mondello, because he didn't like the neighborhood around our hotel. We had no car, so he drove us from one attraction to the next. Sicilian hospitality; it almost makes you feel uncomfortable.

Similarly, Chef Joseph Micieli goes out of his way to help people experience his Sicily. I got his contact info from a Sicilian artist in Amsterdam. I called Joseph, and he immediately agreed to cook with me when I was in town. A few weeks later we were in Punta Secca, an old fishing village in southeastern Sicily with not much more than a lighthouse and a row of houses on the beach. But this hole-in-the-wall village is more famous than you may think: one of the houses in town is in Apple TV's *Detective Montalbano* series. On the terrace of Joseph's trattoria, Cucina Costiera, we ate a shockingly delicious lunch of crudo of red shrimp and langoustines, sardines in lemon sauce, a buttery, smoky barbecued squid, and fatty mackerel in sweet and sour tomato sauce. Joseph slid in with his long, un-Sicilian body and poured a crisp white wine that suggests the Moselle River flows through Sicily. Then he cut loose with his warm baritone voice and talked about his island and the endlessness of its traditional recipes.

Joseph is a kind of Neptune: part fisherman, part chef, and part terroir advocate. Raised among fishing nets, he can read the fish caught close to his restaurants like a book. In his restaurants, he makes *pesce contemporaneo*, which means "contemporary fish," in Italian it sounds way sexier. "Just as a priest knows he belongs in church, I knew from childhood that I was going to be a chef," Joseph says. Among other things, he worked in France and Switzerland and had a career as a television chef. "Now I mainly focus on my restaurants. I feel the need to be present. Travel is fundamental for a chef because it broadens your field of vision, but I know by now that my mission lies here, in Punta Secca." Two blocks away, Joseph has another restaurant, Shabica. There he does other "cheffy" things with fish. As with most Italian chefs, ingredients and season are the starting point of every dish for Joseph. "Together with fishermen, suppliers, and producers, I tell the story of my land, but especially of my sea. The sea is my life." Joseph considers kitchen traditions a kind of guide and an inexhaustible source of inspiration. "For me, traditional Sicilian cuisine is like the lighthouse for my restaurant. It helps me understand where I am and where I want to go."

A day later in his kitchen, we made pasta con le sarde, a classic from Palermo, with sardines, wild fennel, and raisins. This dish is normally a kind of porridge cooked by Palermitan nonnas; Joseph's version leaves the fish intact and is quite elegant. We eat the pasta against the sun-soaked wall of his restaurant overlooking the lighthouse.

Pasta con le sarde

Pasta with sardines, tomatoes, and fennel breadcrumbs

Preparation time:
30 minutes

Serves 4

INGREDIENTS

Fennel breadcrumbs
3 teaspoons pine nuts
1 thick slice stale bread, broken into pieces
1 tablespoon tomato paste
1½ teaspoons fennel seeds
1 teaspoon chili flakes
1 tablespoon not-too-peppery extra-virgin olive oil

5 tablespoons not-too-peppery extra-virgin olive oil, separated
1 small shallot or the white of a spring onion, finely chopped
1 teaspoon chili flakes
4 anchovy fillets, finely chopped
¼ cup (35 g) yellow raisins, soaked in 3 tablespoons white wine
10 ounces (330 g) spaghetti or bucatini
14 ounces (400 g) fresh sardines, de-boned
½ cup (100 ml) white wine
4 small tablespoons tomato purée
1 bunch (½ oz/15 grams) dill leaves

Sicilian Chef Joseph Micieli (see page 139) has several seafood restaurants, and taught me how to prepare pasta con le sarde, among other things. The dish originated in Palermo, where the nonnas traditionally cook the fish into a kind of pasta papposa, which is kind of the consistency of porridge. Instead, Joseph lets the silver sardines fall apart, so you have big chunks of them in the pasta. I chop the raisins completely, so you get a sweet hint throughout, rather than a raisin here and there. In this dish, you can again clearly see the Arabic influences. Sometimes saffron is added, which is also delicious. Pasta con le sarde is made with finocchietto, a kind of wild fennel. This can be difficult to obtain, so I use dill and mix fennel seeds into the breadcrumbs.

Toast the pine nuts in a spacious skillet over medium heat until they are golden brown and then transfer to a bowl to cool down.

Bring a large pot of water to a boil and salt it generously.

To make the Fennel breadcrumbs, grind the bread in a food processor with the tomato paste, fennel seeds, 1 teaspoon of the chili flakes, and 1 tablespoon of the olive oil. Place the mixture into the skillet and sauté until the crumbs are toasted. Place the crumb mixture in a bowl and set aside. Wipe the skillet clean.

Pour the remaining 4 tablespoons of the olive oil into the skillet. Add the shallot and the remaining 1 teaspoon of chili flakes to the cold oil, turn the burner to low heat and sauté the shallot until soft.

Add the anchovies to the skillet. Sauté them over low heat until they melt in the pan. Finely chop the raisins and add them along with the wine they were soaked in.

Add the pasta to the salted, boiling water and cook to al dente.

Meanwhile, add the sardines to the skillet, increase the heat to high, deglaze the skillet with the wine, and simmer until all of the liquid has evaporated. Add the tomato purée and cook gently over low heat for a few more minutes. Next, add the dill leaves.

Using tongs, add the pasta into the skillet with the sardines, add the pine nuts, and mix well. Garnish with the breadcrumbs.

Linguine con pesto di agrumi

Linguine with citrus pesto and bottarga

Preparation time:
30 minutes

Serves 4

INGREDIENTS

Citrus pesto
2 oranges
1 large lemon
Fleur de sel and freshly
    ground black pepper
½ cup (120 ml) not-too-
    peppery extra-virgin
    olive oil
3 ½ tablespoons
    vegetable oil
5 tablespoons capers
½ cup (70 g) toasted
    almonds, coarsely
    chopped
Handful of glasswort or
    samphire, washed well

1 ¼ cups (300 g) linguine
Bottarga, for topping

In Genoa I ate spaghetti with citrus pesto. It was very nice and fresh, but I felt like it was missing something, which turned out, in my opinion, to be bottarga. It's fish roe, and when it's grated over food, it adds a distinctly rich, salty flavor. When I included it in the recipe at home, the dish tasted complete (see page 26 for more info). Pesto di agrumi is not typically Genoese, but Sicilian. There are many variations, including using basil, but I like the way those citrus flavors shine without it. This wonderfully fresh and elegant dish is delicious with a glass of white wine.

Bring a large pot of water to a boil.

To make the Citrus pesto, zest the oranges and lemon and place the zests in a blender.

Remove the pith from the oranges and lemon with a sharp knife. Add the peeled citrus to the blender along with a generous pinch of the salt, a few grinds of pepper, the olive oil, vegetable oil, capers, and almonds. Blend into a thick paste. Taste and season with additional salt and pepper if desired. The pesto will have a strong flavor. Once the pasta is mixed in, the flavor will be milder.

Blanch the glasswort in the boiling water briefly and drain. Add a generous amount of salt to the water and cook the linguine to al dente and reserve some of the pasta water. Combine the linguine and pesto in a large bowl. If it is too dry, add a small splash of pasta water. Not too much, or you'll end up with runny pesto.

Mix the glasswort into the pasta and divide into four shallow bowls. Grate the bottarga over it and serve immediately. *La pasta non aspetta* (the pasta doesn't wait)! Especially this one—it quickly soaks up the sauce.

ABOUT GNOCCHI

"Ridi, ridi, che la mamma ha fatto i gnocchi!" ("Laugh, laugh, your mother made gnocchi!") is an Italian rhyme. It doesn't make much sense, but I don't care, because gnocchi is my favorite. They take some time, so don't make them when you sail in after a long day of work. In that case, use ready-made gnocchi. It's not as tasty as homemade but fine for weekdays. Fry them briefly so they get a crispy coating. Italians don't approve of that, but I do it anyway. Mmm.

GNOCCHI ARE DUMPLINGS Dumplings are eaten all over the world and they can be made from anything: potatoes, starchy vegetables, breadcrumbs, legumes, ricotta, or eggplant. In Italy, besides gnocchi, you also have gnudi, which is in the Tuscan dialect and comes from *gnudo* (naked). They are often made with ricotta and spinach. They are called naked because it uses the filling of ravioli but without the pasta, so it is more like gnocchi. Gnudi are also called *malfatti* (poorly made) in some parts of Italy, and to complete the confusion, in Florence gnudi are called *strozzapreti*. Then there are *gnocchetti sardi*, which is a Sardinian type of pasta (called *malloreddus* in Sardinia). Finally, there are *gnocchi alla romana*, which are large circular gnocchi made of semolina and baked in the oven with butter and Parmesan.

MOISTURE With gnocchi and gnudi, moisture is your enemy. Make sure the ingredients are thoroughly dry. For potato gnocchi, the older the potatoes, the better. The ones with those wrinkled skins are perfect. Always cook them in their skins. Roast squash or celery root in the oven, if you are using those ingredients, so they lose most of the moisture or you will have a problem. For gnudi, you need to squeeze vegetables like spinach very well.

FLOUR As a rule, you use a one-to-four ratio with the weight of the flour to the weight of the potatoes (or vegetables) and usually an egg for binding. I use one part all-purpose flour and one part semolina, but you can also use either one and don't have to mix them. But, don't be tempted to add too much flour, or the dumplings will taste doughy. The exact description of how to prepare gnocchi can be found in the recipes.

STORAGE Place the gnocchi on a surface dusted with semola or a clean tea towel (I use a baking sheet dusted with semola; you can fit a lot of gnocchi on that). Do not store uncooked gnocchi in the refrigerator; they absorb too much moisture and will stick together. Storing them in a dry, cool place with a cloth over them is fine. Cooked gnocchi can be kept in the refrigerator, or even frozen. When you are ready to eat frozen gnocchi, simply cook them in boiling water a few seconds longer than you would cook fresh gnocchi and then finish for a little longer over heat in the sauce of your choice.

SUPPLIES To make the lines on the side of gnocchi, you can purchase a *rigagnocchi* (gnocchi board), but a fork will also do the trick.

Gnocchi con zucchine e gamberi

Gnocchi with zucchini, shrimp and za'atar

Preparation time:
1 ½ hours (45 minutes
with ready-made gnocchi)

Serves 4

___

INGREDIENTS

Gnocchi
(page 365 or store bought)

12 ounces (400 g) large
  shrimp, peeled and
  deveined
Sea salt
2 zucchini (about
  14 oz/400 g)
¼ cup (60 ml) extra-virgin
  olive oil
2 garlic cloves, crushed
⅓ cup (75 ml) white wine
1 teaspoon za'atar

I had some very delicious seafood gnocchi in Chioggia, also known as Little Venice. *"Solo pesce!"* ("Fish only!") the waiter snapped at us upon arrival. I knew the gnocchi was made with fish; I had made a special reservation for it, because I am a serious fish lover. After I ordered all the unusual sea creatures on the menu, the waiter thawed. He must have been frustrated by the hordes of tourists who came in asking for pizza and Fanta after their outing to Venice, which is only a lagoon away. Chioggia may not be as spectacular as La Serenissima, but if you want to experience another authentic fishing village, stay there. However, don't go looking for the za'atar, which of course is my own unorthodox addition. But do drink beer in the bar with the fishermen.

Make the gnocchi and bring a large pot of salted water to a boil.

Cut the shrimp into small pieces and sprinkle with salt.

Halve the zucchini lengthwise and then again, making four long strips. Remove the seeds and cut into slices. Sprinkle with salt.

Heat a large skillet, add the olive oil and sauté the garlic cloves until they are light brown. Add the zucchini and cook until tender, 7 to 8 minutes. Remove half the zucchini from the pan and purée it with 3 ½ tablespoons of water in a blender. Add the shrimp to the pan with zucchini, deglaze with the wine, and cook until the shrimp are just cooked through. It will only take 2 to 3 minutes.

Cook the gnocchi in the boiling water until they rise to the top. Transfer them to the skillet with the zucchini and shrimp. Add the puréed zucchini from the blender and mix everything together. Ladle into shallow bowls, sprinkle with za'atar, and serve immediately.

Gnocchi con porri e zafferano

Gnocchi with creamed leeks, saffron, and hazelnut

Preparation time:
1 hour (15 minutes with
ready-made gnocchi)

Serves 4

___

INGREDIENTS

Gnocchi
(page 365 or store bought)

4 leeks
¼ cup (55 g) unsalted
    butter or 3 tablespoons
    olive oil for a vegan
    version
Sea salt
Saffron threads
¾ cup + 1 tablespoon
    (200 ml) vegetable
    broth (page 357
    or store bought)
¼ cup (30 g) hazelnuts
Few sprigs tarragon,
    leaves removed
Grated Parmesan
    (optional)

The trio of leeks, potatoes, and saffron has proven itself many times before, and this recipe, once again, shows how good the combo is—and it's easy to make it vegan, if you prefer. Homemade gnocchi are decidedly softer than those hearty things from the supermarket, although those are fine too—especially for a weeknight meal. But if you make your own gnocchi, you get fluffy soft pillows. That, combined with a crunchy piece of hazelnut is so delicious.

Make the gnocchi and bring a large pot of salted water to a boil.

Remove the dark green part of the leeks (save for soup or make green sauce with them, see page 40). Cut the white part into rings, washing if necessary as there is sometimes dirt tucked in there. Pat dry if you had to rinse them.

Heat a large skillet and melt the butter. Add the leeks and a pinch of salt. Simmer the leeks until well softened, around 10 minutes. Add the saffron and vegetable broth, simmer for a few more minutes, then purée them in a blender until yellow and smooth, and then return the purée to the skillet.

Cook the gnocchi al dente in the boiling water, spoon them into the pan with the puréed leek cream and mix everything together so that the gnocchi are well coated with the leek mixture.

Next, toast the hazelnuts in a clean skillet and then crush with a mortar and pestle or nut grinder.

Sprinkle the gnocchi with hazelnut crumbs and garnish with the tarragon leaves. You can add grated Parmesan if you would like, but it's not really necessary.

Gnocchi di zucca

Butternut squash gnocchi with browned butter, lime leaf, and shrimp

Preparation time:
2 hours

Serves 4

INGREDIENTS

1-2 large butternut squash
(about 1 pound 10 oz
[750 g])
Sea salt
2 tablespoons mild
olive oil
2 tablespoons grated
Parmesan
1 teaspoon freshly grated
nutmeg
Zest from 1 orange
1 cup + 1 tablespoon
(150 g flour)* (I use
⅔ cup all-purpose
and ⅓ cup whole-wheat)
+ extra
⅔ cup (150 g) salted butter
10 fresh lime leaves
3 tablespoons dried
shrimp
Pinch Aleppo pepper
or other chili flakes

*You need about one-third
ratio of flour to the weight
of pumpkin purée (see also
page 147 for more info).
Whole-wheat flour absorbs
more moisture, and moisture
is your enemy with gnocchi.*

These gnocchi are softer than potato gnocchi. I deliberately use
a small amount of flour so you can taste the flavor of the butternut
squash. Because of the soft dough, it is best to work with two
teaspoons to form the gnocchi.

Preheat the oven to 400°F (200°C).

Peel the butternut squash, cut it in half and remove the seeds and threads
with a spoon. Chop it into cubes. Place on a baking sheet lined with
parchment paper, sprinkle with a pinch of salt, and drizzle with the olive
oil. Roast the butternut squash for about 40 minutes, or until it's soft.
You will be left with about 1 pound (450 g) of roasted cubes.

Transfer the butternut squash to a blender. Season with the Parmesan,
nutmeg, orange zest, and a pinch of salt, and blend until smooth.
Add the flour, little by little, into the warm purée. Be sure all of the flour
is incorporated before adding more. When you feel a lot of resistance,
the dough is ready. Again: the dough will be quite soft and different
from potato gnocchi.

Bring a pot of salted water to a boil.

Line a baking sheet with parchment paper and dust with all-purpose
flour. Separately, sprinkle all-purpose flour into a large plate. Using one
teaspoon, scoop the dough and use a second teaspoon to form it into an
oval shape: smoothing the sides with the spoons until you have a smooth
oval-shaped gnocco. Then, roll it in the flour. Before making more, test it
by cooking the dumpling in boiling water. If it falls apart, you have to add
some more flour to the dough.

Have a bowl of water ready to wet the teaspoons to prevent sticking.
Make the rest of the gnocchi and place them on the baking sheet.
Use a fork or a gnocchi board to press ridges into the gnocchi.
Refrigerate the gnocchi (see page 147 for storage tips).

Brown the butter in a saucepan over medium heat, which can take about
10 minutes. The butter will turn a beautiful caramel color. Once the butter
is brown, tilt the skillet so that it is angled and the white milk solids sink
to one side. Scoop them out with a strainer.

Remove the center vein of the lime leaves and chop the leaves into
narrow strips.

Grind the dried shrimp in a food processor.

Cook the gnocchi in the boiling salted water until they rise to the top.

Using a slotted spoon, scoop the cooked gnocchi from the boiling water
into the skillet with the browned butter. Fry them briefly and then remove
from the heat.

Sprinkle with shrimp, lime leaves, and a pinch of Aleppo pepper.

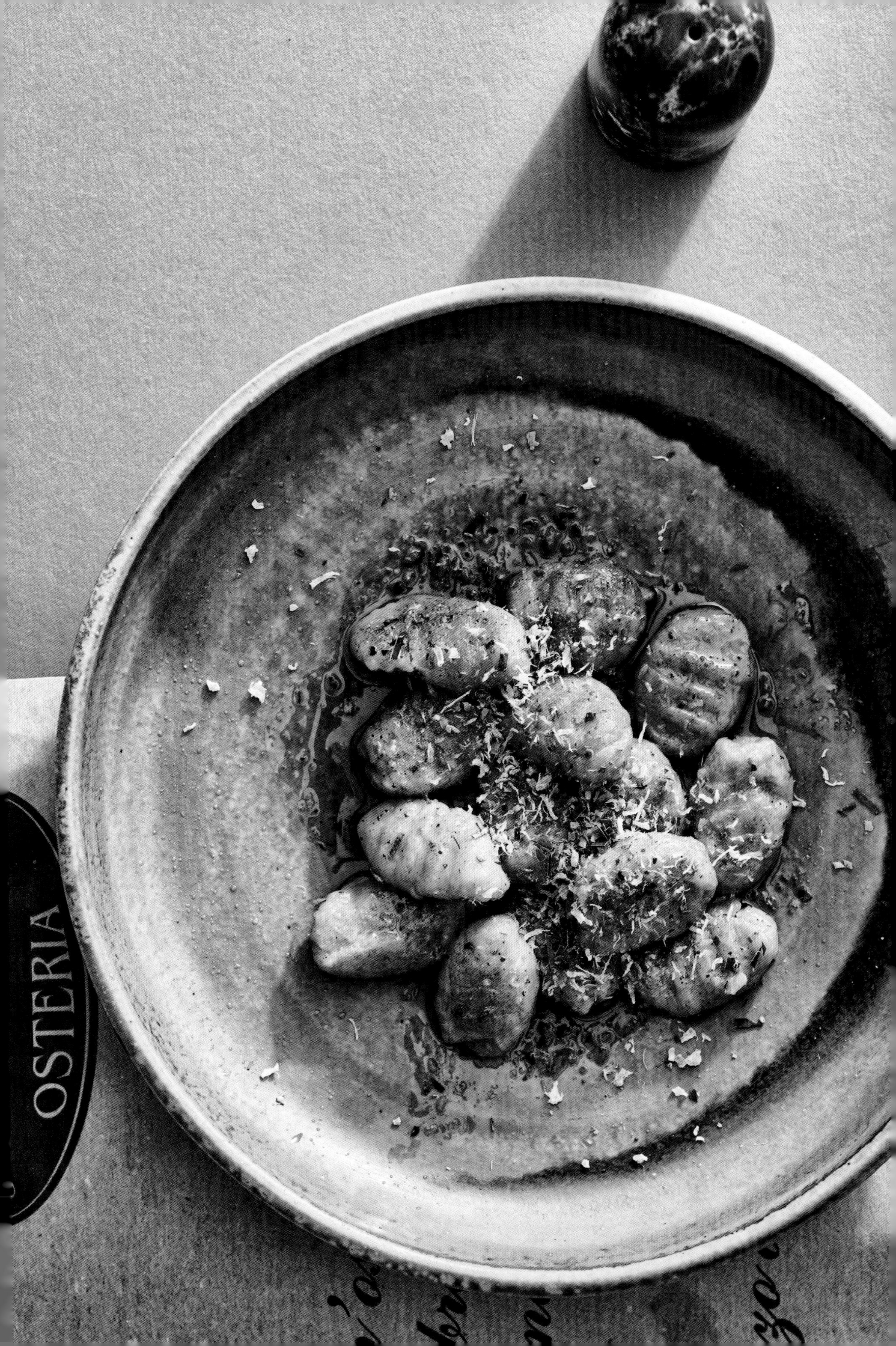
OSTERIA

Gnudi olandesi

Naked pasta with kale and chorizo butter

Preparation:
1 hour + 1 hour drying
(optional)

Serves 4 (makes about
28 gnudi)

———

INGREDIENTS

10 ounces (300 g) kale,
   stems removed and
   leaves finely chopped
2 tablespoons extra-virgin
   olive oil
1 garlic clove, crushed
Sea salt
8 ¾ ounces (250 g) ricotta,
   drained
2 ⅔ ounces (75 g)
   Parmesan, grated +
   extra
Freshly grated nutmeg
1 egg
⅓ cup (45 g) sifted all-
   purpose flour + extra
3 tablespoons unsalted
   butter
A few bay leaves
   (preferably fresh)
1 ¾ ounces (50 g) chorizo
   or other spicy dry
   sausage, removed
   from casings and finely
   chopped

TIPS

You can also use 1 pound
(450 g) of frozen kale.
Defrost and squeeze it
very well before using.
 Do you prefer spinach?
If so, use 1 pound (450 g).

Gnudi are a Tuscan version of stuffed pasta and also a primo, or first course. Gnudi is plural of *gnudo* (naked). The ingredients are the same as the filling for ravioli but without the pasta covering. A pinch of flour is added to make it into the very delicate gnudi. Instead of using the traditional spinach, I make them with kale and spicy chorizo butter. Of course, if you can get your hands on a spicy Calabrese sausage, that's good too.

Bring a large pot of generously salted water to a boil. Cook the kale for 5 minutes. Using a slotted spoon, move the kale to a colander to drain completely. Reserve the pot of cooking water and keep it boiling.

Heat the olive oil in a large skillet and sauté the garlic until it is light brown. Add the kale and a pinch of salt and continue to sauté until most of the liquid has evaporated. Discard the garlic.

Wrap the kale in cheesecloth or a tea towel, and then squeeze out any excess liquid. (If the filling is too wet, it will fall apart.) Place the kale in a bowl with the ricotta, grated Parmesan, a pinch of salt, a pinch of nutmeg, and the egg. Add the sifted flour and mix well.

Line a baking sheet with parchment paper and dust with flour. Separately, sprinkle flour onto a large plate. Using one teaspoon to scoop the dough and the other to form it into an oval shape, smoothing the sides with the spoons until you have a smooth oval-shaped gnudo. Then, roll it in the flour.

Test it by boiling it in some water. If it falls apart, add a little more flour to the dough. Once it is the right consistency, make the rest of the gnudi, roll them in the flour, shape them on the baking sheet, and set them aside to dry (not in the refrigerator, see page 74). The longer they dry, the firmer they will be.

Melt the butter in a large skillet over low heat. Fold up the bay leaf with your fingers to release some of its essence, and add it to the melted butter. Add the chorizo and sauté briefly until the fat runs out. Remove from the heat until ready to use.

Bring the pan with the kale water back to a boil. Cook the gnudi until they rise to the top. Using a slotted spoon, scoop the gnudi into the skillet with the melted butter. Shake the pan so that the delicate gnudi are gently swirled through the butter. Divide among deep plates and serve immediately.

PRINCIPESSA
PUNK

PARTISAN IN THE KITCHEN
Valentina Chiaramonte

Consorzio, in the town of Turin, came up over and over again during my search for restaurants with a contemporary bent. *The New Cucina Italiana* by Laura Lazzaroni lists Consorzio as the archetype of modern trattoria. We went there for lunch with illustrator Gianluca Cannizzo; his drawings adorn the stone-red walls of this particular restaurant and the first page after the endpapers of this book. Through Gianluca, I met Valentina Chiaramonte, the current chef. How this Sicilian ended up in this particular kitchen is actually a mystery to herself. "It happened by chance. I graduated in art history and film studies. Later I was working on a master's that I thought was about the aesthetics of food, but it turned out to be about cooking. I had put a lot of money into it, so then I just finished it." Earning money in the art world is difficult, so Valentina went to work in a restaurant in Catania. So, how did she end up in Turin?

Valentina had also heard about the unique culinary viewpoint at Consorzio, which on the one hand strongly adheres to tradition and on the other is eager for a revolution. "For me, it was the most beautiful place on earth. An authentic place that told the truth about food and wine and worked with the highest quality products, without compromise. That's why I wanted to work for Consorzio." Valentina volunteered, and the restaurant decided to take on the adventure. "It was a mutual bet." Which has gone very well. In addition, she enjoys recognition from culinary platform Identità Golose and was invited to the prestigious Omnivore culinary festival in France. "At Consorzio, the dishes read like a history book about Piedmont. For example, an old dish like *finanziera* (cock's comb stew) is snatched from oblivion and redefined." Conveniently, I ate the same dish earlier in a traditional piola, the Turin equivalent of a trattoria, so I could compare it with Consorzio's take. The meat was tough at the first place I tried, but not so at Consorzio.

They turned it into a buttery ravioli filling, elegant and expertly prepared.

The cuisines of Piedmont and Sicily are miles apart, not just geographically. "Piedmontese dishes are lavish and rich, they are like Botero's sculptures." The risotto with veal stock and the tagliatelle with ragù of heart and butter are divine, but indeed heavy. You recognize Valentina's signature in the acidity she adds. "I use a lot of citrus and vinegar to freshen up dishes." So, the cardoon comes with bagna cauda with grapefruit. She serves sweetbread with apricot and pomegranate, and in season, you can find ceviche of prickly pear.

In Turin, people are very conservative when it comes to culinary matters. Valentina, as a Sicilian, is less bothered by this; her island has traditionally had many outside influences. "I felt I had to reassure people here first. Show respect for regional cuisine and products." Now that she has the public's trust, Valentina is more daring. "Respect for tradition is good, but I am also in favor of cross-pollination." Despite the distance, Piedmontese and Sicilian cuisine also have many similar products. Think tuna, capers, and anchovies. "We are different, but that doesn't mean we can't be harmonious." For Valentina, cooking is also a political act. "I'm for inclusiveness in cooking. And I would like to become more revolutionary in the kitchen. There will be more education, more attention to ingredients. It would be nice if Italian cooks turned into a kind of partisans."

"ITALIAN CUISINE CONSISTS OF MANY REGIONAL CUISINES. BUT DIFFERENT DOESN'T MEAN WE CAN'T BE HARMONIOUS."

ABOUT RISOTTO

Risotto is a classic of northern Italian cuisine that we all know. At least we think we do. As with pasta, it's easy to ruin risotto. A lump of putty is a mile away from a creamy risotto that has nice loose grains with bite. The finesse is in the details. If the base is good, you can start freestyling. This is being done more and more in Italy.

There is a true risotto renaissance going on. The dish is becoming lighter and no longer leans on heavy broths and lumps of butter. At Milan's Ratanà, they cook risotto with tea. Erba Brusca, another restaurant in Milan, makes risotto with smoked ricotta and fermented beet. They are experimenting with new varieties of rice that are inherently creamier. As a result, less butter is needed for the *mantecatura*, the stage when a fat is added to the risotto to make it extra creamy.

Originally the fat added was butter or cheese, but these days it can also be variations very cold whipped oil stirred into the risotto. Risotto in Italy is a primo, or first course. The portions in this book are based on that, too. It is not difficult to make, you just need to know a few basic rules.

WHICH RICE? Different rice grains have different amounts of starches. The starch in the core provides bite and the starch on the outside provides creaminess. What you choose depends on your preference.

Arborio– Most commonly used. Arborio has a lot of starch on the outside, making it well suited for risotto all'onda, a wet risotto. The core of the rice grain does not absorb moisture as quickly, so you need to cook it a little longer. Be careful not to overcook it.

Carnaroli– My favorite and easy to work with. The core contains a lot of starch, which quickly soaks up moisture so the rice doesn't need to cook as long. The grain has less starch on the outside and stays nice and loose, but by stirring, you really do get a creamy consistency as well.

Vialone nano– A small grain that has a lot of starch in the core and less on the outside. As a result, it cooks drier.

FIVE PHASES OF COOKING

Soffritto (Frying)– The seasonings are sautéed over low heat in a small amount of fat (butter or oil) usually with onion, but it can also be a clove of garlic.

Tostatura (Toasting)– An important step and a kind of stress therapy that prepares the grain. The heat changes the structure of the grain; it becomes more resistant and less permeable. As a result, the rice gradually releases its starch, and the grains do not break down. Result: crispy grain and a creamy consistency. Toasting can be done with fat, but also dry. Do not set the heat too high; toast the grains for about 4 minutes until transparent.

Sfumatura (Deglazing)– Depending on the recipe, this can be done with wine or broth.

Cottura (Cooking)– There are several techniques, the most common is *risottare*, which is when you pour a few tablespoons of hot broth on the risotto each time so that it is submerged, repeating the process until all the liquid has been absorbed. After 15 to 20 minutes, the risotto is done. Check by tasting. The core should still have bite. Also keep in mind that the rice is still cooking when you remove it from the heat. Depending on the recipe and your preference, you can choose to serve the risotto drier or wetter. With risotto all'onda, it is so wet that it makes a wavy motion when you move the pan back and forth. There are also recipes where the broth is added all at once and the rice is cooked with a lid on the pan until tender, without stirring. This creates a drier, looser risotto.

Mantecatura (Mixing)– For risotto, if you mix a cold fat into the cooked risotto then letting it rest for 2 minutes creates a creamy, filmy consistency. Because the butter (or other fat) is cold, the fat slowly melts and binds with the cooking liquid to form a creamy emulsion. Mixing is preferably done by pulling the pan forward and backward, causing the risotto to tumble over itself. Resting is ideally done with a tea towel covering the pan. The tea towel ensures that the condensation coming off the rice is absorbed by the fabric and does not rebound into the pan.

TASTE MAKERS Seasonings such as onion are added at the beginning. Then, depending on the recipe, you add other flavorings. The rice is like a sponge that absorbs color and flavor, so if you want the rice to stay white, add the seasonings halfway through. Some seasonings are added at the end.

TYPE OF PAN If possible, use a wide, low pan with a thick bottom that conducts heat well. That way, the rice will heat up evenly and will cook faster. This means you need to stir it less, and there is less chance of breaking the rice and releasing too much starch. If the pan has a handle, that's especially nice. With a pan like that, you can mix well.

Risotto al fondo bruno e midollo

Risotto with veal stock and bone marrow

Preparation time:
25 minutes

Serves 4 as a main dish
or 6 to 8 as a first course

INGREDIENTS

2 cups (475 ml) veal stock
(page 358 or store
bought)
¼ cup (50 g) cold unsalted
butter
1 small onion, chopped
Sea salt and freshly
ground black pepper
1 ½ cups (300 g) carnaroli
rice
½ cup (120 ml) white wine
6 ⅓ cups (1 ½ liters)
chicken broth (page 359
or store bought)
4 beef marrow bones
(or 6 to 8 if serving
as a first course)
3 ½ ounces (100 g)
Parmesan, grated
Zest from 1 lemon

TIP

With the leftovers, you
can make non-traditional
arancini. For example, mix
small pieces of mozzarella,
provolone, or Taleggio
through the rice and
supplement with peas.
See the recipe on page 48
to finish the arancini.

In Turin, everything is coated in vermouth, butter, and Barolo (a luxurious, local wine). You would be as well, if you spent more than a week there. Piedmont cuisine has an aristocratic feel to it, and that, of course, has to do with the royal family that was based in Turin. The Savoyards probably wouldn't have served a marrow bone on the plate; I just think it's a nice touch. This risotto is very rich and heavy. It is inspired by that of Consorzio, the absolute pioneer of neo-trattoria in Turin. (Read more about Consorzio and chef Valentina Chiaramonte on page 160.)

The night before, make the veal stock. Pour the stock in a small saucepan and bring to a boil. Reduce the heat to low and simmer until the stock is reduced down to a thick gravy. Keep warm.

Preheat the oven to 475°F (245°C).

Melt half the butter in a large thick-bottomed skillet. Add the onion and a pinch of salt and simmer over low heat for 5 minutes until soft. Add the rice and toast for about 4 minutes, stirring constantly and until all the grains are coated with fat. Deglaze with the wine and allow the alcohol to evaporate.

Heat the chicken stock and have it on standby. Pour 2 ladlesful of it on top of the rice so that it is completely submerged. Cook the rice over medium-high heat, stirring occasionally until all of the liquid is absorbed and then repeat until all of the stock has been added. The risotto will take about 15 minutes to cook.

Meanwhile, sprinkle the marrow bones generously with sea salt and roast in the oven for 10 to 15 minutes.

When the rice is al dente, add the remaining butter and Parmesan and stir well. Remove the pan from the heat, cover it with a tea towel and let it rest for a few minutes. Ladle the risotto into shallow bowls (give small portions!). Drizzle the veal stock over the risotto and top each plate with a marrow bone. Finish with plenty of freshly ground black pepper and lemon zest. Serve with a small spoon, so your diners can spoon the marrow from the bone over the risotto themselves.

Risotto al nero di seppia e cozze

Squid risotto with mussels and clam-saffron sauce

Preparation time:
45 minutes

Serves 4

INGREDIENTS

2 ¼ pounds (1 kg) fresh
    mussels
3 tablespoons extra-virgin
    olive oil
2 garlic cloves, crushed
Few sprigs parsley, stems
    and leaves separated
5 medium vine tomatoes,
    chopped
½ cup (120 ml) white wine
4 ¼ cups (1 L) fish or
    vegetable broth (pages
    357 to 358 or store
    bought)
1 onion, chopped
1½ cups (300 g) carnaroli
    rice
1 medium russet potato,
    peeled and grated
1 tablespoon squid ink
Pinch saffron threads
1 egg
3 tablespoons lemon juice
Sea salt
¾ cup + 1 tablespoon
    (200 ml) vegetable oil
Chili flakes (optional)

In the movie *Una via a Palermo* (highly recommended) there is a scene in which a family is chowing down on spaghetti with squid ink; everyone has black teeth. Charming it is not, but oh how they are feasting. Squid ink is pitch black, but also very tasty. There is something intimate about getting dirty together.

When it comes to messy food, you indulge unapologetically with people you have loved for a long time. So don't make this squid risotto for a first date, but for the love of your life or close friends. Since most don't necessarily like cleaning a squid, I make this squid risotto with ink sold separately (found at a specialty fish counter or Italian deli) rather than making you get it from the squid itself. It's a quicker, easier version. You can find more about preparing risotto on page 162.

Wash the mussels thoroughly, discarding any with broken shells. Heat 2 tablespoons of the olive oil in a large pan. Add the garlic cloves and parsley stems and sauté, allowing the flavors to infuse into the oil. Add the tomatoes and continue to sauté. Add the mussels, deglaze with the wine, and cook over medium heat with a lid on for about 6 to 7 minutes, until the mussels have opened. Remove the pan from the heat, remove the mussels, and set them aside. Strain the mussel liquid and set aside. Wipe the pan clean.

Heat the stock and have it on standby.

Heat the remaining tablespoon of olive oil in the pan, add the onion, and sauté for a few minutes until translucent. Add the rice and toast it, stirring constantly, for 4 minutes. Add the grated potato and the reserved mussel liquid. Cook over medium-high heat, stirring continuously until the liquid is absorbed.

Pour ½ cup of the stock in a small bowl and add a pinch of saffron. Set aside.

Pour 2 ladlesful of stock on top of the rice so that it is completely submerged. Cook the rice over medium-high heat, stirring occasionally until all of the liquid is absorbed and then repeat until all of the stock has been added. The risotto will take about 15 minutes to cook.

Remove half of the mussels from their shells, and place them in a food processor. Add the egg, lemon juice, and a pinch of salt, and blend. While blending, add the oil in a thin stream. Add the saffron-infused stock and continue to blend. Taste and season further if necessary.

Meanwhile, put the squid ink in a small bowl and stir in just enough stock to make the ink smooth. Once the risotto is fully cooked, add the ink, mix well, and let rest for 2 minutes with a tea towel covering the pan.

Reheat the mussels and broth, if necessary. Ladle the risotto onto plates. On each plate, make nice swirls with the mussel clam sauce and divide the mussels on top, both with and without their shells. Chop the parsley leaves and sprinkle on top with mild chili flakes, if using. Enjoy and get dirty.

"AS WITH PASTA, THERE ARE ALL KINDS OF THINGS TO RUIN A RISOTTO. A LUMP OF PUTTY IS A MILE AWAY FROM A CREAMY RISOTTO THAT HAS NICE LOOSE GRAINS WITH BITE."

Risotto agli asparagi e porcini

Risotto with white asparagus, Taleggio, and porcini breadcrumbs

Preparation time:
40 minutes+ 30 minutes

Serves 4

INGREDIENTS

Porcini breadcrumbs
1 ounce (30 g) dried
   porcini mushrooms
1 slice stale bread
1 tablespoon mild olive oil
1 to 2 coffee beans

5 cups (1.2 L) vegetable
   broth (page 357
   or store bought)
1 ¼ pounds (570 g)
   asparagus
1 bay leaf
Whole nutmeg
5 tablespoons unsalted
   butter
1 onion, chopped
Sea salt
½ cup (120 ml) white wine
   + extra
1 ½ cups (300 g) arborio
   or carnaroli rice
3 ½ ounces (100 g) cold
   Taleggio, sliced

TIP
With the leftovers, you
can make non-traditional
arancini. For example,
mix pieces of ham and
peas into the rice. See the
recipe on page 48 to finish
the arancini.

White asparagus is a seasonal ingredient par excellence. In Italy they are much more militant about cooking with produce that is in season: no pumpkins in the stores in the spring, no broccoli in the summer! Hear hear! Wait for the season, everything tastes much better. Asparagus goes well with earthy flavors like porcini. For a subtle kick, I add a pinch of coffee grounds. Learn more about risotto on page 162.

For the porcini crumbs, soak the mushrooms in lukewarm water for 30 minutes or until soft. Squeeze the porcini well and pat dry with paper towels. Grind with the stale bread in a food processor until fine and well combined. Heat the oil in a skillet and fry the breadcrumbs until crispy. Finely grind the coffee beans and mix into the crumbs.

Heat the stock and have it on standby.

Holding the asparagus by their tips, peel in one motion from top to bottom. Save the peels. Cut off the woody bottoms of the asparagus and save those as well. Cut the rest of the asparagus into slices, (as well as lengthwise if they are thick), but keep the tops whole.

Add the peels and bottoms to the vegetable stock, with the bay leaf and nutmeg. Bring to a boil, turn off the heat, and let stand for 30 minutes. (You can also skip this step, but if you do this, it will infuse your stock with more flavor.)

Melt 2 tablespoons of the butter in a large thick-bottomed skillet. Add the onion and sauté for 5 minutes with a pinch of salt. Add the asparagus slices (keep the tops aside) and deglaze with the wine. Simmer on low heat for 10 minutes. Remove from the skillet and set aside.

Melt another tablespoon of butter in the skillet, add the rice, and toast it over low heat, stirring, until all grains are coated, about 3 minutes. Add the asparagus slices back in.

Pour 2 ladlesful of warm stock on top of the rice so that it is completely submerged. Cook the rice over medium-high heat, stirring occasionally until all of the liquid is absorbed and then repeat until all the stock has been added. The risotto will take about 15 minutes to cook. I like it when the risotto is al dente and all'onda (wet), so I add all the broth.

Add the Taleggio slice by slice to the risotto when al dente, and stir so the cheese melts. Remove the skillet from the heat, cover with a tea towel, and let rest for a few minutes.

Heat the remaining 2 tablespoons of butter in a separate skillet and sauté the asparagus tops. Season with a pinch of salt, deglaze with another splash of wine, and simmer until al dente. Spoon the risotto onto plates, add the asparagus tops, and sprinkle with porcini breadcrumbs. Serve immediately.

Risotto con lambrusco e fichi

Risotto with lambrusco, figs, and Gorgonzola

Preparation time:
30 minutes

Serves 4

INGREDIENTS

1 tablespoon unsalted
  butter
1 shallot, chopped
1 ½ cups (300 g) carnaroli
  or arborio rice
5 cups (1.2 L) vegetable
  broth (page 357
  or store bought)
⅔ cup (160 ml) lambrusco
  secco or another dry
  fruity red wine
½ head radicchio,
  chopped
8 fresh figs
3 ½ ounces (100 g)
  Gorgonzola
5 ¼ ounces (150 g)
  mascarpone
Freshly ground black
  pepper

TIPS

This risotto is also
delicious with sage in it.
Or garnish it with coarsely
chopped basil leaves,
which is also delicious.

If figs are not in season,
you can mix some sausage
meat into the risotto.

As we sat down to tagliatelle with ragù in an air-conditioned restaurant in Bologna on a scalding hot day, I, woman of the world that I am, asked for an ice-cold, dry lambrusco. Remko frowned. "Lambrusco?!" Because what came to mind for him was the sweet lemonade wine we used to drink when we were young, to get drunk as fast as possible. But that stuff has nothing to do with quality lambrusco from Emilia-Romagna. Instead, the real thing is deliciously dry and fruity. It's also perfect for this risotto. To deglaze the dish and to sip on the side.

Melt the butter in a thick-bottomed skillet, add the shallot, and sauté until translucent. Heat the stock and have it on standby.

Add the rice and toast, stirring over low heat, until all grains are coated with butter, about 3 minutes. Deglaze with half of the wine. Allow the alcohol to evaporate.

Pour 2 ladlesful of stock on top of the rice so that it is completely submerged. Cook the rice over medium-high heat, stirring occasionally until all of the liquid is absorbed and then repeat until all the stock has been added. Halfway through, mix in the radicchio and the remaining wine. The risotto will take about 15 minutes to cook.

Cut 6 figs into wedges and add them to the rice mixture for the last 5 minutes of cooking time. Remove from the heat when the risotto is al dente and creamy.

Blend the Gorgonzola and mascarpone into a thick cream.

Divide the risotto onto plates and spoon the cheese mixture onto the risotto, (which is how you do the mantecatura on the plate instead of in the pan). Slice the remaining figs and place them on top of the risotto. Generously top with freshly ground black pepper. Instruct your fellow diners to stir the Gorgonzola cream into the rice before eating.

ABOUT POLENTA

Polenta has long been eaten in Italy. Originally it was made primarily from legumes, but when corn hit the scene in the sixteenth century, corn polenta became staple food numero uno for many regions of northern Italy.

It is comfort food of the highest order, provided you add quite a bit of seasoning. I used to be anti-polenta. It can be a bit bland, and in Italy it often serves as a base. For example, for polenta with a hearty ragù, a tomato sauce, or salty baccalà, all the flavor is in the topping.

My former antipathy also has to do with a past love whom I refer to as *polentone* (a certain swear word that hales from polenta territory). Here's the back story: Before I left for my year in Italy as an au pair, I met one Alessandro from Parma. Dark curls, full mouth, the type to practice Italian on. Unfortunately, I was hired by a family from Rome, and the capital became my place of employment. It could have been worse. Meanwhile, the polentone sent me shiny bracelets and assured me that he would visit me soon. When that didn't happen, I decided to surprise him with a visit to Parma. I sat for hours in Bar l'Orologio waiting for him after a half-day train ride, only to have him never come. When back in Rome, I decided a symbolic gesture was in order to show that I was over him. So, I put a piece of polenta on the road during the morning rush hour. Then all the cars drove over it, which gave me a tremendously satisfying feeling. And now, I like polenta.

DIFFERENT TYPES OF POLENTA You can cook polenta in different ways. Some eat it as a thick porridge, others let it solidify into a thick cake. Firm polenta can be fried or grilled. Which polenta you choose depends on the preparation. Polenta bramata made from corn semolina is the coarsest kind and requires a longer cooking time. As a reward, this polenta has a lot of flavor, and while stirring, you can fantasize about how Italian peasant families used to pour out the steaming polenta on a cloth and sit around it to eat with the whole family. If you're not a romantic, just use quick-cooking polenta *(polenta precotta or polenta istantanea)*. It's ready in a few minutes.

Corn meal is finer than corn semolina and produces a smoother polenta. It is also called *polenta fioretto* or *polenta fine*. In certain parts of northern Italy, buckwheat polenta is also eaten. It's called polenta taragna. There, you buy the mixture pre-mixed. At home you can fake it by mixing some buckwheat flour with the polenta. In Veneto, polenta is made from white corn flour, and is delicious with a seafood stew.

PREPARATION Officially you prepare polenta in a copper skillet, but I do it in a thick-bottomed skillet because polenta can easily cake. For polenta bramata, you have to keep stirring for at least 45 minutes on very low heat. The ratio is about four-to-one for water to polenta, but the coarser the polenta, the more liquid you need. I like a *polenta cremosa* (creamy polenta), so I add lots of liquid so it runs off your plate. Instead of water, you can use broth, or part milk and cream for a more luxurious polenta. And you can infuse flavorings like sage or rosemary into the milk, broth, or cream.

LEFTOVERS You can make gnocchi with leftover polenta. Mix about 2 cups (300 g) of cooled polenta with 1 egg yolk, 1 ½ cups (200 g) of flour, and a few tablespoons of shredded Parmesan. Turn it into gnocchi as described on page 365. Or mix leftover cooled polenta with an egg yolk, chopped herbs, breadcrumbs, and grated cheese, roll it into balls and deep-fry them until crispy. You can also make fries from leftover polenta or grill it with a slice of cheese on top and eat it as toast.

Polenta con cavolo nero e uovo

Parmesan polenta with Tuscan kale, egg, and crispy chili oil

Preparation time:
45 minutes

Serves 4

____

INGREDIENTS

Crispy chili oil (page 370)
1 pound (450 g) Tuscan
    kale, stems removed
    and leaves chopped
2 tablespoons extra-virgin
    olive oil
1 garlic clove, crushed
4 eggs
1 tablespoon white
    vinegar
6 cups (1.4 L) milk or water
    (or a mix)
2 ½ cups (350 g) quick-
    cooking polenta*
Sea salt
3 ¼ ounces (90 g)
    Parmesan or grana
    padano, grated
½ cup (113 g) unsalted
    butter

Quick-cooking polenta is swearing in the Italian church, but we do that anyway in this book. Feel like stirring polenta for an hour? Then see page 174 for preparation instructions.

Polenta calls for hearty flavors: meat ragù, tomato sauce, porcinis. Or, if you think completely outside the box, Chinese crispy chili oil also fits the bill. Polenta is practically made for it. If you keep the chili oil mild, with some Aleppo pepper or other mild chili flakes, you can spoon large amounts of it over the polenta. This is winter comfort food that you eat gratefully after a lot of physical activity in the cold outdoors.

First make the crispy chili oil.

Bring a pot of salted water to a boil, and boil the kale for 5 minutes.

Heat a skillet, add the olive oil and brown the garlic. Transfer the kale from the boiling water into the skillet using a slotted spoon (save the cooking liquid) and sauté for 10 minutes.

Next, bring the kale water to a boil again and pour in the vinegar. Crack one egg into a cup then gently slide the egg from the cup into the water. Swirl the water gently with a fork to twist the white around the yolk. Poach the egg for 3 minutes then scoop it out of the pot with a slotted spoon. Place the egg in a bowl of lukewarm water or on a plate if serving immediately.

Repeat with the remaining eggs. If you are handy, you can poach 2 at a time. (If you find poaching a hassle, you can substitute with hard boiled eggs.)

Next add the water (or milk or a combination of the two) into a saucepan and bring to a boil. Gradually sprinkle in the polenta while stirring. Add ½ teaspoon of salt. Keep stirring until the polenta has absorbed the liquid and become thick. Stir in the cheese and finally the butter. If it thickens too much, you can always add another dash of liquid.

Spoon the polenta into shallow bowls, mix in the kale, and top each plate with an egg. Drizzle the crispy chili oil over it and eat immediately.

Polenta taragna con finferli

Buckwheat polenta with cheese, chanterelles, and porcini brown butter

Preparation time:
1 hour + 20 minutes

Serves 4

_____

INGREDIENTS

5 cups (1.2 L) vegetable
    broth (page 357 or store
    bought) or water
Sea salt
1 cup + 1 tablespoon
    (150 g) polenta*
1 cup + 1 tablespoon
    (150 g) buckwheat flour
7 ounces (200 g) soft
    cheese**
½ ounce (15 g) dried
    porcini
10 ounces (300 g)
    chanterelles (or other
    mushrooms, or a mix)
⅔ cup (150 g) salted
    butter, diced
Few sprigs marjoram
    or oregano, leaves
    removed

*Choose whether to use
bramata, fioretto, or instant
polenta.*

**Use whatever cheese you
want here. Taleggio is a good
option, but I use half fontina
and half clemont rouge
(similar to a mild Brie).*

TIP
Do you have polenta left
over? See page 174 for
what you can do with
the leftovers.

Polenta is an excuse for me to eat a lot of cheese and butter—without it, polenta is boring. I once had buckwheat polenta on the slopes in northern Italy. With lots of cheese, of course, and porcinis. It was great winter food! I love buckwheat, and it adds some fiber and vitamins to the polenta. Chanterelles, porcinis, and marjoram add a chic touch to this peasant polenta.

Preheat the oven to 360°F (180°C).

Bring the broth to a boil over high heat in a thick-bottomed saucepan. (If using water, add a pinch of salt.) Gradually sprinkle in the polenta while stirring.

Sift in the buckwheat flour a little at a time, stirring as you add. The cooking time will vary depending on which kind of polenta you choose. Just before the end of cooking time, dice half of the cheese (I use the fontina) and add it to the polenta. Mix until the cheese is completely melted.

Slice the remaining half of the cheese (I use the clemont rouge). Pour the polenta into a baking dish and top with the sliced cheese. Bake for 15 minutes.

In the meantime, soak the dried porcini in warm water for 10 minutes. Brush the chanterelles clean and cut the larger ones in half.

Melt the butter in a saucepan and brown it over medium heat, stirring constantly for about 10 minutes, until the butter is a caramel color and has a nutty smell. Be careful not to burn the butter. Pour the butter through a fine strainer and discard any burnt ingredients. Wipe the pan clean and pour the butter back in. Remove the porcini from the water. Finely chop the porcini and add it to the browned butter. Leave on very low heat for another 10 minutes and then remove from the heat.

In a separate skillet, sauté the chanterelles in 1 tablespoon of porcini butter over medium-high heat until just tender. It only needs to be brief. Halfway through, sprinkle with salt and season with marjoram leaves.

Remove the polenta from the oven, spoon the chanterelles on top, and sprinkle with marjoram. Not too much; it's a delicious but strong herb. Drizzle the porcini butter on top and serve hot.

SERIOUSLY COSMOPOLITAN
Elisa Rusconi

Bologna's cuisine is famous for its tagliatelle alla bolognese, mortadella, fresh pasta all'uovo, tortellini, *crescentine* (fried bread), and lasagna. It is certainly not the only reason to visit this city, which is also called La Grassa, La Rossa, e La Dotta. *Grassa* (fat) stands for the food, *Rossa* (red) for the red palazzi and political color of the city, and *Dotta* (learned) stands for its university—Bologna has the oldest university in Italy and all of Europe. It is also a solidly built city, with robust medieval buildings and a progressive character. Everywhere you see punkish slouchy Italians with wild hair and girls with rockabilly bangs drinking bottles of beer.

In the historic center sits Trattoria Da Me, with chef Elisa Rusconi at the helm. Her grandfather opened the traditional trattoria in 1937, at the time with Elisa's grandmother as *capocucina* (head of the kitchen). When she was little, Elisa "played restaurant" there, but it was a long time before she started actually working there herself. Elisa first gained experience in other restaurants before taking over the trattoria in 2015. From day one, her "trattoria rivisitata" has been packed.

The décor is a tad fussy for my taste, but the dishes are far from it. We eat fresh, raw(!) sausage with crispy breadcrumbs and homemade sauce. Very flavorful and count on your sausage to be fresh if it is served raw. The cheese ice cream of robiola, Gorgonzola, and stracchino is so good it makes a person weep—creamy, slightly spicy, and surprising. Next comes a kind of deconstructed osso buco. On one of those square slate plates, but who cares, it's so good. Tender stew meat in a bright yellow saffron sauce with a piece of roasted bone marrow on top. Also a favorite: slow-cooked egg with cream of porcinis, crusty bread with Parmesan, and a blueberry sauce. The thinly sliced tongue comes on an insalata russa, what we call hussar salad. "An ode to my girlfriend, who is from Belarus."

I tell her it's fresh and playful. To which Elisa replies, *"L'acidità è fondamentale!"* An acid accent can do wonders for Italian dishes that can sometimes be monotonous. "Take that egg," she says. "Without that sauce of blueberry with it, it would be much too heavy." Elisa has always had an open mind about the cuisine of her region, and that's partly because of her Sicilian roots. After all, Sicilian cuisine has been influenced by other cuisines for centuries. "What also helps is that my father used to take me to starred restaurants all over the world." Elisa's dishes are founded on traditions, but she lets new cooking techniques in.

We talk about the rigidity and conservative nature of Italians in the kitchen. Elisa rolls her eyes and talks enthusiastically. "Italians think the rest of the world can't cook. What nonsense. Of course they can do what we can. In fact, the rest of the world has long surpassed us. The most delicious caponata? I didn't eat it in Sicily, I ate it in California!"

Elisa

"THE MOST
DELICIOUS
CAPONATA?
I ATE IT IN
CALIFORNIA,
NOT IN SICILY!"

VERDURE
VEGETABLES

Caponata con tocco Indonesiano

Sweet and sour Sicilian vegetable stew with an Indonesian touch

Preparation time:
55 minutes

Serves 4

___

INGREDIENTS

2 red bell peppers, halved
with stems and seeds
removed
2 yellow bell peppers,
halved with stems
and seeds removed
6 to 7 tablespoons mild
olive oil
Sea salt and freshly
ground black pepper
2 eggplants, diced
3 tablespoons extra-virgin
olive oil
1 red onion, sliced into
half rings
2 garlic cloves, chopped
2 red chili peppers, crowns
removed and finely
chopped
One (14 oz/400 g) can
cherry tomatoes
3 stalks lemongrass
8 lime leaves
1 teaspoon granulated
sugar
½ pound (225 g) fresh
cherry tomatoes, halved
2 celery stalks, cut into
thin slices
1 tablespoon red wine
vinegar
2 tablespoons capers
2 tablespoons Kalamata
or Taggiasca olives
2 tablespoons pine nuts
Handful basil leaves,
to garnish

TIPS

This dish is very tasty
with farinata (page 54).

You can also use the
caponata as a sauce
for pasta.

Make your caponata with
Burrata—that rhymes and
it's tasty too.

Caponata is one of my favorite Sicilian dishes. There are many versions of it. In Catania they add peppers, and in winter you will find caponata with artichokes. I easily gobble down a whole bowl of these sun-drenched vegetables. In this version, Indonesian flavors sing in the background. It is slightly spicy and aromatic because of the lemongrass and lime leaf. Also, I couldn't resist the garlic because that is used a lot in Indonesian cuisine. I also add extra canned tomatoes for a saucy result. I like to eat my caponata with a piece of farinata, the chickpea pancake from Liguria. A journey from North to South and East to West.

Preheat the oven to 400°F (200°C).

Place the yellow and red bell pepper halves on a large baking sheet, drizzle 2 tablespoons of the mild olive oil over them, sprinkle with a pinch of salt, and place in the oven. Roast for 40 to 45 minutes until the skin is blackened. Every oven is different, so keep an eye on it. Remove from the oven, cover with a clean kitchen towel, and let cool. Remove the skin and cut into strips.

Meanwhile, generously salt the eggplant cubes; use more than you think is needed. Place in a single layer on a baking sheet lined with parchment paper, drizzle with another 2 to 3 tablespoons of the mild olive oil, again more than you think you need, and mix with your hands. Place in the oven and roast for 20 minutes, or until the vegetables are soft and have brown spots here and there. Check occasionally.

Heat the extra-virgin olive oil in a large skillet, add the onion, and sauté until the onion is soft. Add the garlic to the pan, and continue to sauté for a few more minutes.

Add the chopped chili peppers to the skillet. Sauté for a few more minutes, then add the can of cherry tomatoes. Crush the lemon grass and lime leaves and add them to the skillet. Season with a pinch of salt and the sugar and simmer for about 15 minutes. Add the fresh cherry tomato halves to the skillet and sear the tomatoes on the cut surface so that the juice runs out.

Add the celery to the skillet, together with the bell pepper strips and eggplant cubes, and cook for a few more minutes. Then stir in the red wine vinegar, capers, and olives. Taste and season with salt and pepper if necessary.

Toast the pine nuts in a separate skillet and then sprinkle over the top. Using a sharp knife, coarsely tear or cut strips from a handful of basil leaves and garnish the caponata.

Scarola grigliata alla Napoletana

Grilled endive with Neapolitan touches

Preparation time:
10 minutes soaking +
20 minutes

Serves 4

_____

INGREDIENTS

¼ cup (35 g) yellow raisins
3 tablespoons red wine
   vinegar
¼ cup (30 g) capers, finely
   chopped
8 anchovy fillets, finely
   chopped
¼ cup (35 g) pitted
   Kalamata olives, halved
3 tablespoons pine nuts
3 tablespoons extra-virgin
   olive oil + extra
½ cup (250 g) cherry
   tomatoes
1 head endive
Zest from 1 lemon

TIP

Whenever you cook
with anchovy fillets,
make sure you get the
highest quality you can.
You'll taste the difference.

Italians love bitter vegetables and know how to combine them like no other. In Neapolitan scarola alla napoletana, endive is combined with anchovies, capers, olives, and sometimes raisins. Sweet, salty, sour. Cooking with bitter flavors is like mixing a negroni. The trick is to balance the bitterness with other hearty flavors, so that you get an evenly balanced and addictive whole. Instead of boiling or sautéeing the endive, I grill it. That way the leaves don't get slimy, and it gives a pleasant smoky flavor. No tomatoes go into the original, but their juice provides a connection to the other ingredients. You can eat a whole head of this endive in no time. You wouldn't have thought it possible, but in Italy, your wildest dreams come true.

Soak the yellow raisins in the red wine vinegar for 10 minutes and then chop them finely. Combine them with the capers, anchovies, and olives.

Toast the pine nuts in a dry skillet and set aside.

Heat a large skillet, pour in the olive oil and sear the tomatoes on the cut side so that the moisture runs out. Sauté them briefly; they should not fall apart. Add the caper-anchovy mixture, and sauté for another minute, then remove from the heat.

Meanwhile, heat a grill or a grill pan. Halve the endive lengthwise, leaving the underside of the stalk attached. Cut into 8 wedges, brush with olive oil, and sprinkle with salt. Sear the endive wedges until you see nice grill marks and the leaves blister and shrink at the edges. Turn the wedges over and grill for a few more minutes on the other side.

Arrange the endive wedges on a platter or prepare four plates. You can also serve this dish as an appetizer. Spoon the tomato mixture on top, sprinkle with lemon zest and the toasted pine nuts.

Verdure con salsa tonnata

Pan baked asparagus and broccoli with tuna sauce

Preparation time:
35 minutes + overnight
for oil

Serves 4

INGREDIENTS

Parsley oil
1 large bunch (1 oz/30 g)
   Italian parsley
½ cup (125 ml)
   vegetable oil
Lemon wedge

Parsley tonnata salsa
1 pound (450 g) green
   asparagus, trimmed
7 ounces (200 g)
   broccolini, halved
   lengthwise
Handful watercress or
   arugula, to garnish
3 to 4 tablespoons mild
   olive oil
1 shallot, chopped
Sea salt
½ cup (120 ml) white wine
1 ½ cups (350 ml) heavy
   whipping cream
2 bay leaves
One (5 oz/145 g) can tuna
   in olive oil
2 tablespoons capers +
   caper juice
6 anchovy fillets
Juice from 1 lemon

TIP
This sauce is also delicious
with roasted cauliflower
and pointed cabbage.

I love the tuna sauce of vitello tonnato, but I can't be bothered much by the often dry veal meat that it is served with. So, I came up with a variant with crunchy vegetables, a parsley cream salsa tonnata. I bake and steam the vegetables which ensures perfect cooking. They turn out a bit charred, but still beautifully green and al dente. I also use parsley oil which, unlike most green herb oils, actually tastes like parsley. That's partly because you leave it overnight; good things take time. If you don't have that, finely chopped parsley also works well, of course. I serve this as an appetizer; double the quantities if you want to serve it as a salad.

First, make the parsley oil. Pick the parsley leaves off of the stems. Save the stems. Put the leaves in a food processor with the oil and process for at least 10 minutes until completely fine. Put a strainer on a large liquid measuring cup, place cheesecloth or a coffee filter in it and pour the oil over the top. Set the measuring cup with the strainer in the refrigerator overnight, or at least a few hours. Season to taste with a squeeze of lemon juice.

To make the sauce, heat 1 tablespoon of the olive oil in a skillet, add the shallot, and sauté until translucent. Sprinkle on a pinch of salt. Deglaze with the wine. Add the cream, bay leaves, and parsley stems, and simmer until reduced by half. Remove the bay leaves.

In a food processor, grind the tuna with its oil, capers, anchovy fillets, and 2 tablespoons of lemon juice until smooth. Add the cream and blend again until smooth.

Add 2 to 3 tablespoons of the olive oil to a large skillet (enough to cover the bottom of the pan completely) over medium-high heat, and then add the asparagus and broccolini. (You can do this in two batches if they won't all fit in the pan at once.)

Add a pinch of salt and pour in 3 ½ tablespoons of water. Cover and turn the heat to high. Cook for about 5 minutes on high heat. Then remove the lid from the pan, turn the vegetables, and cook for a few more minutes on the other side.

Meanwhile, dress the watercress with a drizzle of lemon juice.

Ladle the sauce onto four plates. Drizzle parsley oil over it, arrange the vegetables and shallots on top, and garnish with the watercress.

Sformatino di carote

Savory carrot cake with lemon-oregano sauce

Preparation time:
30 minutes + 35 minutes
in the oven

Serves 4

INGREDIENTS

Carrot cake
1 pound (450 g) carrots +
    4 extra for the ribbons
2 tablespoons mild olive
    oil + extra for greasing
Sea salt
1 teaspoon coriander
    seeds, crushed
6 tablespoons (100 g)
    mascarpone
3 ½ ounces (100 g)
    Parmesan, grated
1 teaspoon ground
    coriander
Zest from 1 lemon
4 sprigs thyme leaves
2 eggs

Lemon sauce
1 tablespoon butter +
    2 tablespoons cold
    butter, cubed
1 garlic clove, crushed
Juice from ½ lemon
Sea salt and freshly
    ground black pepper
½ cup (120 ml) heavy
    whipping cream
1 tablespoon all-purpose
    flour
Few sprigs fresh oregano

Sformare means to take out of a mold, so a *sformatino* is the delicious food that is prepared in a mold of some kind—whether it's a soufflé, flan, Bundt cake, or something else. If what you are making is on the larger size, it's called *sformato*. These sophisticated, savory dishes are often made from vegetables such as leek, artichoke, zucchini, or spinach, and are so soft that you can eat it with a spoon. For texture and flavor contrast I add carrot crisps and zingy lemon sauce.

Preheat the oven to 360°F (180°C) and line a baking sheet with parchment paper. Bring a pot of salted water to a boil.

Peel 4 carrots into thin ribbons with a vegetable peeler. Place the ribbons in a bowl with the olive oil, a pinch of salt, and the crushed coriander seeds and mix well. Spread the mixture evenly on the prepared baking sheet and bake for 10 minutes, take out of the oven, turn and bake for another 10 minutes until crispy.

Peel the remaining carrots, cut them in cubes, and place them in the boiling water until they are easily pierced with a fork. Purée the cooked carrots in a blender with the mascarpone, Parmesan, ground coriander, lemon zest, and thyme leaves. Beat the eggs, mix them with the purée, and sprinkle with salt.

Grease four large ramekins with olive oil and divide the carrot purée among them. Put the ramekins in an oven-safe dish and add enough water to cover them half way up the sides. Bake for about 35 to 40 minutes or until a skewer comes out clean.

In the meantime, make the lemon sauce. Melt 1 tablespoon of the butter in a skillet over medium heat, then add the garlic. Sauté until the garlic turns light brown.

Add the lemon juice and the cold butter cubes and melt over low heat, stirring continuously with a whisk. Season with salt and pepper, add the cream, and continue to whisk until it's completely combined. Sprinkle the flour and continue to cook for another 5 minutes over low heat. Add half of the oregano leaves and mix well.

Loosen the sides of the ramekins by running a knife along the edges, and then turn them over onto plates. Drizzle the lemon sauce over them, garnish with the roasted carrot strips and the rest of the oregano leaves, and season with pepper.

Peperoni con bagna cauda e burrata

Roasted peppers with bagna cauda and burrata

Preparation:
55 minutes

Serves 4

___

INGREDIENTS

3 red bell peppers, halved
with stems and seeds
removed
3 yellow bell peppers,
halved with stems
and seeds removed
Sea salt
12 anchovy fillets, finely
chopped
½ cup (120 ml) mild
olive oil + extra
4 garlic cloves
3 tablespoons unsalted
butter
Zest and juice from
1 lemon
1 bulb burrata, quartered
Handful basil leaves,
to garnish

Bagna cauda (warm sauce) originated in the Piedmont area. It's predominantly flavored with garlic and anchovies and is often eaten as a dip with raw vegetables, but it becomes something else altogether when it's made with roasted bell peppers.

Because I love them, I have made a study of roasting peppers. The sweet juice from the roasted peppers is divine and melds with the other flavors and the burrata. It's simply addictive. Italians probably won't agree, but in my humble opinion, the rather salty sauce benefits enormously from a sprinkling of lemon zest. Dollop burrata on top, garnish with coarsely chopped basil, and mop it all up with large pieces of bread.

Preheat the oven to 400°F (200°C).

Place the bell peppers skin-side-down on a large baking sheet, sprinkle with a pinch of salt, drizzle with olive oil, and bake for 30 minutes.

Using tongs, empty any liquid from the cavity of the pepper into the baking dish to further caramelise, turn them over and bake for an additional 15 minutes or until they are well charred. Remove from the oven, cover with a kitchen towel, and let cool. Once cooled, peel the skins and discard them.

While the peppers are roasting, place the anchovies in a saucepan. Add the olive oil and sauté over low heat. Next, grate the garlic and add it to the anchovies. Allow the anchovies and garlic to soften over very low heat. Stir in the butter, lemon zest, and lemon juice.

Place the peppers on the plates and pour the roasting liquid over them. Dollop the Burrata over the peppers, generously spoon the anchovy sauce over them, and garnish with basil leaves.

Insalata di cavolini di Bruxelles

Fennel and Brussels sprout salad with bottarga vinaigrette

Preparation time:
30 minutes + 30 minutes
to marinate

Serves 4
_____

INGREDIENTS

8 ¾ ounces (250 g)
    Brussels sprouts
1 large fennel bulb
½ shallot, finely chopped
½ cup (120 ml) fresh
    orange juice
3 ½ tablespoons fresh
    lemon juice
Sea salt and freshly
    ground black pepper
¼ cup (60 ml) not-too-
    peppery extra-virgin
    olive oil + extra
3 tablespoons bottarga*
    + extra
4 large eggs
1 tablespoon white
    vinegar
1 large baguette
5 sprigs Italian parsley,
    leaves removed

*Different types of bottarga
are stronger than others.
Add it slowly, so you don't
put on too much.*

I warned you: I am a fan of bottarga, the dried mullet or tuna roe (see page 26 for more information). It provides a savory, fishy flavor boost that pairs nicely with the robust taste of Brussels sprouts. This salad is delicious as an entrée or as a starter. If you are not a poaching pro, you can easily substitute soft-boiled eggs.

Bring a large pot of water to a boil.

Remove the ends of the Brussels sprouts and slice them very thinly. If you like to keep your fingers, lay the last little bit flat and cut it into thin strips.. If you like your fingers, lay the last bit flat and cut it into thin strips. Cut the fennel in half lengthwise, remove the core and stems, and reserve the leaves. Slice the stems thinly on a mandolin, or use a sharp knife.

Place the shallot in a bowl and add the orange juice and lemon juice. Add a pinch each of salt and black pepper.

Heat the olive oil in a skillet and add the bottarga. Stir to release the flavor and then add to the citrus juice.

Add the Brussels sprouts and fennel to the bowl and marinate for at least 30 minutes.

Add the the vinegar to the boiling water. Crack the eggs into a cup and then gently slide it into the boiling water. Gently stir the egg whites around the yolks with a fork and then poach for 3 minutes. Remove from the water with a slotted spoon and place in a bowl with lukewarm water. Remove any unattached egg whites from the water and then repeat with the remaining eggs. If you are skillful, you can poach two at a time.

Tear the bread into pieces. Heat a skillet, add a dash of olive oil, and toast the bread until crispy.

Drain the vegetables and divide them among four plates, place a poached egg on top, add the croutons, and finish with sea salt on the egg, sprinkled with a pinch of bottarga.

"SIZE MATTERS.
SMALL COURGETTES
ARE THE BEST."

Fagioli corallo grigliati

Grilled runner beans with smoky tomato sauce
and buffalo ricotta cheese

Preparation time:
40 minutes

Serves 4

INGREDIENTS

¼ cup (60 ml) extra-virgin
   olive oil
1 onion, chopped
1 garlic clove, finely
   chopped
1 tablespoon tomato
   paste
1 pound (450 g) ripe vine
   tomatoes, finely diced
1 teaspoon fish sauce
1 teaspoon pimentón
   (Spanish smoked
   paprika)
14 ounces (400 g) runner
   beans, washed
1 ½ tablespoons
   vegetable oil
Zest from 1 lemon
9 ounces (255 g) buffalo
   ricotta cheese
2 tablespoons pistachios,
   finely chopped
Handful basil leaves,
   to garnish

TIP
No buffalo ricotta?
Then use regular ricotta
(cremosa) and mix with
5 ounces (125 g) of feta
in a food processor or
with a hand blender until
you have a creamy, salty
consistency.

In Italy, runner beans are often simmered whole in a tomato sauce. This recipe is a modern twist on that old tradition. The tomato sauce is quick and dirty and is turbocharged with a drizzle of fish sauce and a pinch of smoked paprika. Of course, with flavorful Italian tomatoes, I would never do something so crazy. I can already hear Italians roaring: onion and garlic together? Finely chopped? *Come si permette* (How dare she)! Well, the produce I have on hand requires me to be creative. I grill the green beans for extra flavor.

Heat a skillet and add 2 tablespoons of olive oil and the onion, and sauté until soft. Add the garlic and sauté for a few more minutes. Add the tomato paste and continue to sauté for a few more minutes.

Add the diced tomatoes along with the fish sauce and pimentón. Simmer for about 10 minutes, until most of the liquid has evaporated but the tomato pieces are still intact. Stir in 2 more tablespoons of olive oil. Keep the sauce warm.

Strip the runner beans of their hard undersides. Place the runner beans in a bowl, drizzle with the vegetable oil, and sprinkle lightly with salt. Mix everything so that the oil is well distributed. Heat a grill pan and grill the runner beans over high heat until they blister on the grill side, turn them over and repeat on the other side. Place them in the tomato sauce and simmer them there for a few more minutes.

Mix the lemon zest into the buffalo ricotta.

Serve the runner beans in the tomato sauce with a nice scoop of ricotta on top. Sprinkle pistachio crumbs over the top and garnish with lots of fresh basil.

Zucchine alla scapece con caprino

Sweet and sour zucchini with mint and whipped goat cheese

Preparation time:
35 minutes + 30 minutes marinating

Serves 4

INGREDIENTS

- 1 ½ pounds (675 g) small green zucchini, sliced
- 1 yellow squash, sliced into thick strips
- Sea salt
- ¼ cup (60 ml) extra-virgin olive oil
- 2 garlic cloves, crushed
- ½ bunch (¼ oz/7 g) mint leaves, finely chopped
- 3 tablespoons white wine vinegar
- 8 ounces (226 g) young goat cheese or stracchino (see page 27)
- 3 tablespoons slivered almonds, toasted

Alla scapece is a preparation popular in southern Italy. In Naples, zucchini prepared this way is on the menu everywhere. When I was an au pair, the family I worked for loved this dish, so I learned to make it. In Rome, we always ate it with stracchino, a young creamy cheese. That type of cheese can be difficult to find, so I whip up young soft goat cheese instead. It's delicious as an appetizer or side dish. If possible, use those tasty, small Italian zucchini with light skin. For color, I combine them with yellow squash.

Sprinkle the zucchini and squash slices with salt.

Heat a large skillet, add 3 tablespoons of the olive oil, and fry the zucchini slices until lightly brown on both sides. Do it in portions, so all the slices will get nice brown spots. Drain on a paper towel. Repeat with the squash slices.

Pour the remaining tablespoon of oil into the skillet, add the garlic cloves, and sauté over low heat until they are light brown. Add the mint leaves and white wine vinegar to the skillet. Remove from the heat, pour over the vegetables, and set aside for at least 30 minutes to allow the flavors to meld.

Meanwhile, whip the goat cheese with a blender. Spread on a plate and top with the zucchini and squash. Be sure to drizzle on any of the delicious liquid that remains in the skillet! Sprinkle the toasted almonds to finish the dish.

Panzanella con mango e lime

Tomato and bread salad with mango and lime

Preparation time:
15 minutes + 15 minutes
of resting

Serves 4

INGREDIENTS

1 ¾ pound (800 g) ripe
   tomatoes, cut into
   wedges
Sea salt
½ red onion, cut into
   thin rings
1 tablespoon red or white
   wine vinegar
2 celery stalks
4 snack cucumbers (about
   6 ¼ oz/175 g), sliced
1 ripe mango, peeled and
   cut into cubes or strips
¼ cup (60 ml) lime juice
1 teaspoon honey
2 tablespoons fish sauce
8 tablespoons extra-virgin
   olive oil
One (1-inch/2.5-cm) piece
   fresh ginger, peeled
Pinch chili flakes
2 thick slices stale bread
   (I use sourdough)
Few sprigs Thai basil
   leaves

I'm sure I'll drive Italians nuts with this panzanella variation, but even within Italy, there are lusty variations on this culinary theme. In Sicily, for example, they mix fried eggplant in their panzanella, and on the Tuscan coast they eat bread salad with seafood. I'm writing this to cover myself. Afraid of the rotten tomatoes coming my way from Italy in response to this panzanella with mango, lime, and a drizzle of fish sauce. But when you consider that the Romans embraced *garum* (a fish sauce from the 5th century BCE) and mangoes now grow on Sicily, it's not so crazy. Besides, many tomatoes are not as sweet as Italian ones, so the mango lends them a hand.

Place the tomatoes in a large bowl, and sprinkle with salt.

Mix the vinegar with 1 tablespoon of water and spoon over the onion rings in a large bowl to soak.

Remove the outer strings from the celery and cut the stalks into very thin slices. Bruise the cucumbers with a mortar and pestle, so the dressing can creep in, and add them and the mangos to the bowl with the tomatoes.

In a separate bowl, mix the lime juice with the honey, fish sauce, and 6 tablespoons of the olive oil. Grate the ginger and add it to the bowl along with the chili flakes. Mix well and then pour it over the tomato mixture. Stir well and rest for 15 minutes to allow the flavors to meld.

Preheat the oven to 400°F (200°C).

Tear the bread into coarse pieces, toss with the remaining 2 tablespoons of olive oil, and toast in the oven for 7 to 8 minutes to make croutons.

Divide the tomato mixture among four plates. Divide the onion rings and croutons on top, and garnish with a generous amount of Thai basil.

Porri stufati con salsa verde

Braised leeks with hazelnut salsa verde

Preparation time:
35 minutes

Serves 4

INGREDIENTS

Braised leeks
4 large leeks
Sea salt
2 tablespoons mild olive oil
2 tablespoons unsalted butter
½ cup (120 ml) white wine*

Salsa verde
1 egg
1 ½ ounces (40 g) parsley, finely
   chopped
1 ounce (30 g) mint, finely chopped
⅓ ounce (10 g) tarragon, finely
   chopped
2 teaspoons dill, finely chopped
⅓ cup (40 g) hazelnuts
⅓ cup (80 ml) extra-virgin olive oil
2 tablespoons capers, finely
   chopped + caper juice
3 anchovy fillets, finely chopped
1 ½ tablespoons white or red wine
   vinegar
Sea salt and freshly ground
   black pepper

If you don't have leftover table wine around, 3 tablespoons white wine vinegar will work just as well.

TIPS

Refrigerating the sauce? Put a layer of oil on top and store, covered, in the refrigerator. It will keep for at least 3 days. This is also delicious with roasted beets, fava beans, and celery root, or with a piece of grilled fish, chicken, or meat.

Prefer vegan? Replace the egg with a thick slice of bread soaked in some white wine vinegar. Replace the anchovy fillets with 1 tablespoon of finely chopped green olives.

No big skillet? You can also roast the leeks in the oven.

I usually serve this dish after a primo pasta course alongside a salad.

Salsa verde comes in many forms. In the Florentine trattoria, Casalinga, they add hard-boiled egg to it. Normally salsa verde is made with parsley, but I like to use whatever herbs I have lying around. Tarragon and dill taste very good with leeks, as does hazelnut.

Remove the outer leaves and dark green parts of the leeks. (You can save these and make broth, see page 357.) Rinse away any dirt. Cut off the roots and cut the leeks lengthwise into pieces about 4 inches (10 cm) long. Sprinkle the cut side with a pinch of salt. Heat a large skillet. Add the olive oil and butter and place the leeks, cut side down, in the skillet as soon as the butter begins to bubble. Sear for about 10 minutes over medium-high heat, until they turn a nice brown. Turn them over and sear on the other side. Deglaze with the wine. Reduce the heat to low and braise with a lid on the pan until the leeks are soft and sweet, about 15 to 20 minutes.

Meanwhile, make the salsa verde. Bring a large pot of water to a boil, and cook the egg for 10 minutes.

Scoop all the green herbs into a bowl. Peel the egg and press through a sieve over the bowl of herbs.

Toast the hazelnuts in a dry skillet and coarsely chop. Put them in the measuring cup of a hand blender with the extra-virgin olive oil and grind finely. Add to the herb mixture.

Add the capers, anchovies, and vinegar to the herb mixture. Stir well and season with a pinch of salt and freshly ground black pepper.

Arrange the leeks on a platter, drizzle with the salsa verde, and serve.

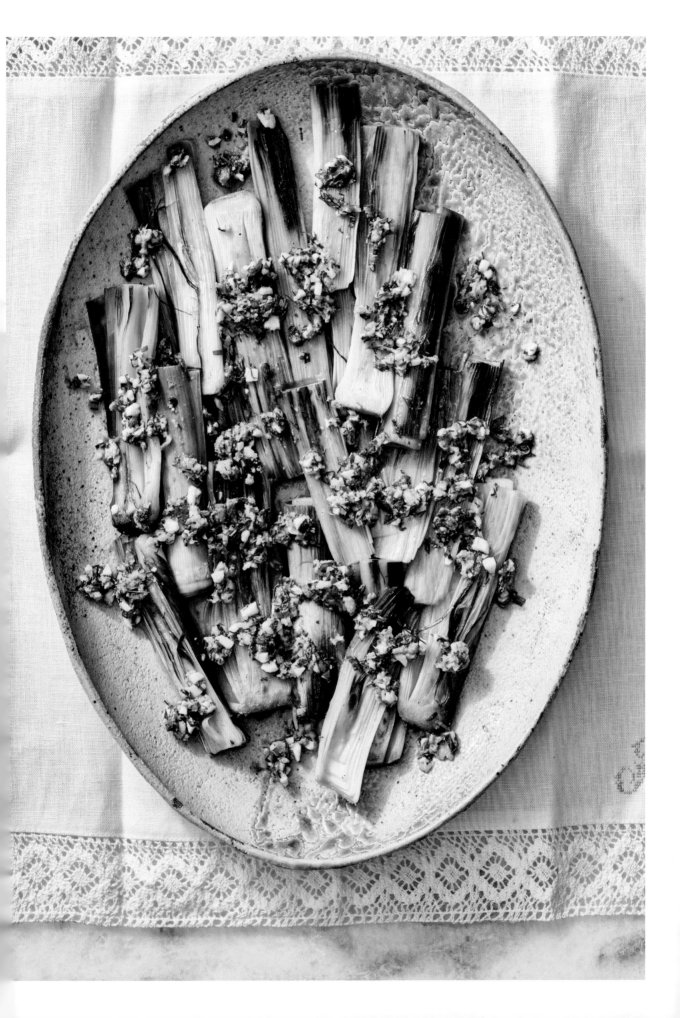

Capunet con funghi XO

Cabbage rolls with XO mushrooms, cream of Taleggio and porcini

Preparation time:
1½ hours

Serves 4 to 6

INGREDIENTS

1 ounce (30 g) dried
    porcini
12 cabbage leaves from
    a green cabbage*
2 shallots, chopped
2 garlic cloves, chopped
2 tablespoons mild
    olive oil
1 pound (450 g)
    mushrooms (for
    example, a mixture of
    shiitake and portobello),
    finely chopped
Sea salt
4 bay leaves
¾-inch (2-cm) piece ginger,
    peeled
1 tablespoon finely
    chopped rosemary
Chili flakes
⅓ cup (50 g) dry
    breadcrumbs
6 black garlic cloves
    (see page 25)
2½ tablespoons balsamic
    vinegar
2½ tablespoons soy sauce
1 egg
1¾ ounce (50 g)
    Parmesan, grated
2 tablespoons vegetable
    broth (page 357 or store
    bought)

Taleggio cream
1 cup (240 ml) heavy
    whipping cream
7 ounces (200 g)
    Taleggio**, diced
Sea salt

*Remove the outer leaves of
the cabbage, which are too
stiff for these cabbage rolls.
You can make cabbage chips
from that, if you want to.*

*If you can't find Taleggio,
you can use Brie or fontina.*

Capunet are cabbage rolls from Piedmont, originally stuffed with leftover meat. For this vegetarian mushroom stuffing, I was inspired by a Chinese umami bomb: XO sauce. I like this veggie capunet even better than the one with meat; there are so many layers of flavor in it. With the cream of Taleggio and porcini, this humble cabbage roll becomes a chic winter meal.

Soak the dried porcini in ½ cup (120 ml) of warm water. Bring a large pot of salted water to a boil.

Cook the cabbage leaves in the boiling water for 5 minutes. Drain and remove the thicker part of the center vein.

Heat the olive oil in a medium skillet and sauté the shallots for 5 minutes. Add the garlic and sauté for another 5 minutes or until soft.

Add the chopped mushrooms to the skillet with a pinch of salt and the bay leaves, and cook over high heat until the mushrooms brown. Grate the ginger into the skillet and mix into the mushrooms.

Finely chop half of the soaked porcini and add to the mushroom mixture along with the rosemary, a pinch of chili flakes, and the breadcrumbs. Cook until most of the liquid has evaporated.

Place the black garlic and the balsamic in a blender and purée until smooth. Add the soy sauce and blend again, then pour into the mushroom mixture.

Continue to sauté until the liquid is absorbed and allow to cool. Remove the bay leaves. Mix in the egg and grated Parmesan.

Preheat the oven to 360°F (180°C) and heat a grill over medium heat.

Using one cabbage leaf at a time, put 3 generous tablespoons of filling on the leaf, fold the sides of the leaf toward the center, and roll it closed. Repeat with the remaining rolls and place them in a baking dish. Once all of the cabbage leaves are assembled and on the baking dish, pour a few tablespoons of broth on top and bake, in the oven for 20 minutes.

Turn on the broiler. Brush the cabbages roles with butter and broil for 5 minutes until nicely browned..

Meanwhile, make the Taleggio cream. Remove the remaining porcini from the soaking liquid. Set a sieve lined with a paper towel or cheesecloth on top of the opening to a blender, and pour the liquid through the sieve into the blender (it should be approximately ¼ cup [60 ml] of liquid). Add the porcini and cream and blend until smooth. Pour into a saucepan, add the Taleggio cubes and allow to melt over low heat. Taste the sauce and season with a pinch of salt if necessary.

Divide the Taleggio cream between the plates and place 2 to 3 cabbage rolls on each plate, depending on the appetite of your diners. A glass of Barbera on the side and your evening can't go wrong.

Insalata di radicchio e sanguinello

Radicchio salad with blood orange and olive crumble

Preparation time:
35 minutes

Serves 4

INGREDIENTS

5 blood oranges
1 egg
1 teaspoon mustard
3 ½ tablespoons red
    wine vinegar
Sea salt and freshly
    ground black pepper
½ cup (120 ml)
    vegetable oil
¾ cup (105 g) pitted
    Taggiasca olives,
    well drained
1 head radicchio

Another salad with radicchio and blood orange? There are already countless variations, but this one is so simple and elegant that it would be incredibly selfish not to share it. I got the idea of boiling a whole orange to make a dressing from my former French restaurant colleague Sophie. The orange gives an awesome flavor to this creamy dressing and is perfect with bitter radicchio. Olive crumble sounds technical, but it amounts to drying out olives in the microwave until they are completely crumbly. The crumbs are like salty bacon pickles, but vegan.

Place 1 whole blood orange, with the peel on, in a pot with a steamer basket placed inside. Add water until just submerged. Boil for 20 minutes until soft. Transfer to a food processor. Add the egg, mustard, red wine vinegar, and a generous pinch of salt. Blend, adding the oil in a slow stream until it forms a lumpy dressing. Taste and season with the pepper and more salt if desired.

Peel the remaining 4 oranges. Once the peels are removed, either slice the oranges, or cut them into segments. Sprinkle the orange slices with sea salt.

Coarsely chop the olives and place them on a plate. Put them in the microwave for 5 to 7 minutes on the highest setting. (If you don't have a microwave, you can dry out the olives in the oven. Set the oven to 175˚F [80˚C], spread the well-dried olives out on a baking sheet lined with parchment paper, and bake for 1½ hours.) Allow to cool for 10 minutes and chop finely.

Tear the leaves of the radicchio into bite-sized pieces and place in a large bowl. Pour in dressing and gently toss the leaves with your hands until everything is evenly coated with dressing.

Grab a nice plate and arrange the radicchio leaves on it. Place the orange slices on top and sprinkle with the olive crumbles.

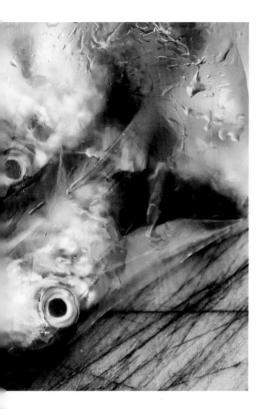

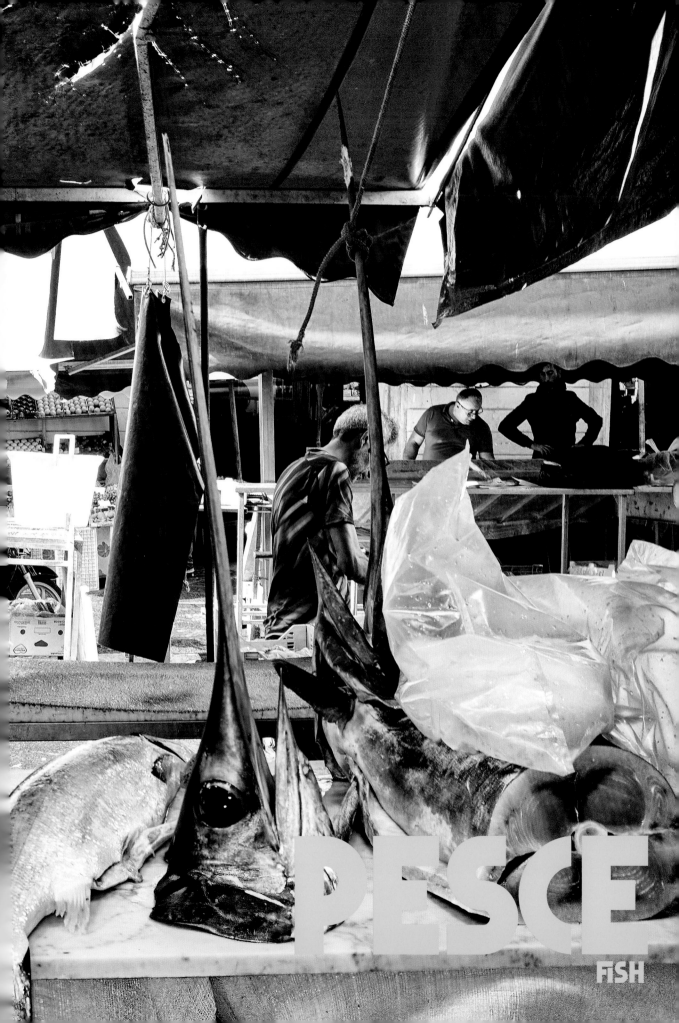

PESCE
FiSH

Fagioli con cime di rapa e spigola

Sea bass with chili-saffron beans and cime di rapa

Preparation time:
30 minutes

Serves 4

INGREDIENTS

4 dorado or sea bass
   fillets, at room
   temperature
Sea salt
Lemon mayo (optional;
   page 368)
1 pound (450 g)
   cime di rapa*
¼ cup (60 ml) extra-virgin
   olive oil
2 garlic cloves, crushed
1 ⅔ cups (400 ml) chicken
   or vegetable broth
   (pages 357-359 or store
   bought)
Two (15-ounce/440-g) cans
   white beans, drained
1 pinch saffron threads
1 teaspoon chili flakes
Vegetable oil
Zest from 1 lemon

*Learn more about cime
di rapa, where to get the
vegetable, and what to
substitute it with on page 26.*

Cime di rapa is a tasty, popular Italian vegetable similar to broccoli rabe. These vegetables have flavor and character. If you can't get ahold of it, you can use broccoli rabe, of course, or spinach. Swiss chard is also delicious paired with the creamy beans and fried fish. The lemon mayo with it may sound crazy, but it completes this dish. In Italy it is perfectly normal to serve fish with a dollop of mayo.

Sprinkle each sea bass fillet with a pinch of salt and set them aside. Now make the lemon mayo, if serving it.

Cut the florets from the cime di rapa and coarsely chop them so they cook evenly. Cut the stems into small pieces and finely slice the leaves.

Heat a large skillet and add the extra-virgin olive oil. Sauté the garlic until light brown, swirling the pan if necessary so that the oil runs to one side and the garlic is submerged and releases its flavor. Add the cime di rapa with a pinch of salt and sauté for a few minutes over medium-high heat. Lower the heat, add the broth and cook the vegetables for 10 minutes.

Add the beans, saffron, and chili flakes, and cook for an additional 5 minutes or until the vegetables are soft.

Next, heat another large skillet. For crispy fish skin that does not stick to the pan, add a drizzle of vegetable oil to the pan and place a piece of parchment paper in it so the paper will stick to the pan. Now add another drizzle of oil on top of the paper. Add the fish fillets, skin side down. Fry over medium-high heat until the skin is nice and crisp and the edges of the fish look cooked. Then flip and cook the other side briefly, for about 1 minute more. Then remove from the heat.

As an alternative, you can bake the fish in an oven preheated to 350°F (180°C). If you bake it, first brush the fish fillets with vegetable oil on the skin side, place them skin side down on a baking sheet, and bake for 10 minutes.

Meanwhile, mix the lemon zest into the vegetables. Spread them evenly on a platter and place the cooked fish fillets on top. Serve with the lemon mayo, if desired.

Carpaccio di polpo con gremolata

Octopus carpaccio with lime-coriander gremolata

Preparation time:
45 minutes + 1½ hours
stewing + 1 night
chilling + 30 minutes
in the freezer

Serves 4

—

INGREDIENTS

Octopus carpaccio
1 octopus (about
    2 pounds/900 g),
    cleaned and thawed
3 tablespoons olive oil
3 garlic cloves, crushed
Juice from 1 lemon
Sea salt
3 bay leaves (preferably
    fresh)

Gremolata
Zest and juice from
    2 limes
½ chili pepper, sliced
    into thin rounds
Sea salt
½ bunch (¼ ounce/7 g)
    cilantro, stems and
    leaves separated
3 ½ tablespoons
    extra-virgin olive oil
1 fennel tuber
1 lemon wedge

TIP
You'll need a clean,
cylindrical, plastic water
bottle, 16 to 20 ounces
(475 to 600 ml). Cut off
and remove the top third
and poke a few holes in
the bottom.

Nice and tender octopus carpaccio! I have tried every method of cooking octopus, from dipping the tentacles in boiling water to cooking it with a cork or potato, but it did not necessarily result in tender octopus. Freezing does help, and now most octopus is frozen immediately after being caught. But I have found that octopus is most delicious if you stew it in its own liquid. How long depends on the size, but count on about 1 to 1 ½ hours per 2 pounds (900 g). As for the cilantro, it's blasphemy in Italy, but the flavors taste great together. Plus wine bar Tannico in Milan serves shellfish with cilantro, so I feel justified!

Usually octopus has already been cleaned and the intestines and ink sac removed. If you have to remove the mouth, you'll find it in the middle of the tentacles. Cut loose with a sharp knife and remove.

To make the Octopus carpaccio, rinse the octopus clean and pat dry. Heat a large casserole dish and pour in the olive oil. Add the octopus along with the garlic, bay leaf, half of the lemon juice, and a scant pinch of salt. Not too much; octopus is salty by itself. Put a lid on the pan and stew the octopus over low heat for 1 to 1 ½ hours until tender. Check with a knife; if it slides through, the octopus is done.

Remove the octopus from the pan and cut into large pieces. You won't use the sauce left in the pan in this recipe, but it tastes delicious mixed through pasta or risotto.

Place the modified plastic bottle vertically in a bowl. Now place the ctopus pieces tightly into the bottle. Next, press the octopus toward the bottom of the bottle with a pestle or spoon; liquid will drain out at the bottom. Using kitchen shears, make four evenly spaced vertical cuts in the top of the bottle, stopping right before you get to the octopus. Fold the four strips you cut from the top of the bottle over the octopus as if you were closing a package. It will further compact the octopus and all of the liquid will run out. Wrap plastic wrap all around it, place the bowl in the refrigerator with something heavy on top, and chill for at least 8 hours and up to overnight.

Remove the octopus from the refrigerator, take it out of the plastic bottle, and place in the freezer for another 30 minutes.

To make the gremolata, zest the limes and place the zest into a bowl. Next, squeeze the juice from the limes into the bowl. Add the chili pepper rounds plus a pinch of salt. Finely chop the stems of the cilantro and add these as well. Add the olive oil, whisk the ingredients together, and then set it aside to allow the flavors to meld.

Cut paper-thin slices of the fennel, using a mandolin or sharp knife. The thinner, the more luxurious it tastes. Season the fennel with a squeeze of lemon juice and a pinch of salt.

Cut the octopus into thin slices, place on a large platter or individual plates. Place a portion of fennel in the center and spoon the gremolata over it. Finish with the cilantro leaves.

Scampi con zabaglione di bottarga

Langoustines with bottarga zabaglione

Preparation time:
25 minutes

Serves 4

___

INGREDIENTS

8 crisp fresh langoustines
(or large prawns)

Bottarga zabaglione
4 egg yolks
Sea salt
1 to 2 tablespoons grated
bottarga (see page 26)
Zest from 1 lemon
2 tablespoons white wine

Few chives, finely chopped

TIPS
The bottarga zabaglione
is also very tasty with a
piece of white fish or with
grilled vegetables, such
as pointed cabbage.
Or serve with pasta and
spicy endive.

This dish is for my friend Pietro. We met during our college days. Crazy things always happen with Pi, as if he attracted them. Once, when I visited him in Florence, I wanted to go to the beach. He agreed, but kept procrastinating as the day went on. Italians are masters at it. First, we had to go to an antique market, then he ran into an acquaintance, and it was the afternoon by the time we were on our way in his parents' car. But then the car broke down. Pi was yelling at his father through the phone. I was amazed at the tone he took with his father in a country where *la famiglia* is sacred. We waited in the red-hot heat for a tow truck, then we were dropped in a village where we waited in vain for half an hour for a bus. Finally, we hitchhiked. By that point, we could almost smell the beach. Finally, a car stopped. The Neapolitan behind the wheel was willing to take us but first had to take a tray of langoustines to a restaurant on the coast. By the way, didn't we want to buy his car? He was selling it. I didn't want that car. I wanted those langoustines!

Rinse the langoustines well under running water and pat them dry. With a sharp knife, cut them lengthwise all the way from the head, so that they unfold. Remove the intestinal tract. It is usually near the tail.

Preheat a grill over medium-high heat.

To make the bottarga zabaglione, put the egg yolks in a bowl that fits on a saucepan. Fill the pan one-third full with water and bring to a boil.

Beat the yolks with a pinch of salt until frothy. Place the bowl on the pan of boiling water and keep whisking while you add the wine. (By the way, I use the hand blender with the whisk attachment for this. Manual whisking is also possible, but more labor intensive.) Beat until a thick cream forms. Turn off the heat when the zabaglione is nice and thick. Add the bottarga and lemon zest and mix well. Remove from the heat, continue whisking for a few more minutes, and set the zabaglione aside.

Grill the langoustines for a few minutes on the shell side. Carefully turn them over and cook for an additional minute on the other side. Really only briefly.

Place them on a large platter, stir the zabaglione again, spoon it over the langoustines and garnish with the chopped chives.

Crudo di spigola

Raw sea bass with samphire citrus salsa and orange zest

Preparation time:
15 minutes

Serves 4

INGREDIENTS

14 ounces (400 g) fresh
   skinless sea bass fillet
Zest and juice from
   1 orange
Handful Gaeta olives
   (or other tasty black
   olives such as Kalamata
   or Taggiasca)
3 ½ ounces (100 g)
   samphire*, washed well
Juice from 1 lemon

* If you can't find samphire,
substitute with thin
asparagus.

Simple dish, great effect. Make sure you get really fresh, high quality sea bass. You can eat many types of fish raw, as long as the fish is extremely fresh. That reminds me of a legendary eatery in Gallipolì, at the southern tip of Puglia. The first time I was there, about twenty years ago, I was amazed. A beautiful town and absolutely zero tourism. How different it is now. The last time Remko and I were there with our children, we fled the crazed historic center. On the way to the car, close by the port, we stumbled upon a fish market where two scruffy types were opening crisp shells. They were preparing huge platters of seafood, all served raw. From clams to shrimp to all sorts of native shells. The food was served outside. If you wanted a bottle of wine, you had to knock on the door of the neighboring, groggy pizza restaurant. It was a great experience. Be sure to stop by Pescheria Fratelli Quintana if you're in the area. For now, make this crudo of sea bass. I purposefully use olives with pits. They have more flavor. Please don't get those black rubber things from the can. The crudo salsa is fresh and salty and delicious with fish. Don't make the sauce until the last second, because it loses color quickly.

Cut the fish crosswise into thin slices. (You can do this ahead of time if you are having a dinner party and want to prep. Store the fish in the refrigerator until you are close to serving, then allow it to come to room temperature before plating the food.)

Bring a large pot of water to a boil and set a bowl of ice water nearby.

Peel the orange rind with a vegetable peeler, making sure not to take the bitter white pith with it. Then cut the peel into gossamer-thin oblong strips and set aside for garnish.

Gently hit the olives with the bottom of a glass or mug so that they split. This way you can easily remove the pits then finely chop the olives.

To make the sauce, place the samphire in boiling water for 1 minute and then transfer to the ice water. Drain well in a colander. Squeeze approximately ⅓ cup (80 ml) of orange juice. Next, squeeze about 2 tablespoons of lemon juice. Purée the samphire with the orange and lemon juices in a blender until creamy.

Divide the sauce among four plates or two bowls. Place the sea bass slices on top and finish with the olives and orange zest. Serve immediately.

Fave e cicoria con calamaretti fritti

Fava bean purée with chicory and fried squid

Preparation time:
soaking overnight +
45 minutes

Serves 4

___

INGREDIENTS

Fava bean purée
14 ounces (400 g) dried,
    double shelled fava
    beans*
2 bay leaves
½ teaspoon sea salt

1 pound (450 g) baby
    octopus or baby squid
1 bunch (about 14 oz/
    400 g) chicory (more info
    on page 26)
3 tablespoons extra-virgin
    olive oil
2 garlic cloves, crushed
1 teaspoon chili flakes
Vegetable oil, for frying
1 cup (140 g) all-purpose
    flour or semolina
4 lemon wedges,
    to garnish

** You can also use other
beans, even canned ones,
like lima beans or Spanish
butter beans. Learn more
about dried fava beans on
page 26.*

Fave e cicoria from Puglia is *cucina povera* (peasant food) of the highest order. Creamy purée of dried fava beans with chicory, a leafy vegetable from southern Italy with a hearty flavor. Adding crunchy squid turns it into a fancy dish. I used baby arrowtail squid, but baby octopus can also be used, which is often already cleaned and quicker to prepare. Even clams or shrimp would work; they all taste great with fava bean purée. If you prefer not to deep-fry, you can also grill the squid. Serve this as an appetizer, snack, or side dish.

To make the fava bean purée, rinse the fava beans in water and then place them in a pot and submerge them in water. Add the bay leaves and salt and bring to a boil. Lower the heat and simmer until soft, about 25 minutes. Drain the beans, but save the cooking liquid in a separate bowl. Purée the beans until smooth in a blender, adding as much cooking liquid as needed until you have a smooth purée, then set aside.

Bring a pot of salted water to a boil.

Baby octopus are usually already cleaned, squid often need cleaning. Check at your fish counter. I cleaned the baby squids and cut them into pieces: the more crispy surface, the bigger the feast. But see for yourself what you like. Pat the cleaned octopus or squid dry with paper towels, sprinkle with salt, and set aside.

Pull the leaves from the chicory stalks and wash them. Cut into pieces about 3 inches (7.5 cm) long. Add the chicory to the boiling water and cook for 3 minutes.

Next, heat a skillet, add the extra-virgin olive oil, and sauté the garlic cloves until they are light brown. Add the chili flakes. Using a slotted spoon, transfer the chicory from the boiling water to the skillet. Season with a pinch of salt and sauté for a few more minutes. Remove from the heat.

Fill a pan with a layer of vegetable oil that will allow the squid to be completely submerged. (You can also use a deep fryer.) Check if the oil is hot enough by dipping in one piece of squid. If the oil bubbles, you can get started.

Sprinkle the flour in a shallow bowl and roll the squid in it. Shake off as much of the flour as possible and lower it into the hot oil one piece at a time. Deep-fry for a few minutes, until light brown and crispy. Remove from the oil with a slotted spoon and drain on a paper towel-lined plate while you fry the rest.

Reheat the fava bean purée and chicory, divide among four plates and top with the squid. Serve with the lemon wedges.

Fagioli con baccalà mantecato

Yvette's beans with cod brandade and 'nduja croutons

Preparation time:
12 hours of soaking + at least
1 ½ hours of stewing

Serves 4

INGREDIENTS

Baccalà mantecato
(optional; page 59)

Fagioli
3 cups (480 g) dried beans
  (white, cannellini,
  or black-eyed)
Sea salt
5 to 6 garlic cloves, crushed
1 to 2 small vine tomatoes, coarsely
  chopped
Few thyme or oregano sprigs
Extra-virgin olive oil
2 ½ cups (50 g) arugula
7 ounces (200 g) spinach
1 lemon
1 tablespoon 'nduja
2 slices stale bread,
  torn into crouton-sized pieces

TIPS

These beans lend themselves to a variety of dishes. For example, grate bottarga over them and serve the beans with a piece of cod or scallops. Or serve the beans with grilled cabbage and a dot of ricotta or with spicy Tuscan kale and sausage.

A word about salting beans: many cooks say that immediate salting makes the beans tough, but that myth has long been debunked by culinary scientist Harold McGee. Whether or not beans become tough depends more on age. I personally salt them at the beginning. I had leftover baccalà (see page 59). It's similar to brandade and is a divine combo with beans. But a side of fried cod is just as tasty. Use what you have on hand. Those 'nduja croutons are mandatory, though. Viciously delicious.

The advantage of cooking your own beans is that they come with free soup—the cooking liquid. You don't have to explain that to Italians. For example, fagioli al fiasco is an ancient Tuscan method of cooking beans in an urn with water, garlic, herbs, and a dash of olive oil. These ceramic jars used to be placed in the embers of the baker's fire where the beans cooked low and slow. My friend and Dutch cookbook author's beans are fagioli al fiasco times a thousand. She also cooks them slowly with garlic, herbs, and a dash of oil, but she goes one step further. She adds tomatoes, and at the end she reduces the cooking liquid, seasons it with a dash of vinegar or lemon juice, and pours it back over the beans. Because I think everyone should learn about this preparation in Italy, I included Yvette's beans in this book.

Soak the beans in a bowl of water for 12 hours. Drain them, place them in a saucepan, and cover them with clean water. Bring to a boil, then turn the heat low. Add a pinch of salt, the garlic cloves, the tomatoes, and a few sprigs of herbs.

Pour a generous splash of the olive oil, and cook over low heat until tender. Exactly how long depends on the age of the beans; it varies between 1 to 2 hours. Taste them periodically to check for tenderness, and add salt to taste.

When the beans are cooked, ladle out the cooking liquid and simmer it until it has been reduced by half in a separate pot. Season with lemon juice and then pour the liquid back over the beans.

Heat 1 tablespoon of the olive oil in a skillet and sauté the arugula and spinach with a pinch of salt until just wilted. Finish with a squeeze of lemon juice. Remove from the pan.

Heat the remaining tablespoon of the olive oil in the frying pan and add the 'nduja. Once the 'nduja is melted, add the bread pieces, and fry until crispy.

Spoon the beans into bowls, top with the shredded vegetables and a dollop of baccalà, if using. Finish with the 'nduja croutons.

If you serve the beans with baccalà mantecato, make that first and keep in mind that the fish needs to desalt for 24 hours.

€ 4,50
CASTRA

CARNE
MEAT

SPACCIO CARNI 5

MAIALE

SPALLA	(5.99)	€\kg
COSCIA INTERA\METÀ	(4.99)	€\kg
ARISTA	(5.99)	€\kg
COPPA	(5.99)	€\kg
PANCETTA con COSTINA	(5.99)	€\kg
COSTINE	(5.99)	€\kg
BRACIOLE di MAIALE	(5.99)	€\kg
SALSICCIA	(5.99)	€\kg
FRATTAGLIE	( )	€\kg
PORCHETTA SARDA	( )	€\kg

Polpette al sugo e crema di formaggio
Meatballs in tomato sauce with Parmesan cream

Preparation time:
1 hour + 30 minutes cooling

Serves 4 (makes about
16 to 18 balls)

_____

INGREDIENTS

Meatballs
2 thick slices stale bread
  without crust or 1 ½ cups
  (200 g) dry breadcrumbs
Milk
2 pounds (900 g) ground veal
  or half ground beef and half
  ground pork
3 eggs
8 ¾ ounces (250 g) cheese
  (half pecorino and
  half Parmesan, or just
  Parmesan), grated
2 garlic cloves, peeled
1 large bunch (¾ oz/20 g)
  of parsley leaves, finely
  chopped
1 teaspoon chili flakes
Sea salt
Sunflower oil, for frying

Tomato sauce
1 onion
1 carrot
1 celery stalk
2 tablespoons extra-virgin
  olive oil
4 ¼ cups (1 L) tomato sauce

Parmesan cream
1 cup (240 ml) heavy whipping
  cream
2 pounds (900 g) Parmesan,
  grated
Sea salt
Freshly grated nutmeg
Freshly ground black pepper

Handful basil leaves,
  to garnish

TIPS
If you would rather not deep-
fry the meatballs, you can
use an air fryer, or brush the
balls with oil and cook until
browned on all sides. Deep-
frying sears the balls and
keeps them juicy inside.

Bono gets out of bed for these meatballs. Yes, the one from U2. We ate them at Mimì alla Ferrovia, an iconic family restaurant in Naples right by the train station. Celebrities come here—that's widely publicized with the many photos on the wall. There is a jovial atmosphere and the décor is chic. In other words: meatballs and table linens. In addition to classics like those buttery balls and caprese, there are also modern dishes, like langoustine tartare and potato croquette with kimchi of cime di rapa. Chef Salvatore was good enough to share the recipe for his polpette; I adapted it to a home-made version. Ideal for when a group of people are coming for dinner, because who doesn't love a fancy ball?

To make the meatballs, soak the stale bread in enough milk to be submerged.

In a large bowl, mix the ground meat with eggs and cheese. Grate the garlic cloves on a fine grater over the bowl. Mix in the parsley, chili flakes, and 1 teaspoon of salt.

Squeeze the milk from the bread, add to the meat mixture, and mix well. Form the mixture into large balls, about 2 inches (5 cm) in diameter. Cover and place in the refrigerator to firm.

To make the tomato sauce, finely chop the vegetables. Heat the olive oil in a skillet and sauté the vegetables until soft. Add the tomato sauce and season with a pinch of salt. Let simmer for 20 minutes.

In a deep saucepan, pour the sunflower oil deep enough to deep-fry the meatballs. Deep-fry the balls in batches until lightly browned. Scoop the cooked meatballs from the oil with a slotted spoon and drain on a plate lined with paper towels. Add to the tomato sauce and cook over low heat for another 20 minutes.

Meanwhile, make the Parmesan cream. Warm the cream in a saucepan. Add the cheese and allow it to melt. Season generously with salt, freshly grated nutmeg, and freshly ground black pepper. Do not let it boil. If you would like to add stripes of cream on the meatballs to impress, pour the Parmesan cream into a piping bag and zig zag across the balls. Garnish with basil.

Cotoletta di pollo con puntarelle

Breaded chicken with anchovy mayo and puntarelle salad

Preparation time:
45 minutes

Serves 4

___

INGREDIENTS

Anchovy mayo
(page 369)

1 bunch Catalonian
   chicory*
2 large whole chicken
   breasts
Sea salt and freshly
   ground black pepper
1 bunch red endive, thinly
   sliced
1 cup (140 g) all-purpose
   flour
1 large egg
1 cup (60 g) panko or dry
   breadcrumbs
1 ¾ ouces (50 g) Parmesan,
   grated
Sunflower oil
2 blood oranges, peel and
   pith removed and cut
   into segments
Lemon wedges

*More info on page 26.
If you can't find Catalonian
chicory, substitute with red
endive.*

TIP

If you don't want to
make the Anchovy mayo
from scratch, blend 8 to
10 anchovy fillets with
1 ¼ cups (300 g) of
mayonnaise and season
with lemon juice
and pepper.

Puntarelle are typical winter vegetables. They are the shoots of what later becomes chicory, a bitter leafy vegetable. Italians love bitter, a taste you learn to appreciate if you know how to cook with it. Puntarelle are traditionally prepared with anchovies; the salty balances the bitter. But bitter also likes fat. Enter: breaded chicken Parmesan.

First make the mayonnaise.

Remove the outer dark leaves from the chicory. (Discard them or blanch these and stir-fry them with garlic and chili pepper to eat separately.) From the lighter, inner shoots, remove the hard bottom and cut the shoots lengthwise into very thin strips. Place them in a bowl of ice water for 30 minutes. They will curl nicely and become milder in flavor. Drain and pat them dry.

Cut the chicken breasts in half lengthwise into four cutlets. Place plastic wrap or wax paper on top of the chicken and then, using a meat mallet or frying pan, hit them until the fillets become thin. The thinner they are, the faster they will cook and the more tender they will be. Remove the plastic wrap and sprinkle the fillets with salt. Set aside.

Prepare two flat plates and one deep plate, like a pie dish. Sprinkle the flour on one of the flat plates, whisk the egg with 1 tablespoon of water in the deep plate, and sprinkle the other flat plate liberally with the panko. Mix the Parmesan into the panko. Place the fillets first in the flour, press well, and turn over. Then place them in the egg, press, and turn again. Finally, place them on the panko-Parmesan mixture, press, flip, and press on the other side.

Heat a spacious frying pan over medium-high heat and add a generous amount of sunflower oil. Once the oil is hot, fry the fillets on both sides for a few minutes per side until golden brown. Drain on a paper towel-lined plate.

Place the chicory, endive, and orange segments in a bowl, dollop on some of the Anchovy mayo (you won't need all of it), and mix.

Serve the chicken with lemon wedges and the chicory salad. Grind black pepper on top.

Spezzatino di agnello

Lamb stew with fava beans and mint labneh

Preparation time:
4 hours draining +
1 ½ hours stewing

Serves 4

INGREDIENTS

- 2 cups (480 g) Greek yogurt
- Sea salt and freshly ground black pepper
- 2 pounds (900 g) lamb shoulder (may be substituted with veal shanks or shoulder)
- All-purpose flour, to dust the meat
- 3 tablespoons mild olive oil
- 1 large onion, chopped
- 1 ½ tablespoons fennel seeds, crushed
- 1 carrot, grated
- 2 celery stalks, thinly sliced
- 2 garlic cloves, crushed and chopped
- ½ cup (120 ml) white wine
- 4 ¼ cups (1 L) vegetable or chicken stock (pages 357, 359 or store bought)
- 1 sprig rosemary
- 3 sprigs sage
- 2 sprigs thyme
- 2 bay leaves
- 1 lemon
- 2 pounds (900 g) fava beans, in the pods
- 1 bunch (¾ oz/20 g) mint leaves, finely chopped

TIP

You'll also need cheesecloth or a clean tea towel and kitchen twine.

Spezzatino is an Italian stew. It's often made from veal, but it can also be made with other types of meat. For this recipe, I used lamb and paired it with fava beans, which is a typical spring dish in Italy. Yogurt is a no-go in Italian cuisine, but this thick, drained labneh pairs perfectly with the rich lamb. I was inspired by a dish I once ate with Belgian chef Kobe Desramault, who served stewed lamb with very fresh cheese and fava beans. Just try it, this is divine.

Put a strainer on a bowl, place a cheesecloth or clean tea towel in it. Spoon in the Greek yogurt, mix with a pinch of salt, and allow to drain for at least 4 hours.

Cut the meat into chunks—the chunks will shrink so don't cut them too small—and sprinkle with salt and flour. Heat the olive oil in a large pot. Once the oil is hot, add the lamb pieces, and brown the meat all around. Remove from the pot.

Add additional olive oil to the pan if necessary, and braise the onion in the pot. Add the fennel, carrot, celery, and garlic to the pot. Return the meat to the pot and deglaze with the wine over high heat. Lower the heat and add the broth. Tie all of the herbs together with kitchen twine, cut the lemon peel off of the lemon in strips, and add the herbs and lemon peel to the pot. Simmer over low heat with the lid halfway on the pan for about 1 ½ hours.

Time to shell the fava beans, which is a bit of a chore. You can do this ahead of time, or use child labor if you have a cooperative kid on hand. Remove the beans from their pods. Blanch them, rinse cold and then remove from their individual shells: slice them open with your thumb nail and gently squeeze so they will pop out of their jackets. Very little ones don't need to be removed from their individual shells.

Mix the mint leaves into the drained yogurt. Season with pepper and more salt if necessary. Serve the meat with the fava beans and labneh.

Porchetta con insalata di lenticchie

Porchetta with lentil salad and roasted beets

Preparation time:
35 minutes + 1 night
brining + 3 to 4 hours
of cooking (count on
1 hour per 2 pounds
[900 g] of meat)

Serves 10

INGREDIENTS

Porchetta

7 ¾ pounds pork (3.5 kg)
   (the belly with the piece
   of boned rib and rind
   attached)*
Coarse sea salt
3 ½ tablespoons extra-
   virgin olive oil
2 tablespoons white wine
   vinegar
¾ ounce (20 g) rosemary
   sprigs, leaves removed
   and finely chopped +
   3 extra sprigs
1 ounce (30 g) sage leaves,
   finely chopped
¼ cup (25 g) fennel seeds
8 garlic cloves
3 ½ tablespoons fine
   sea salt**
Zest from 3 lemons
1 ¾ ouces (50 g) dill,
   finely chopped

Lentil and beet salad

2 ¼ pounds beets
2 lemons
2 ½ cups (500 g) small
   green lentils
1 teaspoon granulated
   sugar
½ teaspoon sea salt
2 tablespoons balsamic
   vinegar
¼ cup (60 ml) extra-virgin
   olive oil
3 ¾ cups (75 g) arugula

* The rind is the thick skin that
will later become nice and
crispy.

** Count on 1 tablespoon salt
per 2 pounds (900 g) of meat.

During my time in Florence, I was dating a pork aficionado named Lorenzo. On special occasions he would bring porchetta from Siena. It was the most divine giant porchetta, juicy inside, full of spices and a crispy rind. Liver was also cooked inside, and often a whole arista—a kind of pork loin—went in as well. That's too much for a home recipe, so I adapted it to an achievable version. In Lazio, porchetta is flavored with rosemary, among other things; in Tuscany with *finocchietto* (wild fennel). I use my own blend of herbs. Porchetta looks impressive, and it's a serious crowd-pleaser. And the funny thing is that it's not hard to make at all. The only key thing is to order a good piece of meat from your butcher.

For the Porchetta, lay the piece of pork in front of you and butterfly it with a fillet knife, if it's thick. To butterfly, cut the piece of meat horizontally and flip it open. This doesn't have to be precise; you won't see any of it later anyway. Now turn the meat with the rind up. Sprinkle the rind generously with coarse sea salt and let stand while you prepare the stuffing.

In a saucepan, heat the olive oil with the white wine vinegar, turn off the heat, and add 3 sprigs of rosemary. Set aside.

Finely crush the fennel seed in a mortar with a pestle, add the garlic cloves and fine sea salt and grind until mashed. Mix with the chopped sage and rosemary. Add the lemon zest and dill.

Pat the rind dry and turn the piece of meat over again. Rub the meat all over with the rosemary-infused oil. Then spread the spice mixture on top and massage it in. Grind black pepper generously over the top.

Cut 4 to 5 pieces of kitchen twine long enough to wrap around the porchetta once it's rolled. Roll the meat tightly, starting at the thinnest part and tie the roll with kitchen twine. Cut the rind deeply here and there. Place the porchetta uncovered in the refrigerator overnight. This will allow the rind to dry out and become even crispier. You can also cook the porchetta immediately, but if you do, brine the meat beforehand, making it juicier and more flavorful (the salt binds the moisture in the meat).

When you are ready to cook the meat, preheat the oven to 300°F (150°C).

Wrap the sides of the roast with aluminum foil and place the meat on a rack in a roasting pan. Pour water into the roasting pan so it comes up the sides 1 inch (2 ½ cm) and slide into the oven. Now go and do something else for 3 hours. Occasionally pop back into the kitchen to pour some more water into the drip tray. After 3 hours, check the temperature of the meat. It's done when the inside is around 140°F (60°C).

TIPS

You'll need kitchen twine and a meat thermometer.

Leftover porchetta is great to eat in a sandwich the next day. Delicious with mostarda (see page 367) or sweet and sour vegetables.

This lentil salad goes well with the porchetta, but is also delicious with a baked sausage or grilled tomino cheese.

You can also make a decadent autumnal porchetta with truffle, porcini, and Tuscan kale. For this you will need: 2 ¾ ounces (80 g) dried porcini rehydrated in water and finely chopped, 4 ½ ounces (120 g) of truffle tapenade, and 2 bunches of cavolo nero (black cabbage), center veins removed and then blanched. In addition, use sage, rosemary, garlic, and salt as described on the prior page.

Meanwhile, make the lentil and beet salad. Roast the beets (without covering them in foil) in the oven. I roast them along with the porchetta because the oven is on anyway. You can roast them with the meat for about 3 hours. If you cook them separately, it can be done more quickly and at a higher temperature: about 1½ to 2 hours at 400°F (200°C). Cut the lemons in half and roast them in the oven for the last 30 minutes. Remove from the oven, allow to cool, and peel the beets.

Now take the roasting pan out of the oven, remove the roasting rack, discard the foil, and place the porchetta directly in the drippings. Raise the oven temperature to 450°F (230°C) and turn on the convection setting, if you have one, and crisp the porchetta in the oven for another ½ to 1 hour or until the core temperature reaches 150°F (65°C). Roll the porchetta a little bit at a time so that all sides of the rind are blistered and crispy. When the porchetta is done, leave to rest for 15 minutes. When you are ready to serve, cut nice thick slices with a large, sharp knife.

Rinse the lentils under cold water and cook according to package directions until al dente. Squeeze the juice from the roasted lemons into a bowl, add the sugar, salt, balsamic vinegar, and a generous amount of freshly ground black pepper. Add olive oil until the mixture is the consistency of salad dressing.

Drain the lentils and mix them into the dressing while they are still warm. Cut the beets into wedges and add to the lentils with the arugula.

Serve the porchetta with the salad.

VEGETARIAN WITH MEAT DNA
Sarah Cicolini

Sarah Cicolini is combative and serious, always looking to improve, constantly open to innovation, and cooks her balls off. And when she's not cooking? "Then I'm busy with bureaucracy," the thirty-five-year-old restaurant owner says with an ironic grin. It's nine in the morning. With a punishingly strong thimble of coffee and phone in hand so she can work while we talk, we begin our conversation.

Sarah, who hails from Abruzzo, has now been adopted by the city where she has lived for many years, Rome. In the San Giovanni district, not far from the neighborhood where, as a nineteen-year-old au pair, I babysat a baby and a four-year-old child during the day and made Rome unsafe at night, Sarah runs her neo-trattoria. At Santo Palato, you need to make a reservation weeks in advance. By noon, the joint is packed with culinary tourists, among them a young chef on an inspirational visit and a hip Israeli couple. Beside us, Romans feast on Sarah's buttery porchetta with an ethereal hint of wild fennel, the perfect blend of Abruzzo and Lazio.

Sarah is pretty much vegetarian. Still, she cooks a lot with the less common parts of animals in search of more ethical meat consumption. "If you cook with animals, use them completely." It's the adage of Roman cuisine, but it was also instilled in her with the Abruzzese nurture. "If my grandmother had wrung ten chickens' necks, she was stuck with the entrails; she then made a kind of scrambled eggs with that."Sarah shows how she adapted that dish. From the livers she makes a pâté and the "scrambled eggs" becomes a soufflé. Her dishes are edgy, including a savory oxtail pie, a riff on a traditional Roman stew.

A whole *romanesco aglio olio peperoncino* (cauliflower with olive oil and peperoncino pepper) comes to the table. Smoky, spicy, and perfect. The dishes that come out of the kitchen are true to the gastronomic tradition of Central Italy while evoking a subtle evolution. You can tell and taste she has cooked in starred restaurants. "I soon understood that that type of restaurant was not for me."

Inspired by the bistronomy trend in Paris and taking neo-trattoria pioneer Consorzio in Turin as an example, Cicolini started her own business in 2017. It is a tumultuous era in which much is changing. The rise of natural wine and the philosophy surrounding it, more attention to the origin of products, and through social media, a whole new world is unfolding for Sarah and chefs of her generation. They exchange ideas and enrich each other's fields. "During the Covid outbreak, I did all kinds of collaborations. In Taiwan in China, Los Angeles, Canada, Australia. It has broadened my view and changed my perspective."

At Santo Palato, eighty percent of the dishes are based on tradition. "Traditional dishes are usually about seasonal produce, about endurance, and as little waste as possible." Yet you'll also find flavorings like katsuobushi, miso, or algae. "Everything to get the best flavor out of our dishes." She is clear about one thing: *i primi non si toccano* (the primi should be left alone). They are good the way they are. Then to conclude less adamantly, "I am never finished. There is always something to learn, my restaurant is a work in progress."

"ITALIAN CUISINE IS SO FAMOUS BECAUSE WE MAKE EATING THE MOST IMPORTANT TIME OF THE DAY."

Coda alla vaccinara rivisitata

Pithivier with Roman oxtail and parsley-lime salsa

Preparation time:
1 hour + 3 to 4 hours
of stewing

Serves 4

___

INGREDIENTS

3 ½ pounds (1.5 kg) oxtail
Sea salt and freshly
   ground black pepper
¼ cup (60 ml) extra-virgin
   olive oil
8 celery stalks
1 onion, chopped
2 carrots, grated
1 tablespoon tomato
   paste
⅔ cup (160 ml) red wine
Puff pastry sheets
   (1 pound/450 g)
4 garlic cloves
1 ½ cans (1 ⅓ lb/600 g)
   peeled tomatoes
½ tablespoon cocoa
   powder
1 tablespoon fish sauce or
   colatura di alici
   (see page 26)
Zest and juice from 1 lime
1 egg, beaten
2 tablespoons yellow
   raisins, soaked in water

Parsley-lime salsa
(page 368)

Romans are experts at using all parts of animals. Americans often find using the cuts that don't come in plastic wrap from the grocery store off-putting, which is why I have an entry-level recipe for you all to try for your first attempt at branching out: oxtail. It's delicious and makes excellent gravy. In the classic coda alla vaccinara, oxtail is simmered with cloves and celery, among other things. Chef Sarah Cicolini (see page 246) turns it into something truly phenomenal. For you, I came up with an easy-to-make homemade savoury oxtail pie. The amount of oxtail seems like a lot for four, but there usually isn't much meat on it.

Sprinkle the oxtail with salt and pepper. Heat 2 tablespoons of the olive oil in a large pot. When the oil is hot, add the oxtail, and brown on all sides. If necessary, do this in portions. Remove from the pot.

Finely chop 3 of the celery stalks. Sauté the celery, onion, and carrots in the remaining 2 tablespoons of olive oil along with the tomato paste. Add the oxtail and deglaze with the wine. Add the garlic and the tomatoes and enough water to submerge the meat. Season with salt, cover the pot, and simmer for 3 to 4 hours or until the meat is ready to fall off the bone.

Remove the oxtail and allow to cool. Pick the meat off the bones and set aside. Sift the cocoa powder into the pot. Mix in ½ tablespoon of the fish sauce. Taste and season further if necessary. Mix in the lime zest. Strain the gravy and return the meat to the pot. Pour the gravy over the meat and cook until the gravy is completely absorbed by the meat. Set aside to let cool. Defrost the puff pastry while the oxtail cooks.

Preheat the oven to 400°F (200°C). Cut out rounds with a diameter of about 5 inches (11-12 cm). Notch half of the rounds from the center with a sharp knife and make a fan pattern (see photo).

Divide the cooled meat between the puff pastry rounds without the fan pattern. Cover with the notched rounds of puff pastry and press along the edges so that the tarts close. Brush with the beaten egg. Bake the pithiviers in the oven for 30 minutes or until nicely browned.

Thinly slice the remaining celery and place in a bowl. Squeeze the lime juice and drizzle the fish sauce over the celery. Chop the soaked raisins and mix into the salad.

Make the parsley-lime salsa and serve the pithiviers with the salsa and salad.

Torta rustica con cipolle e salsiccia

Galette with sausage, caramelized onion, and mostarda

Preparation time:
1 hour + 30 minutes to
rest (with ready-made
dough 50 minutes total)

Serves 4
———

INGREDIENTS

Dough

2 cups + 2 tablespoons
(300 g) flour (I use half
all-purpose and half
whole wheat)
1 tablespoon fresh
rosemary leaves,
chopped
1 teaspoon sea salt
½ cup (120 ml) mild
olive oil
1 egg, at room
temperature, white and
yolk divided
½ cup (120 ml) ice cold
water

Filling

3 tablespoons unsalted
butter
8 onions, cut into half rings
Sea salt
1 bunch sage (½ oz/15 g),
chopped
7 ounces (200 g) pork
sausage, casings
removed
¼ cup (60 g) mascarpone
or other cream cheese
½ head radicchio
2 tablespoons balsamic
vinegar
1 tablespoon extra-virgin
olive oil

Quince mostarda
(page 366)

TIP

Instead of sausage, you
can finely chop 6 anchovy
fillets and mix them into
the caramelized onions.

This savory tart becomes extra delicious with sharp-sweet mostarda from quince pear, a condiment from Lombardy that you often eat with cheese and meat. It takes a few days to make mostarda, so keep that in mind. There is also ready-made mostarda, for sale at Italian delis or online. But those are usually too sweet, so making your own pays off, as always.

Make the quince mostarda several days in advance.

To make the dough, put the flour in the food processor. Add the rosemary and salt. With the machine running, incorporate the olive oil, egg yolk, and ice cold water. (Add the water slowly because you may not need to use it all. Give the dough time to form. If it doesn't, add some more water. Whole-wheat flour soaks up a lot of moisture.) Feel the dough. It's right if it feels a little wet to the touch. Form it into a ball and place covered in the refrigerator for 30 minutes.

Preheat the oven to 400°F (200°C).

To make the filling, heat the butter in a frying pan and add the onions and a pinch of salt. Cook over low heat for 20 minutes. Stir occasionally and allow the onions to caramelize. Add most of the sage to the caramelized onions, keeping some leaves for garnish.

Divide the meat into small pieces and set aside. Set on a paper towel-lined plate to cool.

Roll the dough into a thin sheet on a piece of parchment paper. Transfer the dough (still on the paper) onto a baking sheet. Add a layer of mascarpone and top with the caramelized onion and sausage meat. Fold the dough in at the edges and brush the edges with the egg white.

Place into the oven and bake for 20 to 25 minutes until the edges are light brown.

Meanwhile, tear the radicchio into bite-sized pieces and place in a bowl. Add a pinch of salt, the balsamic vinegar, and the olive oil, and mix so that all the leaves are coated.

Remove the tart from the oven. Garnish with the remaining sage leaves and radicchio and serve with mostarda. It's delicious with green vegetables, such as green beans with roasted hazelnuts.

Lingua di vitello con barbabietola

Veal tongue with roasted beets and green sauce

Preparation time:
25 minutes + 2 hours
of cooking

Serves 8

INGREDIENTS

8 equally-sized beets
1 veal tongue (about
    1 ¾ lbs/ 800 g)
Coarse sea salt
3 celery stalks, coarsely
    chopped
1 large carrot, coarsely
    chopped
1 onion, coarsely chopped
Few bay leaves, crushed
1 tablespoon peppercorns
1 teaspoon sea salt
Green sauce (page 370)
Turnip greens or other
    fresh lettuce (optional)

TIP

You can also brine the tongue before you cook it. Not a must, as the meat has plenty of flavor on its own, but brining gives it another boost. Dissolve 5 ounces (140 g) of salt in 3 quarts (2.8 L) of water and let the tongue brine in this for 10 hours, covered. Then place the tongue in fresh water for 1 hour to de-salt it.

Many readers will not (dare not) make this dish, yet here it is. First of all, it is seriously tasty and makes a flavorful broth. It's also easy to prepare, is an Italian classic, and is a chance to be adventurous and use the less popular parts. I'm a fan of using said parts and wish they were more popular. This is already the case in Italian cuisine, and even in Indonesian cuisine, the organs are eaten right up. Even I grew up eating them. When I lived in Florence, I used to frequent Casalinga, a wood-paneled trattoria where the staff would ask with a flat Florentine accent if they could sit with you at the table for a moment to calculate a few table checks. I always ate lingua with green sauce there. It's a hearty dish that tastes great with a chilled Chianti. Last summer, out of nostalgia, I went there again. My version of this dish with colored beets and French green sauce is a bit more international. It is an ideal group dish, because you can't finish such a huge tongue by yourself.

Preheat the oven to 400°F (200°C).

Roast the beets in their skin (without aluminum foil, without oil, without salt) in the oven for 2 hours. The skin will look like dried clay, but you can peel it off easily, and the beets will have a smoky, sweet flavor after those 2 hours. Cut the beets into wedges and set aside.

Meanwhile, rinse the tongue well, and place in a large pan. Add the celery, carrot, onion, and crushed bay leaves to the pan.

Pour in water until everything is submerged, add the peppercorns and salt, and cook over low heat for 1 ½ to 2 hours, until the meat is tender. The exact time depends on the size of the tongue.

While the tongue is simmering, make the green sauce.

Check if the tongue is cooked by poking it with a sharp knife. If the meat feels tender, it is ready. Let rest in the boiling water for another 15 minutes (save the broth for soup or sauce, it is divine!) and peel the tongue while it is still warm. (To peel the tongue, face it upwards and cut lengthwise into the outer flesh. Dig your fingers into the slit and peel off the outer skin. It's important to do this while the tongue is still warm or it won't separate well.) Cut the tongue into slices. The front part is the leanest, towards the back, the meat becomes fattier. Serve each person slices from both sides.

Garnish the tongue with wedges of beet, a nice dollop of sauce Gribiche, and some turnip greens.

PIZZA

ABOUT PIZZA

Do you have to go to Naples for the very best pizza? What can I say? In Kyoto and Portland these days, they make rock-solid pizza too. Anyone who has watched Netflix's *Chef's Table* knows that hyper-focused freaks exist in several places around the world who dedicate their lives to the perfect pizza. Naples is the birthplace, but pizza only became famous after Italian immigrants started making pizza in America. Until the 1950s, few Italians outside of Naples had even seen a pizza up close. You can eat good pizza everywhere these days—bad pizza too, for that matter—but it's still terribly fun to eat the original pizza in Naples. I did so as a nineteen year old at Da Michele in Naples. I thought it was hilarious that there was only cola, beer, marinara, and margherita to be had. By now the whole world knows that's how it is, courtesy of cliché and cringe movie *Eat, Pray, Love* and mass tourism. Last year Remko and I went back to Naples with our children. Twenty years ago, I wouldn't have ventured into this urban jungle without clinging to a trusted local, but the once infamous city has become quite accessible. From Sodom and Gomorrah to foodie enclave.

We ate a lot of pizza. From traditional pizza right out of the wood oven to puffy *pizza fritta* (fried pizza) and even gourmet pizzas. Neapolitan pizza from the oven is not crispy, but soft and bread-like with a smoky flavor, with a *cornicione alto* (high crust) and a wafer-thin base with little filling. You cut the pizza into quarters, grab the crust, fold it in half, and bite the tip right off. If you take the pizza out on the street, it folds up like a purse. It is called *a portafoglio*, or *a libretto*. The somewhat conservative Associazione Verace Pizza Napoletana has established strict regulations that a Neapolitan pizza must meet. My pizzas definitely don't meet them; I suspect the bulk of Netflix's pizzas don't either. And even in the rest of Italy, they make pizzas that would not pass the Neapolitan balloting. That doesn't mean they aren't delicious, just different. In Rome, the crust is thinner and crispier. You also have *pizza a taglio*, rectangular slab pizza that is thicker and more heavily topped. Near Noto, Remko and I made *lumera* with a Sicilian family. Lumera is a local pizza where the edges are folded over the filling, and the pizza cooks longer in the wood-fired oven.

With the instructions in this book, you can certainly make a tasty pizza, but also realize that a home pizza does not have the magic of a smoky, wood-fired, oven-baked pizza with big bubbles and juicy ingredients. Although we have come a long way!

REQUIREMENTS FOR A TASTY PIZZA A pizza oven that gets really hot. Keep in mind that a wood-fired oven reaches 840°F (450°C), and the pizza only bakes in it for a few minutes. A regular oven often doesn't get that hot so the pizza has to stay in the oven longer, which dries it out and loses some magic. If you do make pizza in a regular oven, turn the oven to the highest setting and use a pre-heated pizza stone, which is a thick tile that allows the pizza to get plenty of contact heat from below. Put the stone in the oven an hour in advance so it can get really hot. The thicker the stone, the longer it stays hot, and the more pizzas you can bake on it.

A pizza peel for sliding pizza into the oven if you have a pizza oven.

Semola di grano duro (see page 73) or fine cornmeal to dust your work surface.

A dough scraper to cut the dough into pieces.

Pizza con zucchine alla scapece

Pizza with squash, zucchini, and herb butter

Preparation time:
15 minutes + 10 minutes
rest + 5 to 10 minutes
of baking

Serves 4

———

INGREDIENTS

Basic pizza dough ball
(page 366 or store bought)

Herb butter
½ garlic clove
½ cup (113 g) salted
   butter, cut into small
   cubes
A handful of green herbs
   (mint, basil, tarragon,
   dill, whatever you have)
Sea salt and freshly
   ground black pepper

Toppings
1 zucchini
1 yellow squash
Sea salt
¼ cup (60 ml) olive oil
1 garlic clove, crushed
   and peeled
3 tablespoons white wine
   vinegar
½ bunch (¼ oz/7 g) mint
   leaves, finely chopped
1 8-ounce ball raw
   mozzarella, sliced
2 tablespoons peeled
   pistachios
2 tablespoons extra-virgin
   olive oil

TIP
The dough needs 4 hours
to rise + 24 hours in
the refrigerator, so plan
accordingly.

At Pizzeria Concettina ai Tre Santi in Naples, I ate great pizza with zucchine alla scapece. It was fluffy and smoky with fresh squash and zucchini for contrast. I tried to recreate it at home, but it lacked mojo. Then again, I haven't dedicated my entire life to the perfect pizza dough. So, for this home version, I added herb butter, cheese, and some chopped pistachio and mint. Also delicious! You'll have some squash, zucchini, and herb butter left over. Eat the leftovers as a side dish or incorporate into a salad. In any case, never overcrowd your pizza, it won't taste any better! The dough will not get cooked, and it will be too wet.

First, make the dough 28 hours in advance. Remove the dough ball from the refrigerator and set on the counter to come to room temperature.

Place a pizza stone in the oven and preheat the oven on the hottest setting 1 hour before you are ready to bake the pizza. (Don't use the convection setting unless you like parched pizza).

To make the herb butter, add the garlic, butter, and green herbs to a food processor. Process until minced, then season with salt and pepper. Store in a refrigerator until you are ready to use it.

Slice the squash and zucchini into long wafer-thin slices on the mandolin or with a cheese slicer. Sprinkle with salt.

Add the olive oil to a large skillet then add the garlic and sauté until light brown. Add the squash and zucchini slices and continue to sauté, stirring gently, for a few minutes. If necessary, do it in two parts.

Deglaze the squash mixture with the white wine vinegar. Add most of the mint (keeping some aside for garnish) and continue to sauté for 2 minutes to allow the flavors to infuse.

Roll the pizza crust onto a lightly floured surface. Spread with herb butter and top with the squash and zucchini strips and mozzarella. Bake for 5 minutes (wood fire oven) or 10 minutes (for regular oven). Transfer your pizza to a large cutting board.

Mix the remaining mint leaves and pistachios with the extra-virgin olive oil and drizzle it over the pizza. Slice and enjoy!

Pizzetta con 'nduja e uovo

Pizza with 'nduja and thinly sliced Brussels sprouts

Preparation time:
10 minutes + 5 to
10 minutes of baking

Serves 4

INGREDIENTS

2 basic pizza dough balls
(page 366 or store bought)

Toppings
3 to 4 Brussels sprouts
Lemon wedge
Sea salt
1 8-ounce ball mozarella,
   grated
2 tablespoons
   tomato sauce
3 tablespoons 'nduja
2 eggs
Few dill sprigs (other
   green herbs such as
   parsley, tarragon,
   or basil will also work)

TIP
The dough needs 4 hours
to rise + 24 hours in
the refrigerator, so plan
accordingly.

With 'nduja it is easy to win, because even dirt becomes tasty with this spicy spread from Calabria. I pair the greasy, smoky 'nduja with a soft boiled egg and fresh thinly sliced Brussels sprouts and dill. Tarragon would also be delicious with this. The quantities below are for two medium-sized pizzas, adjust as needed for appetite size.

First, make the dough 28 hours in advance. Remove the dough balls from the refrigerator and set on the counter to come to room temperature.

Place a pizza stone in the oven and preheat the oven on the hottest setting 1 hour before you are ready to bake the pizza. (Don't use the convection setting unless you like parched pizza.)

Cut the Brussels sprouts into gossamer-thin slices with a sharp knife or mandolin. Lay the last bits of Brussels sprouts a little flat to spare your fingers and cut into thin strips. Mix the Brussels sprouts in a bowl with the lemon juice and a pinch of salt, and massage briefly so that the flavors sink in.

Roll the pizza crusts onto a lightly floured surface; spread the tomato sauce and top with the mozzarella. Spread the 'nduja on top and slide into the oven.

Bake for 5 minutes (wood fire oven) or 10 minutes (for regular oven). Halfway through, remove the pizzas from the oven, crack an egg onto each pizza, and cook for a few more minutes until the whites are set and then remove again.

Sprinkle with the chopped Brussels sprouts and dill, then serve hot.

Pizza con scarola piccante e taleggio

Pizza with spicy endive and taleggio

Preparation time:
10 minutes + 5 to
10 minutes of baking

Serves 8 to 12

INGREDIENTS

**2 to 3 basic pizza
dough balls**
(page 366 or store bought)

Toppings
2 tablespoons extra-virgin
  olive oil
1 garlic clove, crushed
  and peeled
Sea salt
14 ounces (400 g) endive,
  sliced
1 teaspoon chili flakes
  + extra
3 ½ ounces (100 g)
  Taleggio, sliced
Zest from 1 lemon

I love endive so much, and the Italian name sounds like a bell: *scarola*. Admit it, it sounds a lot more cheerful than endive. It makes your mouth water just by saying it. In Naples, endive often goes in a calzone, but what goes in can also go on top. The slightly bitter taste of the endive is perfectly balanced by the fatty Taleggio. So delicious. This topping is good for two to three pizzas. Never top your pizza too thick or the bottom won't cook properly, which is sad after all the work you put into it.

First, make the dough 28 hours in advance. Remove the dough balls from the refrigerator and set on the counter to come to room temperature.

Preheat the oven to the hottest setting 1 hour before you plan to bake your pizza, and place a pizza stone in it so it will be nice and hot. (Don't use the convection setting unless you like parched pizza.)

Heat the olive oil in a skillet and brown the garlic. Add the endive, a pinch of salt, and the chili flakes, and sauté until just wilted. Remove from the heat.

On a lightly floured surface, roll the pizza dough into rounds and top with the endive and slices of Taleggio. Bake for 5 minutes (if you are using a wood fire oven) or 10 minutes (if you are using a regular oven). Transfer your pizza to a large cutting board.

Grate the lemon zest over it, add more chili flakes if you dare, and slice.

Pizza con patate e salsa di acciughe

Pizza with potato and anchovy-fennel sauce

Preparation time:
15 minutes + 1 night
brining + 5 to
10 minutes baking

Serves 8

INGREDIENTS

2 basic pizza dough balls
(page 366 or store bought)

Toppings
2 medium potatoes
1½ tablespoons coarse
 sea salt
1 tablespoon fennel seeds,
 finely chopped
1 chili pepper, seeds
 removed and chopped
½ garlic clove
7 anchovy fillets, chopped
6 tablespoons extra-virgin
 olive oil
3 ½ ounces (100 g)
 ricotta cheese
1 sprig fresh rosemary

TIPS
The dough needs 4 hours
to rise + 24 hours in
the refrigerator, so plan
accordingly.

You can brine more
potatoes and use them as
a topping on a casserole
dish. Or place leftover
potato slices together in
a baking dish, drizzle on
olive oil and seasonings
such as garlic and herbs,
and bake in a preheated
oven at 400°F (200°C) for
about 1 hour until crispy.

I used to think it was weird for Italians to eat carbs on carbs. But now we know who is really weird: someone who doesn't like pizza with potato! I put the potato slices in wet brine overnight, which gives them flavor and crispness by washing away the starch, which is a tip I got from sourdough baker Florence Gramende of Levain et le vin in Amsterdam. I love anchovies, but they often get too dried out on a pizza. That's why I came up with an anchovy sauce that you drizzle over the pizza after baking. The quantities below are for two pizzas (you'll have some sauce leftover, but I'm sure you know what to do with it).

First, make the dough 28 hours in advance. Remove the dough balls from the refrigerator and set on the counter to come to room temperature.

Using a mandolin or cheese slicer, cut the potatoes into very thin slices. Dissolve the sea salt in 4 ¼ cups (1 L) of water, and brine the potato slices overnight or for at least 6 hours.

Preheat the oven to the hottest setting 1 hour before you plan to bake your pizza, and place a pizza stone in it so it will be nice and hot. (Don't use the convection setting unless you like parched pizza.)

Meanwhile, add the fennel and chopped chili pepper to a bowl and then grate the garlic over it. Add the anchovies and then drizzle in olive oil until you get to the taste you like.

Remove the potato slices from the brine just before use—otherwise they will discolor—and pat dry.

Roll the pizza dough out on a lightly floured surface. Then top with ricotta and potato slices. Sprinkle with rosemary. Bake for 5 minutes (if you are using a wood fire oven) to 10 minutes (if you are using a regular oven). Remove from the oven and drizzle the anchovy sauce on top. Serve hot.

Pizza fritta
Deep-fried pizza

Preparation time:
1 hour + 30 minutes rest

Serves 4

INGREDIENTS

**½ basic pizza
dough ball**
(page 366 or store
  bought)

Sunflower or peanut oil,
  for frying

Basic filling
8 ¾ ounces (250 g)
  ricotta cheese
3 ½ ounces (100 g)
  scamorza affumicata
  (smoked cheese) or
  mozzarella (not buffalo
  mozzarella!), in cubes
Freshly ground
  black pepper

**More topping
suggestions**
Caramelized onions,
  sage, and anchovy
Sautéed garlic and
  endive with olives,
  capers, and raisins
Cubes of cooked ham
  or mortadella
Halved cherry tomatoes
  with basil
Grilled vegetables and
  gremolata
Nutella and crispy
  pancetta
Spicy tomatoes
  and arugula

The *Sciasciona* (pronounced shashona) is the symbol of Naples. With long jet-black hair, a sultry gaze, heavy breasts, soft flesh, and a mermaid's tail, the plump mermaid is an ode to the well-endowed (a tad vulgar) Napoletana combined with the mermaid Parthenope from Greek mythology. Sciasciona comes from the Italian word *ciccia*, or fat. Fat that you can give a good squeeze, fat that represents the good life. The Sciasciona can be found on every Neapolitan street corner. As a painted icon on peeling walls, and the incarnate version spins by with her cloned friends as they descend the city stairs. What does this have to do with fried pizza? Well, it's just as sexy as the Sciasciona. Voluptuous and hot. Deep-fried pizza sounds heavy, but is surprisingly light.

This pizza once originated as an inexpensive alternative to pizza from the wood-fired oven. You can use the basic pizza dough ball recipe (page 366) and cut it in half. I do a quick rise here, but you can also stick to the long rise, which benefits the taste and the dough. Usually one part ricotta and one part mozzarella or smoked scamorza creates a base. You can expand that further with fillings you love. I give some suggestions below, go wild, but make sure the filling is not too wet. You can fill fried pizza like a calzone or put the filling on top, "raw," when the dough comes out of the fryer. The smell is strong, so once they notice the scent, you may have to invite the neighbors.

To do the quick rise, make the dough 8 hours in advance, but do not place it in the refrigerator. After the dough has risen for 2 hours at room temperature, divide it in half. Place it in the refrigerator to let rise overnight and use for another pizza.

Divide the dough into four pieces, form into balls, and place about 2 inches (5 cm) apart in a container with a lid. Secure the lid and let rise for about 4 hours in a warm place (75 to 80°F [25 to 28°C]). I do this in an oven that is off, but with the light on).

Pour the oil in a large saucepan until it comes up the sides about 3 inches (7.5 cm) so the pizza can be submerged, and heat to 360°F (180°C).

Roll the balls into rounds about 6 inches (15 cm) in diameter on a floured work surface (see page 366). Cover half of the dough with filling and fold closed to form a crescent. Press the edges closed tightly so the toppings won't escape while they're frying. Using a spatula, pizza peel, or bench scraper, scoop the pizzas loose and grab at both ends to create a sort of hammock.

Deep-fry the pizzas individually for a few minutes per side until golden brown. If the pizza cannot be completely submerged in the oil, use a ladle to carefully spoon the hot oil over the top. Remove from the oil with a slotted spoon, drain on a paper towel-lined plate, and sink your teeth into it. Be careful, it's hot!

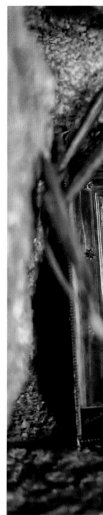

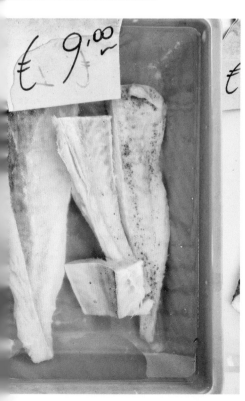

€ 9.00

NAPOLI 1926

DOLCI SWEETS

Fragole con balsamico e ricotta

Strawberries with balsamic and buffalo ricotta cheese

Preparation time:
10 minutes | 30 minutes
to marinate

Serves 4

_____

INGREDIENTS

14 ounces (400 g) ripe
   strawberries, hulled
   and halved
¼ cup (60 ml) balsamic
   vinegar (see page 25
   for more info)
1 pound (450 g) buffalo
   ricotta
¼ cup (50 g) granulated
   sugar
1 teaspoon black
   peppercorns
1 teaspoon anise seed

TIPS

Search for "Borgo del
Balsamico" and you will
find sites where you can
buy this balsamic online.
Of course, any other tasty
balsamic is also good.

If you can't find buffalo
ricotta, then use regular
ricotta (cremosa) and mix
in 5 ounces (125 grams)
of feta in a food processor
or with a hand blender
until you have a creamy,
salty consistency.

Good balsamic vinegar has nothing to do with that syrup from the supermarket, as Italophiles like you and me know. But even with good balsamic vinegar, you have the crème de la crème. Il Borgo del Balsamico is a fairytale bed and breakfast in the countryside between Modena and Parma. In the middle of an Italian garden lies a brick-red mansion with pouty chic guesthouses, vineyards, and an acetaia, where the balsamic vinegar matures. The borgo is run by two sisters, whom I once interviewed for a glossy magazine. As thanks, I received a bottle of their black gold. Their balsamico is addictive and maddeningly delicious with strawberries, buffalo ricotta, toasted pepper, and anise.

Mix the strawberries with the balsamic vinegar in a bowl and allow to marinate for 30 minutes.

Whip the ricotta with the sugar. (I do this in a food processor, but a hand mixer or blender will also do the trick.)

Toast the black peppercorns and anise seed in a dry skillet for a few minutes over high heat. Grind in a mortar—it does not have to be completely fine, a little coarse is just right.

Divide the buffalo ricotta between bowls, spoon the strawberries with balsamic on top, and finish with a pinch of toasted pepper and anise.

Panna stracotta con mostarda

Panna cotta with citrus mostarda

Preparation time:
45 minutes | 4 hours
to rise

Serves 6

INGREDIENTS

Citrus mostarda
(page 366)

3 cups (715 ml) heavy
    whipping cream
1 vanilla pod
⅓ cup (65 g)
    superfine sugar
1½ sheets gelatin*

** The panna cotta will be silky
smooth this way, if you prefer
a slightly stiffer panna cotta,
add 2 sheets of gelatin.*

Everything has already been done with this classic dessert from Piedmont. Pandan panna cotta, panna cotta with saffron, panna cotta with orange, with caramel, with coffee, with coffee-caramel. So, I settled on the perfect texture and an unorthodox condiment to go with it. The citrus mostarda provides an exciting kick. As for that perfect texture, all credit goes to Caffè Toscanini in Amsterdam. They beat in whipped cream and use less gelatin. In addition to that, they cook the cream all the way through, hence *stracotta* (cooked through). This is the tastiest panna cotta on Earth, you glide through it.

Make the citrus mostarda a couple of days in advance.

In a saucepan, heat 2 cups (475 ml) of the cream with the sugar. Cut open the vanilla pod and scrape the seeds into the cream and add the pod to the cream as well. Simmer for 30 minutes until the cream is yellow and reduced by half. Remove the vanilla pod and let cool a bit.

Soak the gelatin in cold water for 10 minutes. Squeeze the water out and stir the gelatin well into the still-warm cream so that it dissolves completely.

Whip the remaining 1 cup (240 ml) of cream until softly whipped and mix into the reduced vanilla cream until the texture is smooth.

Pour into the ramekins, leave to cool completely and let set in the refrigerator for at least 4 hours.

Before serving, place the ramekins in a layer of hot water for a few seconds and immediately release the panna cottas onto plates. Loosen with a knife if necessary. Spoon the citrus mostarda on top and serve.

Ricotta di bufala con prugne e saba

Vanilla ricotta with saba plums

Preparation time:
25 minutes

Serves 4

INGREDIENTS

4 plums (not too ripe), halved and pitted
Juice from 1 large orange
2 tablespoons granulated sugar
1 tablespoon finely chopped rosemary
3 tablespoons saba + extra
12 ¼ ounces (350 g) buffalo ricotta
1 vanilla pod
2 tablespoons powdered sugar
2 tablespoons unsalted butter
⅓ cup (40 g) walnuts

If you can't find saba, you can substitute with good balsamic.

If you can't find buffalo ricotta, substitute with 8 ¾ ounces (250 g) of mascarpone and 5 ¼ ounces (150 g) of crème fraîche mixed well.

TIP
If plums are not in season, use red grapes.

At an Italian wine bar in London, we had a bowl of thick, fat buffalo ricotta with saba for dessert. Saba, also known as mosto cotto, is concentrated grape juice that has a thick, syrupy texture and is the residual product of aceto balsamico. I love lazy desserts like this, where the produce does all the work for you. If you can get your hands on buffalo ricotta, I would definitely use it. Otherwise mix mascarpone with crème fraîche. Saba has a dark caramel-like, but also fruity, flavor. The better the quality, the better this is to eat.

Preheat the oven to 360°F (180°C).

Cut the plums into wedges. If you have riper plums, you can roast them in halves, otherwise they will be too soft.

Pour the orange juice into a baking dish. Mix in the sugar, rosemary, and saba. Place the plums in and cook in the oven for 15 minutes, until the juice is syrupy and the plums are soft but still intact. If the juice is still too liquidy, remove the plums from the dish and allow the juice to boil down more.

Place the buffalo ricotta in a large bowl. Cut the vanilla pod in half and scrape out the seeds over the buffalo ricotta. Add the powdered sugar, and mix everything together into a thick cream.

Melt the butter in a skillet and sauté the walnuts until fragrant, then chop coarsely.

Divide the ricotta among four bowls, spoon the plums with sauce on top, pour some more saba over it, and sprinkle with the walnuts.

Bunet con caramello di miso

Silky chocolate pudding with miso caramel

Preparation time:
30 minutes + 40 minutes
in the oven + cool for at
least 3 hours

Serves 4

INGREDIENTS

Miso caramel
½ cup + 1 tablespoon
   (120 g) granulated sugar
1 tablespoon shiro miso
   paste

Pudding
1 cup + 2 teaspoons
   (250 ml) milk
1 vanilla pod or
   1 tablespoon vanilla
   extract
2 tablespoons small pieces
   dark chocolate
   (75% cocoa)
1 tablespoon rum
2 tablespoons espresso
3 eggs
¼ cup (50 g) granulated
   sugar
3 tablespoons cocoa
   powder
Sea salt
7 ounces (200 g) amaretti
   cookies + some extra
Crème fraîche or whipped
   cream, to top
1 tablespoon coarsely
   chopped hazelnuts,
   to garnish

TIPS

You'll need 4 ramekins
or molds 3 ½ inches
(9 cm) wide and at least
1 ½ inches (4 cm) tall.

Instead of dark chocolate,
you can also use ¼ cup
(70 g) of Nutella for a
flavor that is slightly less
intensely chocolatey.

Bonet or *bunet* is a dessert from Piedmont. It is a kind of chocolate crème-caramel with amaretti and a drop of rum, cooked au bain-marie. The amaretti float to the top and provide a distinct layer. Sometimes bonet is firm as a brick, other times creamy and soft. The Piedmontese Jasmin, who taught me how to make bonet makes it in a pan on the stove, following her grandmother's recipe. Her bonet is very light and wobbly, and obviously Jasmin's favorite. My favorite is a little bit creamier. That's why I add a tiny bit of chocolate. And I make the caramel with miso—the saltiness makes you keep eating it. But I guess they wouldn't agree with that in traditional Piedmont.

First, make the miso caramel. Melt the granulated sugar with 2 tablespoons of water over low heat in a thick-bottomed saucepan. The sugar will first bubble and then gradually turn a beautiful color. In Italy they keep the caramel for bonet very light, I let it caramelize a little further. When the caramel has the color of—you guessed it—caramel, turn the heat down low. Add the miso paste, stir until smooth, and pour the caramel into the molds. Do it quickly, before the caramel hardens.

Preheat the oven to 325°F (165°C).

Pour the milk in a saucepan. Cut the vanilla pod in half, scrape the seeds into the saucepan, and bring to a boil. Add the chocolate to the saucepan, and let it melt. Remove the saucepan from the heat and pour in the rum and espresso.

To make the pudding, beat the eggs in a large bowl until they are frothy, then add the sugar. Stir in the cocoa powder and beat again until the color is even.

Pour the milk mixture into the egg mixture, season with a pinch of salt and crumble in the amaretti cookies. Using a large ladle, pour the mixture into the ramekins. Place them in a baking dish and fill with water until it reaches halfway up the ramekins. Cover with aluminum foil and bake for about 40 minutes. They may still be a little wobbly. If they are too wobbly-wobbly, cook uncovered for another 5 minutes.

Remove from the oven and cool completely in the refrigerator, at least 3 hours, but overnight is better so the caramel has enough time to soften again. Use a knife to loosen the edges around the bonet and then turn them over onto plates.

Garnish with a dollop of whipped cream or crème fraîche. Sprinkle with coarsely chopped hazelnuts and crumble the extra amaretti cookies over the top.

PASTRY MAGIC
Salvo Lioniello

It was not my intention to portray Italian chefs outside of Italy. The country already suffers from brain drain, which is precisely why I went looking for game changers in Italy itself. But I hadn't spent a minute talking to Neapolitan pastry chef Salvo, before I knew he belonged in this book. Salvo owns a bakery in Amsterdam with his wife Limau, where he bakes Italian sweets like Sicilian cannoli, Roman maritozzi, and Neapolitan pastries, as well as international goodies like Japanese chocolate mousse with pistachios.

When I lived in Rome, maritozzi (Italian cream buns) didn't interest me. I found them boring, soft, and sweet, but now they are internationally hyped and Salvo's maritozzi are worth it. His are elegant and light as a feather. There are hints of citrus and the cream is perfectly whipped and not too sweet.

> **"We have fantastic products. You won't find our sheep's milk ricotta anywhere else in the world. But we can do more with it."**

Salvo is self-taught. In Naples he worked in the hotel industry behind the bar, but because of his obsession with baking, he could not stand to be away from the kitchen. He apprenticed with Neapolitan pastry chefs then later moved to London where he worked at the Savoy Hotel, among other places. There he asked the pastry chefs every question imaginable, or as Salvo puts it, "li ho ammazzati con domande" ("I killed them with questions"). Because he wants to know and understand everything.

He teaches me how to make his famous maritozzi. First he mixes the flavors without letting them come into contact with the flour. He mixes orange and lemon zest with sugar and lets me smell the scent from his dough scraper. He lets me feel how wet the dough is—tremendously wet!—and shows me how he briefly knocks air into it by passing through it as if he were stroking someone's butt. And then he leaves it alone for 24 hours, because dough wants to rest. The flavors soak in better that way.

The décor in Salvo's bakeshop is crisp white and blue, with not a green-white-and-red ornament to be found. "That's deliberate," explains Limau, who runs the front, "because we are more than an Italian bakery." Some Italian guests find that awkward, but if you do things differently, you chase Italians away.

Salvo: "We have fantastic products in Italy; you won't find our sheep's milk ricotta anywhere else in the world. But we can do more with it. We need to move forward." I understand what he is saying and show Salvo and Limau a picture from our book, pasta filled with sauerkraut and Parmesan cream. Limau said, "Beautiful photos." And then with a wink, "But Italians are going to hate you." I'll just have to take that risk.

Salvo is more cautious, claims that he does not have the borrowed wisdom, and just does what pleases him. That's to his credit, but such modesty is out of place. Everything he does speaks of experience, precision, and love.

Salvo has already made a batch of the maritozzi dough and is now showing me how to turn the dough into balls. "There shouldn't be too much air, or you'll end up with bubbles." He presses his finger onto a ball of dough that springs back nicely. "Perfect. Now brush with egg yolk and bake in the oven."

We cut open the golden-brown clouds and see how beautifully the dough has risen. Salvo, meanwhile, has whipped cream and adds powdered sugar at the last minute. "About 10 percent on 1 liter." He intuitively adds a little more anyway. Limau, who stands among these things the whole goddamn day, is nevertheless tempted. "These do look very tasty." We bite simultaneously, an inevitable dot of whipped cream on our noses. What a tasty maritozzi. Let Salvo tweak that tradition.

Maritozzi
Roman cream-filled rolls

Preparation time:
30 minutes + 1 night
and 1 hour of rising +
15 minutes of baking

Makes 14 to 15

INGREDIENTS

1 pound (450 g) manitoba
   flour*
½ cup (90 g) granulated
   sugar
½ teaspoon sea salt
Zest from 1 orange
Zest from 1 lemon
1 tablespoon vanilla extract
2 eggs + 2 yolks
2 ½ ounces (70 g) olive oil
   + extra
½ ounce (15 g) fresh yeast
   (or 1 ⅔ teaspoons [5 g]
   dried yeast)
1 cup + 2 teaspoons
   (250 ml) whole milk

Fillings
**Balsamic cream with
crispy pancetta**
(page 375)

**Parmesan mascarpone
cream with sweet
tomato sambal**
(page 374)

Ricotta-pistachio cream
(page 375)

** Manitoba flour is available
at Italian grocery stores. It
is a refined flour used for
cakes and brioche. You can
substitute with another flour
with a protein percentage
above 12%.*

For the romantics among us: the story goes that fiancees would hide an engagement ring in the mountain of whipped cream inside the roll. So be careful if you bite into one, because before you know it, someone might want to marry you. When I lived in Rome, I never ate maritozzi. Not that I was afraid of an engagement (okay, that too), but I'm more of a savory and crunchy lover. So, at first, I wanted to make a crispy maritozzo, like a French puff where there is another layer of butter and sugar over the puff batter that gets crispy. But, once I made the rolls with pastry chef Salvo (see page 288) and he taught me how to get maritozzi nice and fluffy, I gave up on the crispiness, afraid of being cuffed by the maritozzi police. Besides, you learn to appreciate dishes more when you make them yourself. You taste in a different way, and in the end, I actually appreciated the softness. Could I have finally grown up?

If you are working by hand, pour the flour onto a clean work surface and make a large circle. That way, you can place the other ingredients in the center of the circle without allowing the ingredients to come into contact with the flour.

Add the sugar and salt in the center. Grate the zest of the orange and lemon on top of the sugar and salt. Next pour the vanilla on top and mix well. Add 1 whole egg and 1 yolk and mix into the sugar with clean hands. Then add the olive oil and mix again until the mixture is uniform.

In a small bowl, mix the fresh yeast with the milk. Pour the mixture into the sugar-egg mixture and mix again gently with your hands. Now you can mix in the flour little by little using a dough scraper. It will be a wet mess, and that's fine. Briefly knead air into the dough by making a rotating motion with your hands through the dough several times.

If you prepare the dough in a stand mixer, use the dough hook attachment. Crumble the yeast into the milk and set aside. Combine the flour, sugar, salt, and citrus zests in the bowl of the stand mixer. One at a time, mix in 1 egg, 1 yolk, the oil, and the yeast-milk mixture. Run for a few minutes until a sticky, wet dough forms.

Put the dough in a greased spacious bowl, cover loosely with plastic wrap and let rest overnight in the refrigerator. You could also let the dough rise for a shorter time (say a few hours, depending on the temperature) at room temperature until it has doubled in volume. But for flavor and texture, it is better if the dough is given time to rise slowly.

SALVO

Once the dough has risen, take it out of the refrigerator and dump it on a lightly floured work surface. Have a bowl of oil and a scale ready. Rub your hands with oil so the dough won't stick to them and cut pieces of dough weighing about 2 ounces (55 g) each, "For a cute maritozzo," says Salvo. Turn the dough into balls. Best to check out my Instagram page on how to do that.

Place the balls (with space in between) on a baking sheet lined with parchment paper and let them rise again at a temperature between 82 and 86°F (28 and 30°C) until they have doubled in volume. You can place them close to the heater, or in an oven that is off but with the light on. The time depends on the temperature, but I would say 1 hour.

Meanwhile, make a filling of your choice, or several fillings.

Preheat the oven to 360°F (180°C).

Beat the second egg plus the second yolk and brush the buns with it.

Bake them in the oven for 15 minutes until golden brown. Turn off the heat and open the oven door to allow cold air to flow in. Then, after a few minutes, remove the buns from the oven. Let them cool on a rack, then cut them across the middle, but not all the way through. Using a spatula, fill generously with the filling of your choice. Again, look on Instagram to see exactly how to do this.

"IF YOU DO IT DIFFERENTLY, YOU'LL SET THEIR TEETH ON EDGE."

Pastiera Napoletana

Neapolitan Easter cake with ricotta, citrus, and orange blossom water

Preparation time:
1 hour and 20 minutes +
1 hour and 20 minutes
of baking + 1 night
for rising

Serves 12

___

INGREDIENTS

Dough
2 ⅔ cups + 2 tablespoons
  (300 g) wheat flour
¾ cup (175 g)
  superfine sugar
Sea salt
½ cup + 1 tablespoon
  (130 g) cold unsalted
  butter, in cubes + extra
3 egg yolks

Rice cream*
½ cup (100 g) carnaroli rice
1 ⅔ cups (400 ml)
  whole milk
Pinch ground cinnamon
1 teaspoon superfine
  sugar
Sea salt
Zest from 1 lemon
2 tablespoons unsalted
  butter

Ricotta cream
1 pound (450 g) ricotta,
  drained
1 cup + 2 tablespoons
  (230 g) superfine sugar
1 orange
1 lemon
6 eggs
1 teaspoon vanilla extract
1 teaspoon orange
  blossom water
Sea salt
3 ½ ounces (100 g)
  candied fruit (optional)
Powdered sugar

*In Italy they use cooked
wheat grains; you buy
them ready-made there.
To reduce the preparation
time I use rice.*

Pastiera is now eaten year-round in Naples, whereas it was traditionally served at Easter. The cake is full of symbolism, and according to legend, it was conceived for the mermaid Parthenope, the icon of Naples. The Neapolitans brought her seven gifts: flour for wealth, ricotta for abundance, eggs for fertility, grain cooked in milk as a symbol of the union of the animal and plant kingdoms, orange blossom as the perfume of the surrounding landscape, spices as a toast to all people, and sugar to celebrate her sweet siren song. The seven strips of pastry crust on the cake are said to represent the different streets of ancient Naples. But that may all be fake: I read it on the site napolike.it, and the number of streets may not be correct either. Which means the story of Parthenope may not be true either. But seven is a magic number, and Neapolitans are superstitious as hell, so I am sure to include seven strips of crust on the top in a cross-weave pattern. Make this cake when you have visitors because it is delicious but also very filling.

To make the dough, place the flour, sugar, and a pinch of salt in a bowl. Mix in the cold butter with your fingertips until coarse crumbs form. Add the egg yolks one at a time and add some ice-cold water if the dough needs more moisture to hold together. Once the dough is formed, knead it minimally. Wrap it in plastic wrap and let it rest in the refrigerator for at least 1 hour.

You can also make it in a food processor with a dough blade. In that case, start with the dry ingredients; add the yolks and 2 to 3 tablespoons of ice-cold water until the dough forms. If it doesn't hold together, add some more water. Wrap it in plastic wrap and let it rest in the refrigerator for at least 1 hour.

Meanwhile, make the rice cream. Place the rice in a saucepan with the milk, cinnamon, sugar, a pinch of salt, the lemon zest, and butter. Cook the rice for about 25 minutes, stirring constantly, until tender. Add a splash of water if it becomes too dry. It should eventually have the consistency of creamy risotto. Remove from the heat and allow to cool. Blend half of the cream until smooth with a hand mixer and then combine it with the rest of the rice.

For the ricotta cream, mix the drained ricotta in a large bowl with the sugar and the citrus zests. Remove the whites from the citrus with a sharp knife and cut out the flesh from between the membranes. Blend the citrus with a hand blender and mix into the ricotta. (This step is my own addition, because I wanted to incorporate the citrus.) Next beat in the eggs one at a time. At the end, add the vanilla and orange blossom water with a pinch of salt.

Then, with careful strokes, mix the rice cream into the ricotta cream.

Traditionally there would be candied fruit. I leave it out because I don't like it. To please the superstitious Neapolitans, I put those 7 strips of dough on the cake in a crossweave pattern to compensate. If you do like candied fruit, chop it finely and mix it into the cream. Preheat the oven to 360°F (180°C) and grease a 9-inch (23-cm) springform pan with butter.

Take the dough out of the refrigerator. Set aside enough for the strips of dough to go on top. On a lightly floured work surface, roll out the rest into a thin, round piece ⅛ inch (3 mm) thick (about the height of two pennies). If the dough tears, you can place it between 2 sheets of parchment paper while you roll it. Fold the dough loosely so you can move it easily, place in the springform pan and unfold again. Trim the excess dough from the edges. Pour in the filling.

Roll out the remaining dough and cut 7 strips about ½ inch (13 mm) wide. Place them on top in a crossweave pattern, pressing the dough well at the edges.

Place the cake in the oven and bake for 20 minutes. Then reduce the temperature to 325°F (160°C) and bake for about 50 to 60 more minutes.

Let the cake cool completely and set overnight in the refrigerator. Dust lightly with powdered sugar before serving.

A "SALVO CONDEMI"
gli Amici dei Gradini S. Barbara
ti Ricordano con Affetto.

"che Dio ti abbia in Gloria"

Risolatte con rabarbaro e salvia

Rice pudding with rhubarb and sugared sage

Preparation time:
40 minutes

Serves 4

INGREDIENTS

Sugared sage
¼ cup (30 g) powdered
    sugar
1 tablespoon lemon juice
Few sprigs sage, leaves
    removed

Rhubarb compote
1 pound (450 g) rhubarb
Zest and juice from
    1 orange
¼ cup (50 g) granulated
    sugar
6 green cardamom pods

Rice pudding
4 ¼ cups (1 L) whole milk
1 vanilla pod
1 cinnamon stick
Zest from 1 lemon
½ cup (100 g) granulated
    sugar
Sea salt
1 cup (200 g) arborio rice

TIPS
You can make the rice
pudding ahead of time.
Then, when you are ready
to use it, add a small
splash of water or milk
and warm over low heat.
Stir well until the liquid is
absorbed and you have
wet rice. For a vegan
version, replace the milk
with almond or oat milk.

In Rome, we stopped by Santo Palato, the restaurant of feisty Sarah Cicolini, an Abruzzo-born chef with a penchant for hip-hop (see page 246). Sarah learned to cook at home in Abruzzo from her nonnas at an early age, later ending up in starred restaurants. You can taste it all in the sophistication of her trattoria food. For example, she served a risolatte with rhubarb, strawberry, and basil oil, and the taste was incredibly complex. It's very inspiring, because rice pudding is normally something more basic to be made at home. This is my interpretation of her risolatte. This dessert is easy to make and so comforting. Eat the leftovers for breakfast.

For the sugared sage, mix the powdered sugar and the lemon juice into a paste. Brush the leaves on both sides with the mixture and dry on a wire rack.

For the rhubarb compote, wash the rhubarb stalks, remove the lower part and cut into small pieces. Place in a saucepan with the orange zest and juice and bring to a boil. Add the sugar and dissolve. Crush the cardamom pods with a mortar, pick out the black seeds (discard the green pods and any brown and dry seeds) and grind them to a powder. Add to the pan with the rhubarb. Soften over low heat for about 10 minutes.

To make the rice pudding, pour the milk into a thick-bottomed saucepan. Cut open the vanilla pod and scrape out the seeds, and add the seeds and the pod to the milk along with the cinnamon stick, lemon zest, sugar, a pinch of salt, and the rice. Now cook over low heat, stirring constantly, until the rice is tender and has absorbed most of the milk, about 15 to 20 minutes. Remove from the heat when the rice is still a little wet.

Spoon the rice onto small plates or into bowls. Don't make the portions too large if you want to keep it elegant. Spoon the rhubarb compote on top and garnish with the sugared sage leaves.

Torta di polenta e sanguinelli

Polenta cake with blood orange, Campari, and rosemary syrup

Preparation:
1 hour + 15 minutes

Serves 4

INGREDIENTS

Polenta cake
¾ cup + 1 tablespoon
(200 ml) mild olive oil
+ extra
8 ¾ ounces (250 g) ricotta
cheese
4 to 5 blood oranges
½ teaspoon sea salt
1 cup (200 g) granulated
sugar + 1 tablespoon
extra
4 eggs
100 g corn flour
½ cup + 1 tablespoon
(100 g) all-purpose flour
2 teaspoons baking
powder

Blood orange, Campari, and rosemary syrup
6 blood oranges
½ cup (120 ml) Campari
1 cup (130 g) granulated
sugar
Few sprigs rosemary

Every year I look forward to the arrival of the Sicilian *sanguinella* or *arancia rossa* (blood oranges). I immediately buy a whole box, snack on them throughout the day and use them for dressings, salads, and in this polenta cake. During blood orange season, you see this cake popping up everywhere. Mine is different. Instead of baking it upside down, I let the oranges caramelize. I also pour a syrup of blood orange, Campari, and rosemary on top and use olive oil to keep it moist. You will end up with more syrup than is needed for the cake, but I trust you can find something to do with it.

Preheat the oven to 360°F (180°C) and grease a 9-inch (24-cm) round cake pan with a little olive oil.

To make the polenta cake, mix the olive oil with the ricotta in a large bowl. Zest 3 oranges over the bowl, and squeeze the juice of 2 oranges and add that, too. Add the salt and 1 cup (200 g) of the sugar, then whisk in the eggs one by one. Add the corn flour, all-purpose flour, and baking powder and stir to make a smooth batter. Pour into the cake pan.

Peel the remaining 2 oranges. To do this, first cut a piece from the bottom with a sharp knife so that you can set the orange down. Also cut the cap off the top. Then with the knife, cut off the peel from top to bottom, following the curve of the orange, ensuring you cut the piths off as well. Cut into slices and top the cake with them. If 2 oranges are not enough to cover the whole cake, use one more. Sprinkle the cake with the remaining tablespoon of sugar and place in the oven.

Bake the cake for about 50 minutes, then turn on the broiler to allow the oranges to caramelize and get a little crispy. Keep an eye on it, some broilers are hotter than others.

Meanwhile, make the blood orange, Campari, and rosemary syrup. Squeeze about 1 ⅓ cups (330 ml) of orange juice from the oranges. Pour the juice into a saucepan with the Campari, sugar, and rosemary sprigs then bring to a boil. Lower the heat and simmer for about 20 minutes until you have a thick syrup. Allow the syrup to cool, remove the rosemary, and pour into a clean bottle. The syrup will keep in the refrigerator for weeks, but before it spoils, it's bound to have ended up in drinks or desserts.

Pour the syrup on at the last minute and serve.

Zabaglione con caffè
Zabaglione with palm sugar and coffee

Preparation time:
15 minutes

Serves 4

———

INGREDIENTS

6 egg yolks
4 tablespoons palm sugar
   or superfine sugar
Sea salt
¼ cup (60 ml) marsala
   or other sweet wine
   (medium sherry will
   also do)
4 hot espressos

TIPS
From the egg whites you
can make Almond cookies
(page 371), they taste
great with this. Or make
fluffy Jasmine gelato with
them (page 320). The rest
of the egg whites can be
frozen, or you can add
them to scrambled eggs
or omelets, or use it to
make meringues or
Italian foam.

Fourteen years ago, in a social housing apartment the North part of Amsterdam, I had a tattoo done on my back by an Iranian-Italian artist who was staying with a Neapolitan friend with Rasta hair. The apartment was furnished as you might expect: saris on the couch, Nepalese flags and Hindu Om signs everywhere. While tattooing, the two sat around smoking weed, and so we (or rather they) spent a convivial afternoon. It wasn't the smallest of tattoos, so I was gritting my teeth a bit at one point. When my tattoo was finished, the Neapolitan asked if I wanted coffee. He grabbed the percolator and began preparing the drink with great care.

I marveled at the domestic scene—almost surreal in this setting. The moment the creamy layer of coffee flowed, he poured some into a glass with a scoop of sugar. He stirred it fanatically with a long spoon, which created a light, frothy cream. Then he poured in the rest of the coffee. I was completely surprised. He told me that in Naples they made it even richer by adding egg yolk to the sugar. It gave me the idea of coffee and zabaglione, and I told myself that someday I would do something with that.

That moment is now. I add palm sugar to the zabaglione, which has coffee notes, and it makes it extra tasty. The only disadvantage of zabaglione is that after dinner you have to leave your guests at the table for a moment to go back into the kitchen. That's why I make this one ahead of time and serve it cold. It's also delicious with hot espresso.

Put the egg yolks in a bowl that fits on a saucepan. Fill the saucepan one-third full with water and bring to a boil.

Beat the yolks with the sugar and a pinch of salt until frothy. Place the bowl on the pan of boiling water and keep whisking while you add the marsala—I use the hand blender with the whisk attachment for this, but it does splash a bit. Manual beating is also possible, but is a little more labor intensive. Beat for about 7 to 8 minutes until you have a thick cream (say yogurt thickness) while you let the eggs cook. Remove from the heat and continue beating. Allow to cool slightly, cover with plastic wrap, poke a few holes in the top and refrigerate until use. The zabaglione will stay stiff for at least 3 hours; if you make it the day before, you may need to whip it again before serving.

Divide the espressos among four glasses and spoon the zabaglione on top.

Tiramisesamo

Tiramisù with sesame cookies

Preparation time:
1½ hours + 3 hours to rise

Serves 4

___

INGREDIENTS

Reginelle
(page 373)

4 eggs, yolks and whites
   separated
6 tablespoons granulated
   sugar
1 pound (450 g) mascarpone,
   at room temperature
¼ cup (60 ml) marsala or
   other sweet wine, such
   as sweet sherry
¾ cup + 1 tablespoon
   (200 ml) espresso
Cocoa powder, to sprinkle
   on top
1 tablespoon sesame seeds,
   to sprinkle on top

TIPS

You may be able to find
ready-made reginelle at
Italian specialty food stores.

I always make tiramisù with
fresh raw eggs (without
cooking the yolks) and never
get sick. If pregnant women,
old people, or young
children are eating with you,
you can beat the yolks au
bain-marie (in a bowl over a
simmering pot of water) to
cook them and then mix with
the mascarpone.

For the whites, in a
saucepan heat the sugar
with 3 tablespoons of water
until it becomes hot syrup
and reaches 250°F (120°C).
Separately, beat the whites
until frothy, and while
beating, gradually add the
hot syrup until you have stiff
peaks. Mix the whites into
the mascarpone cream.

Agostino, my ex Lorenzo's home cook, made the most delicious
tiramisù on Earth. His tiramisù was not a stiff drizzle, but rather
the sloppy *je-ne-sais-quoi* type. "With pavesini, not savoiardi,"
Lorenzo then said proudly. "In Italy you're either in the pavesini
camp or the savoiardi camp." It's not as interesting a debate here,
because we only have one type of lady finger cookies to edge
tiramisù. Because I find those pretty dull, I replaced them with
Sicilian sesame cookies, reginelle. They have some orange zest,
are brittle, and are the perfect texture for tiramisù—they don't
get soft and soggy. The downside is that you have to bake
them yourself.

Make the reginelle. Or, for a quicker version, skip the reginelle
and just use lady fingers. For the sesame flavor mix in a couple
of tablespoons of tahin into the mascarpone egg cream.

Beat the yolks until they are light yellow (see tip if you prefer to
cook the yolks) with 3 tablespoons of the sugar and mix with the
mascarpone and 2 tablespoons of the marsala. Beat the whites
until frothy, add the remaining 3 tablespoons of sugar and beat
to stiff peaks. With a spatula, fold the egg white mixture into the
mascarpone mixture.

Pour the espresso into a deep dish and mix with the remaining
2 tablespoons of marsala. Place the cookies one by one in the
espresso mixture, leave for a moment so they can soak in the
espresso, then place in the bottom of a not-too-deep dish.
Drizzle some more espresso over them and spoon half of the
mascarpone mixture on top. Cover with another layer of espresso-
soaked cookies and spoon the rest of the mascarpone mixture
on top. Cover with cling film and refrigerate for a few hours so it
becomes firm. (Chill for 2 to 3 hours for sloppy tiramisù, longer
for a firmer version.)

Remove from the refrigerator and sprinkle with cocoa powder
through a sifter. Toast the sesame seeds in a dry frying pan and
sprinkle the tiramisù with them.

Peramisù

Tiramisù with espresso-braised pear

Preparation time:
1 hour + 45 minutes +
2 to 3 hours to rise

Serves 4

_____

INGREDIENTS

Braised pear

4 small cooking pears
⅔ cup (130 g) granulated
  sugar
2 tablespoons vanilla extract
3 bay leaves (preferably fresh),
  bruised
5 tablespoons espresso
  powder

Gluten-free almond cake

1 cup (100 g) almond flour
⅓ cup + 1 tablespoon
  (45 g) cornstarch
1 teaspoon baking powder
Sea salt
¼ cup (55 g) unsalted butter,
  at room temperature
4 ½ tablespoons granulated
  sugar
4 eggs
8 ¾ ounces (250 g)
  mascarpone, at room
  temperature
Cocoa powder, for dusting

TIPS

I always make tiramisù with
fresh raw eggs (without
cooking the yolks) and never
get sick. If pregnant women,
old people, or young children
are eating with you, you can
beat the yolks au bain-marie
(in a bowl over a simmering
pot of water) to cook them and
then mix with the mascarpone.

For the whites, in a saucepan
heat the sugar with
3 tablespoons of water
until it becomes hot syrup
and reaches 250°F (120°C).
Separately, beat the whites
until frothy and while beating,
gradually add the hot syrup
until you have stiff peaks.
Mix the whites into the
mascarpone cream.

Because I am so fond of tiramisù, here's another variation on
this formidable dessert (see page 307 for sesame tiramisù).
This one is with pear simmered in coffee, vanilla, and bay
leaves, and a gluten-free almond cake instead of lady finger
cookies. The flavors are pretty much the same, but with the
fruity addition of coffee pear.

It may surprise you in the land of pizza and pasta, but you can eat
delicious gluten-free food in Italy these days. Every restaurant
has gluten-free options and traditional recipes are adapted too!

To make the braised pears, peel the pears with a sharp knife or
peeler, leaving the stem attached. Cut off the bottom crown and
place them in a large saucepan. Add ⅔ cup (130 g) of the sugar, the
vanilla, bay leaves, and espresso powder to the pan. Fill the pan with
water until the pears are just submerged. Stew them over low heat,
covered, for about 1 hour or until soft. Remove the pears from the
cooking liquid and reduce the liquid to a thick syrup. Remove from
the heat and allow to cool. (For an exciting flavor, mix some finely
ground cardamom seeds with the coffee syrup.)

Meanwhile, make the gluten-free almond cake. Preheat the oven
to 350°F (180°C). Place the almond flour in a bowl, and add the
cornstarch through a sifter. Add the baking powder and a pinch
of salt.

In a large bowl, beat the butter and 2 ½ tablespoons of the sugar
until pale yellow. Mix in 2 eggs, one at a time, then the almond
flour mixture. Beat until you have no lumps. Spoon the batter into
four heatproof bowls (between 4 ½ and 5 inches [11 and 13 cm]
in diameter).

Press the stewed pears into the center of the batter. Bake for 20 to
25 minutes or until the cake begins to color at the edges. Remove
the trays from the oven and let cool completely.

Separate the 2 remaining eggs. Beat the yellows with the remaining
2 tablespoons of sugar until frothy, then mix into the mascarpone
(see Tip if you prefer to cook the yolks). Beat the whites until stiff
in a clean bowl and mix into the mascarpone mixture.

Prick holes in the almond cake with a skewer and pour the coffee
syrup over it.

Evenly divide the mascarpone cream on the individual cakes and
set them in the refrigerator for 2 to 3 hours. Dust with cocoa powder
before serving.

GELATO E GRANITA

ABOUT GELATO

Italians conquered the world with their artisanal gelato, and I'll say it right away: I'm a snobbish gelato bitch. I eat it when it's really good, and otherwise not at all.

By good gelato, I don't mean technically perfect, but made with fresh ingredients and flavors that are a little challenging. Gelato parlors that make artisanal gelato can be recognized by their use of seasonal produce. If they don't have bubble gum flavor, that is also a good indicator—by the way, my kids think otherwise. In Turin last winter, at my daughter Reva's request, Remko ordered a strawberry gelato at Mara dei Boschi, where they also do innovative things with coffee and chocolate. "Strawberries?!" Everyone in the store turned their heads. "We don't have those right now, sir," was the measured reply. Remko was mortified. If you are in a gelato parlor like that, then you're in the right place.

The great thing about making your own gelato is that you can go wild with your favorite flavors. You can add spices and herbs, nuts, tea, savory ingredients—anything goes with gelato. Making gelato is addictive and fun.

Do you need an ice cream maker? It does make it easier, but it can be done without one. If you make gelato by hand, you have to whisk the gelato every so often in the freezer. Once I cooked for groups of people at a yoga retreat in Crete. I made gelato with fresh Greek sheep's milk and some thyme I had picked from the mountain earlier in the day. Every so often, I ran to the freezer to whip the gelato so it would be perfectly creamy for the guests. It was mighty delicious. With attention, time, and love, you can get far even when you are doing it by hand. Want to make lots of gelato? Then an ice cream maker comes in handy. There are self-freezing machines and machines with a cooling element that must be put in the freezer the night before. The first machine is the easiest, because you can make gelato right away. The disadvantage is that it is more expensive and larger, so you must have the space for it. Not all ice cream makers are the same: Mine holds 4 ¼ cups (1 L) and turns gelato in 30 to 40 minutes, while other machines may take longer.

You can freeze anything, so there are many types of gelato. Gelato is made with dairy such as milk and cream. Depending on the recipe, eggs are added to the cream base, in which case it is called gelato alla crema, and it starts with a kind of custard base. Eggs bind and make the gelato creamier and fuller in flavor. Making gelato with eggs takes more time because you have to pasteurize—or heat—the eggs and then refrigerate them again. As a reward, however, you do get delicious gelato. Instead of eggs, locust bean gum, also known as carob flour, is used as a thickener in Italy. It is made from the beans of the carob tree, *il carrubo* in Italian.

Sorbet is water-and-fruit-based. It's delicious when it's very hot outside. *Semifreddo* (semi-cold) is the Italian name for parfait. It is not churned like "normal" gelato, but poured into a mold and frozen. Helpful if you don't have an ice cream maker. Semifreddo consists of more fats, which don't freeze as hard and keep the texture soft and creamy, despite not having an ice cream maker. To learn more about granita, see page 324.

Gelato di albicocche e rosmarino

Apricot gelato with rosemary and almond cookie

Preparation time:
45 minutes + 30 to 40
minutes in an ice cream
maker (5 to 6 hours
without an ice cream
maker)

Serves 4, makes about
4 ¼ cups (1 L)

INGREDIENTS

1 pound (500 g) ripe
  apricots, pitted and
  cut into pieces
1 ⅓ cups (320 ml) whole
  milk
⅓ cup (80 ml) heavy
  whipping cream
⅔ cup (130 g) granulated
  sugar
Juice from 1 lemon
1 ½ tablespoons carob
  flour or locust bean
  gum*
1 sprig rosemary

Almond cookie
(page 373)

* Available at health food
stores (see page 26 for more
info).

TIP
You can also make this
recipe with other fruits
such as strawberries, or
a combination of red
fruits, like cherries,
raspberries, etc.

During Italian summers, you get bombarded to death with apricots and peaches. That gave me the idea to make gelato with them. It's deliciously fresh, tart, and herbal. For this gelato, I work with carob flour. The flour is made from carob tree beans, found in many places in Italy. The flour causes fewer ice crystals to form, keeping the gelato soft in texture.

If you have an ice cream machine that needs to be pre-frozen, put it in the freezer the night before. Machines vary, so the churning time also varies. In some machines, you have to churn the gelato in parts.

Put the apricots in a large saucepan along with the milk, cream, sugar, lemon juice, and carob flour or locust bean gum. Purée everything with a hand blender until smooth. Add the rosemary sprig and bring to a boil. Then turn off the heat and let steep for 15 minutes.

Pour the gelato base through a fine sieve into a large pitcher. Press well so that as much apricot pulp as possible passes through the sieve. Allow the mixture to chill in the refrigerator for 1 hour.

Meanwhile, make the almond cookie.

Pour the mixture into the ice cream maker, and follow the instructions for your ice cream maker, since they are all different. If you don't have an ice cream maker, put the mixture in a sealed container in the freezer for about 5 hours. Remove the lid and stir every 30 minutes, until it's frozen but still creamy.

Serve the gelato with pieces of almond cookie on top.

Gelato di gorgonzola con fichi

Gorgonzola gelato with figs and balsamic vinegar

Preparation time:
30 minutes + 1 hour cooling + 40 to 50 minutes in an ice cream maker (5 to 6 hours without an ice cream maker)

Serves 4, makes about 4 ¼ cups (1 L)

INGREDIENTS

1 ¼ cups (300 ml) whole milk

¾ cup + 1 tablespoon (200 ml) heavy whipping cream

¼ cup (50 g) granulated sugar

10 ounces (300 g) Gorgonzola

1 tablespoon locust bean gum or 1 tablespoon carob flour*

4 fresh figs, cut into wedges

Balsamic vinegar

Few sprigs basil, to garnish

Flatbread or crackers, to serve (see page 26 for more info on Sardinian flatbread)

Carob flour and locust bean gum are available at health food stores. See page 27 for more info.

When we ate chef Elisa Rusconi's cheese gelato (see page 182) at Trattoria Da Me in Bologna, We didn't know what to expect, but were mind blown. Creamy, slightly sweet, salty, and a little spicy. If you are a cheese freak, this cheese board disguised as gelato will make you very happy.

If you have an ice cream maker that needs to be pre-frozen, put it in the freezer the night before. Machines vary, so the churning time also varies. In some machines, you have to churn the gelato in batches.

Heat the milk in a saucepan over low heat with the cream and sugar. Add the Gorgonzola to the cream mixture and gently melt. Stir in the locust bean gum, allow to thicken slightly, and remove from the heat. Cover and cool completely in the refrigerator.

Pour the mixture into the ice cream maker, and follow the instructions for your ice cream maker, since they are all different. If you don't have an ice cream maker, put the mixture in a sealed container in the freezer for about 5 hours. Remove the lid and stir every 30 minutes, until it's frozen but still creamy.

Spoon the gelato into bowls, garnish with the figs, and top with a splash of the very best balsamic you can find. Garnish with basil leaves and serve with a piece of crispy flat bread or crackers.

Pêche Elba

Peaches in wine with peach gelato

Preparation time:
45 minutes + 1 hour
chill in refrigerator +
40 minutes in an ice
cream maker (5 to 6
hours without an ice
cream maker)

Serves 4, makes about
4 ¼ cups (1 L)

INGREDIENTS

6 ripe peaches
2 ⅔ cups (600 ml) sweet
  red wine, such as
  aleatico passito or
  a light port
1 ¼ cups (250 g)
  granulated sugar,
  separated
¾ cup + 1 tablespoon
  (200 ml) heavy whipping
  cream
¾ cup + 1 tablespoon
  (200 ml) whole milk
Lemon wedge
4 egg yolks
Few sprigs thyme, leaves
  removed

TIPS

If you are making gelato
without an ice cream
maker, you can soften
it with a hand mixer
and then put it back in
the freezer for another
10 minutes to get the
delicious texture of
fresh gelato.
You can also make a
semifreddo out of this.
To do that, beat the
whipping cream until firm
and mix into the cooled
peach mixture. Substitute
the milk with mascarpone,
pour the base into a cake
pan, and freeze for
6 hours.

The Indonesian-Italian Angelina was a friend of my father's (Angelina is still around, my father sadly no longer). Her family has a house on the ridge of the village of San Pietro, on the island of Elba. During summer vacations, we often visited her in my father's ancient Mercedes bus. We helped in the garden, went to the beach, hiked in the mountains, or did nothing at all. Angelina made doing nothing sweeter by soaking ripe peaches in a heavy sweet wine: aleatico, named after a grape from which they also make wines in southern Italy. After the fruit soaked up the wine, my brother and I slurped it and got even lazier. They still soak peaches in wine on Elba, often accompanied by a scoop of vanilla gelato. Peach gelato seemed more delicious to me, and so the Pêche Elba was born.

If you have an ice cream machine that needs to be pre-frozen, put it in the freezer the night before. Machines vary, so the churning time varies. In some machines, you have to churn the ice cream in parts.

Cut 2 peaches into pieces and distribute them between four pretty glasses. Pour a layer of wine over them and soak the peaches in the wine for 1 hour.

Meanwhile, prick 4 peaches with the tip of a knife and blanch them in boiling water. Remove them from the water, allow them to cool until they can be handled then peel them. Remove the pit and cut the flesh into coarse pieces.

Combine the peaches with 1 cup + 2 tablespoons (230 g) of the sugar, the cream, and milk in a saucepan. Squeeze the juice from the lemon wedge into the saucepan and stir over low heat until the sugar dissolves. Blend with a hand mixer until creamy and smooth.

In a bowl, beat the yolks until they're frothy with the remaining 2 tablespoons of sugar, and transfer to a saucepan. Add the peach mixture, and heat over low heat until the substance thickens. If you are using a kitchen thermometer; the temperature should not exceed 185 °F (85 °C). Check the thickness by dipping a wooden spoon into the mixture and then scrape a line across the spoon; if the line remains and the substance does not run off, it's thick enough. Remove from the heat and allow to cool completely in the refrigerator.

Pour the mixture into an ice cream maker, and follow the instructions for your ice cream maker, since they are all different. If you don't have an ice cream maker, put the mixture in a sealed container in the freezer for about 5 hours. Remove the lid and stir every 30 minutes, until it's frozen but still creamy.

Scoop dollops of peach ice cream into the glasses and finish with thyme leaves. Sip and slurp your Pêche Elba on a warm summer evening.

Gelato nuvola di gelsomino

Jasmine gelato with almond-jasmine crumble

Preparation time:
1 to 2 days of steeping
+ 50 minutes + 30 to 40
minutes in an ice cream
maker (5 to 6 hours
without an ice cream
maker)

Serves 4, makes about
4¼ cups (1 L)

INGREDIENTS

2 ounces (50 g) dried
   jasmine flowers*
4 egg whites
⅔ cup (150 g) superfine
   sugar
2 tablespoons rum

Fregolotta
(page 372)

*You could also use jasmine
tea, but it's a bit more bitter.*

TIPS

Instead of jasmine
flowers, you can use
other flowers or floral
syrup: for example,
elderflower or lavender.

You'll need a kitchen
thermometer for
this recipe.

You can put the fresh
egg yolks to use by
making pasta carbonara
(page 101).

This gelato is like a delicate cloud. Unlike most gelatos, it is made with egg whites instead of yolks and is very light and airy. Originally in Sicily, this was made with the flower of the scursuni plant, but over time, this was changed to jasmine. Jasmine also reminds me of Indonesia. You can smell lush jasmine flowers everywhere there. Since, like me, I expect you don't have bunches of fresh, unsprayed jasmine flowers at your disposal, I use dried jasmine flowers. For a crunchy contrast, I top the gelato with *fregolotta*, a kind of crumb cake made with almond flour. I also mix in coconut, as a nod to Indonesia.

If you have an ice cream machine that needs to be pre-frozen, put it in the freezer the night before. Machines vary, so the churning time also varies. In some machines, you have to churn the gelato in batches.

In preparation, steep the jasmine flowers in 2 cups (475 ml) of water for 1 to 2 days. Strain the water through a fine sieve.

Beat the egg whites in a clean, large bowl, and set aside.

Next, bring the sugar and 3 ½ tablespoons (50 ml) of jasmine-infused water to a boil. Use a kitchen thermometer to monitor the temperature. Continue to boil the sugar mixture until it reaches 245 °F (118 °C) and forms a syrup. Whisk the syrup into the egg whites. It will foam and increase in volume, which is why it's important to use a large bowl. Continue to beat the syrup-egg white mixture until stiff peaks form.

Whisk in more jasmine infused water, 2 tablespoons at a time, until the mixture is thick and creamy. Add the rum, pour it into an ice cream maker and follow the instructions for your ice cream maker, since they are all different. If everything does not fit into the bowl of the ice cream maker, place the extra in a sealed container in the freezer and beat it every 20 minutes until it's frozen but creamy.

If you don't have an ice cream maker, put the mixture in a sealed container in the freezer for about 5 hours. Remove the lid and stir every 20 minutes, until it's frozen but still creamy. In the beginning it may separate a bit. It has to be vigorously mixed more frequently than other types of gelato.

In the meantime, make the fregolotta.

Spoon the gelato into bowls and sprinkle with fregolotta. Enjoy it on a hot day.

Gelato di riso con torrone di riso
Saffron rice gelato with nougat

Preparation time:
30 minutes + 1 hour
cooling + 40 minutes
in an ice cream maker
(5 to 6 hours without an
ice cream maker)

Serves 4

—————

INGREDIENTS

½ cup (100 g) carnaroli rice
3 cups + 3 tablespoons
    (755 ml) whole milk
1 cup (240 ml) heavy
    whipping cream
Zest from 1 orange
Zest from 1 lemon
1 teaspoon orange
    blossom water
Sea salt
½ vanilla pod or 2
    teaspoons vanilla extract
3 egg yolks
⅔ cup (130 g) granulated
    sugar
Javanese long pepper,
    grated (optional)

Torrone
(page 372)

TIP
Stir the leftover egg
whites into an omelet or
scrambled eggs or use
them to make Jasmine
gelato (page 320). Too
cold for ice cream? Eat the
custard as rice pudding.

Gelateria Fassi in Rome has been around since 1880. History seeps from the walls of this gelato palace. In the huge hall, framed newspaper articles give inside information about who has licked gelato here. D'Annunzio for example, a fascist poet; Mussolini too, he needs no explanation; and Italo Balbo, wasn't he, too, a fascist? Further on, I read that when Hitler came to Rome in 1938, the Nazi regime ordered Fassi to make a huge strawberry cake, completely decorated with a swastika. Believe it or not, as we read this in line for gelato, it is April 25, Liberation Day in Italy. While all over the city the liberation from Nazism is being celebrated, here, while (consciously or unconsciously) fascism is again being flaunted. Italy in a nutshell. Not only because of these contradictions will I never forget Fassi, but they also had surprisingly delicious rice gelato there. Because people from Arab nations introduced rice to Sicily, I give it an Arabic twist with saffron and orange blossom.

If you have an ice cream machine that needs to be pre-frozen, put it in the freezer the night before. Machines vary, so the churning time varies. In some machines, you have to churn the gelato in parts.

Place the rice in a saucepan with the milk, cream, orange and lemon zests, orange blossom water, and a pinch of salt. Slice the vanilla pod open with a sharp knife, remove and scrape the seeds into the cream mixture, and drop the pod in as well. Cook, stirring constantly, until the rice is tender, about 20 minutes. Remove the citrus zests and vanilla pod. Remove 3 tablespoons of rice from the mixture and set aside. Blend the rest finely with a hand blender.

Place the egg yolks and sugar into a separate bowl and beat them until creamy. Add it to the saucepan with the blended rice mixture and cook over low heat. Stir the mixture until it forms a thick custard. Do not let it boil, as this will scramble the eggs. If you have a kitchen thermometer, remove the pan from the heat once the mixture reaches 185°F (85°C).

Refrigerate the mixture while you make the torrone.

Next, pour the mixture in an ice cream maker. The exact time depends on your ice cream maker. During the last 10 minutes, add the 3 tablespoons of rice you had set aside. If you don't have an ice cream maker, you can fabricate one yourself (read how Giovanna does it on page 324). Or, you can put the mixture in a shallow lidded container in the freezer and stir it loose with a fork every hour for 5 to 6 hours. You'll get bigger chunks, and it won't be as creamy but it's still delicious.

Scoop the gelato into bowls, serve with chunks of torrone, and finish with some grated Javanese long pepper, if desired.

GRANITA GURU
Giovanna Musumeci

Giovanna Musumeci taught me how to make granita in the village of Randazzo, a commune built on black lava rock on the north flank of Mount Etna. Giovanna is a master gelato maker and pastry chef who has won all kinds of awards for her sublime work. Giovanna's father was also a pastry chef and ice cream maker, and she took over his gelateria. We first tasted a whole flight of granitas: persimmon, pistachio, tangerine, strawberry, and chocolate. They were creamy and soft and melted away pleasantly on our tongues. A Sicilian granita is different from a "regular" granita—one of those slushy-like ones with artificial fruit syrup from a machine. Nice for brain freeze, but they don't live up to the Sicilian granitas that Giovanna creates. Hers are made from fresh fruit or nuts and follow the same method as for gelato: an icecream maker is used so very tiny ice crystals are formed resulting in super creamy and smooth granita.

Next I tasted an almond. Creamy, crunchy. Hello! What a difference from one of those raw tart almonds from the health food store! For almond granita, we first make a panetto, a kind of paste made from ground almonds and sugar. Another secret goes into it. Giovanna opens a jar with cinnamon sticks into which she has previously poured boiling water. This creates a kind of cinnamon juice with an insane cinnamon smell, which strangely also has something almondy about it. She pours a few drops into her granita mixture.

The rest of the staff stands rolling brioche dough. Granita with brioche is a widely eaten breakfast in Sicily. Here the brioche (*brioscia* in Italian) has a kind of bun on top. You break it off and scoop granita into the hole. It's the perfect heat wave breakfast.

Routinely, two ladies stand to *pirlare* (quibble) good-naturedly as their arms roll the dough simultaneously and gracefully from the outside in, reminding me of Balinese dancers. Then they roll a tail on small balls of dough making a kind of dough commet. This is pushed on top of the larger sphere and forms the "top knot" of the brioche.

Meanwhile, Giovanna manually fabricates an ice cream machine. Of course they have a professional one there, but she wants to show how it used to be done and that you can also make granita without an ice cream maker. She grabs two aluminum bowls, the largest of which she fills with ice cubes and salt. Then she puts the smaller bowl in it, which she will now freeze. This way you create an ice wall to chill the granita. She pours the mixture into the bowl then stirs until the whole thing freezes and becomes a beautiful *granita liscia*: a smooth, still-somewhat-liquid granita. Giovanna says, "In Catania the granita is *molto asciutta* (drier). They spin it longer there. In Messina, on the other hand, the granita is more liquid. In Randazzo they are in between; both geographically and in terms of granita texture.

Giovanna's father was already experimenting

> "I welcome innovation and experimentation in the kitchen. But if we just finished grape picking, I want pasta al forno—food that nourishes and comforts."

with interesting flavors in the 1990s. "He did use too much sugar, we always had discussions about that." Giovanna points to a photo of papà Musumeci with tears in her eyes. Does Giovanna stick to traditional recipes or does she dare to experiment? "Both. In the *pasticceria* (pastry shop), I restrain myself. The village people come here for their breakfast as well, they don't want too much craziness."

With her colleague Ida, she has a mobile gelato parlor where they prepare gelato in front of you. A kind of chef's table of two Sicilian gelato mistresses. At events, Giovanna goes wild with funky flavors. "Crostino with butter gelato, salty anchovies and lemon zest or shrimp with strawberry granita." Gelato is a great flavor carrier and you can go in any direction with it. With her solid technical base and her open-minded brain, the sky is Giovanna's limit.

Granita al caffè e datteri

Coffee granita with cardamom and cream

Preparation time:
15 minutes + 30 minutes cooling + 20 to 25 minutes in an ice cream maker (4 hours without an ice cream maker)

Serves 4

INGREDIENTS

2 cups (475 ml) brewed coffee or 1 cup (240 ml) very strong espresso with 1 cup (240 ml) water
1 tablespoon granulated sugar
2 ½ cups (200 g) pitted dates
8 to 10 green cardamom pods*
½ cup (120 ml) heavy whipping cream
1 tablespoon powdered sugar

If you prefer less cardamom, you can reduce the amount by half. It comes through really well. Can you also use cardamom powder? You can, but the powder is sometimes stale and less flavorful because the pods are ground along with it.

TIP

I deliberately make small quantities of this granita because it uses strong coffee and because it's best if you eat it as soon as it's ready. In Sicily, they have special equipment to refrigerate granitas. At home, if you have to store the granita in the freezer before serving it, remove it from the freezer 15 minutes before serving. But, if possible, finish it and serve it so that it's *á la minute!*

Master ice cream maker Giovanna from Randazzo (see page 324) taught me how to make creamy Sicilian granitas. This is my version of granita al caffè, sweetened with dates and flavored with cardamom, a match made in the Middle East. The Sicilians eat this for breakfast when it's scorching hot, but as dessert or an afternoon treat on a languid hot day is also a possibility, of course.

If you have an ice cream maker that needs to be pre-frozen, put it in the freezer the night before. Machines vary, so the churning time varies. In some machines, you have to churn the granita in batches.

Begin by mixing the hot coffee with the sugar. Add the pitted dates and blend with a hand blender until it's puréed.

Put the cardamom pods in a mortar. Crush the pods, pick out the black seeds, and discard the

. Fresh cardamom seeds are dark and shiny, so for the best taste, discard seeds that are dried and light brown. Grind the seeds finely. You should be left with about 1 teaspoon. If you don't know cardamom very well yet or don't like it, use ½ teaspoon.

Add the finely ground cardamom seeds to the coffee mixture and it cool completely. Taste it, and if it is too strong, add some water. I brewed coffee and added 3 ½ tablespoons of water, and it was perfect. Pass the mixture through a fine sieve and press firmly to get all the flavor from the cardamom and dates. Let the mixture cool completely in the refrigerator.

Pour the mixture into an ice cream maker and turn it into a creamy granita in about 20 minutes. The exact time depends on your ice cream maker. If you don't have an ice cream maker, you can fabricate one yourself (read how Giovanna does it on page 324, plus you can watch a video about it in my highlights on Instagram). Or, you can put the mixture in a shallow lidded container in the freezer and stir it loose with a fork every hour for 4 hours. You'll get bigger chunks and it won't be as creamy as a granita from the ice cream machine, but it's still delicious.

Meanwhile, whip the cream until soft peaks begin to form. When it begins to thicken, add the powdered sugar and continue to whip it until it is thick. Divide the granita between four small bowls or glasses and finish with a dollop of whipped cream.

Granita di mandorle

Almond granita with toasted brioche

Preparation time:
15 minutes + 30 minutes
cooling + 20 minutes in an
ice cream maker (4 hours
without an ice cream maker)
+ 1 to 2 days steeping

Serves 4

———

INGREDIENTS

1 ½ cups (200 g) of raw,
  peeled almonds
⅔ cup (120 g) superfine
  sugar
Few drops cinnamon water*
4 brioche rolls**
¼ cup (55 g) unsalted butter
2 teaspoons ground
  cinnamon

* For the cinnamon water,
pour boiling water on, say,
10 cinnamon sticks in a Mason
jar. Break the sticks if they are
not submerged. Seal and let
steep for at least 1 day.

** In Sicily, they swear by a
brioche bun with a kind of bun
on top, but any brioche will
work. Or, make the rolls for the
Maritozzi (page 290).

TIP

I deliberately make small
quantities of this granita
because it's best if you eat
it as soon as it's ready. In
Sicily, they have special
equipment to refrigerate
granitas. At home, if you
have to store the granita
before serving it, remove it
from the freezer 15 minutes
ahead of time. But if
possible, finish and serve
it so that it's *á la minute!*

The almond granita from Giovanna of Gelateria Musumeci is creamy, not too sweet, and without almond extract so the flavor is authentic and delicious. To pick up the almond flavor, Giovanna has a trick; it's below. Granita is often eaten with a brioche bun for breakfast. My first granita breakfast is still vividly in my mind. It was during a date with a guy from Catania who had a sports car and wore pink shorts. After a wild night, he treated me to granita with brioche. I thought that was an odd breakfast choice at the time, but I ate it, sitting on his hood, overlooking the harbor and the rising sun, knowing that this was my first and last breakfast with the pink shorts.

If you have an ice cream machine that needs to be pre-frozen, put it in the freezer the night before. Machines vary, so the churning time varies. In some machines, you have to churn the granita in batches.

Put the almonds in a food processor with the sugar and grind into a thick paste. At first it will be coarse, but continue until the nuts release their fat and become sticky. Scrape the nuts from the wall of the food processor back to the blade each time. If you don't have a blender, you can use a good hand blender. With the food processor running, gradually pour in 2 ⅓ cups (550 ml) of water. Season with a few drops of cinnamon water—the amount depends on how long the cinnamon sticks were steeped in the water. The flavor should be subtle and only enhance the almond flavor. Start with a small amount.

Pour the mixture into an ice cream maker and turn it into a creamy granita in about 20 minutes. The exact time depends on your ice cream maker. If you don't have an ice cream maker, you can fabricate one yourself (read how Giovanna does it on page 324; in my highlights on Instagram you can watch a video about it). Or you can put the mixture in a shallow lidded container in the freezer and stir it loose with a fork every hour for 4 hours. You'll get bigger chunks; and it won't be as creamy as a granita from the ice cream machine, but it's still delicious.

Meanwhile, cut open the brioche buns. Heat a large frying pan, melt 2 tablespoons of butter and add 1 teaspoon of cinnamon. Toast 2 buns over high heat on the cut edges until brown and crispy. Repeat with the remaining 2 buns. Let them cool.

Fill the brioche balls with granita and eat immediately.

Granita di anguria

Watermelon granita with a Mexican touch

Preparation time:
10 minutes + 30 minutes
in an ice cream maker
(4 hours without an ice
cream maker)

Serves 6

INGREDIENTS

2 pounds (900 g)
  watermelon, seeds
  and rind removed
  and chopped
5 tablespoons lime juice
¾ cup (150 g) granulated
  sugar
2 teaspoons Mexican tajín

Watermelon granita comes in handy during heat waves. Because of the high water content in the fruit, the sugar dissolves on its own so you don't need to make a syrup for it separately. I add a pinch of Mexican tajín—a mixture of dried lime, chili powder, and salt. It gives the granita an exciting kick. You could also serve it as a cocktail with a splash of mezcal in it. ¡Arriba!

If you have an ice cream machine that needs to be pre-frozen, put it in the freezer the night before. Machines vary, so the churning time varies. In some machines, you have to churn the granita in batches.

Place the watermelon pieces in a food processor or blender with the lime juice, sugar, and tajín, and blend until smooth.

Pour the mixture into an ice cream maker. The exact time depends on your ice cream maker. If you don't have an ice cream maker, you can fabricate one yourself (read how Giovanna does it on page 324; you can watch a video about it in my highlights on Instagram). Or, you can put the mixture in a shallow lidded container in the freezer and stir it loose with a fork every hour for 4 hours. You'll get bigger chunks, and it won't be as creamy as a granita from the ice cream machine, but it's still delicious.

Granita di pomodoro e basilico

Tomato granita with basil

Preparation time:
10 minutes + 30 minutes
in an ice cream maker
(4 hours without an ice
cream maker)

Serves 6

INGREDIENTS

2 pounds (900 g) very ripe
    cherry tomatoes, halved
2 teaspoons olive oil
1 tablespoon sea salt
3 tablespoons
    granulated sugar
2 to 3 sprigs basil,
    leaves removed

Giovanna of Gelateria Musumeci (see page 324) taught me how to make granita, but not before she had first filled us up completely with an extensive variety of flavors, from persimmon to tangerine, from coffee to pistachio. Finally, we made a tomato granita with basil. Since I don't have a sweet tooth by nature, I found this one quite tasty. Think of a refreshing gazpacho on a hot day, but creamier and more elegant.

If you have an ice cream machine that needs to be pre-frozen, put it in the freezer the night before. Machines vary, so the churning time varies. In some machines, you have to churn the granita in batches.

Add the tomatoes, olive oil, salt, sugar, and basil into a food processor or blender and purée until smooth.

Pour the mixture into an ice cream maker. The exact time depends on your ice cream maker. If you don't have an ice cream maker, you can fabricate one yourself (read how Giovanna does it on page 324; you can watch a video about it in my highlights on Instagram). Or, you can put the mixture in a shallow lidded container in the freezer and stir it loose with a fork every hour for 4 hours. You'll get bigger chunks, and it won't be as creamy as a granita from the ice cream machine, but it's still delicious.

Giovanna serves this granita on slices of fried eggplant and garnishes them with basil leaves. Enjoy this as a refreshing *merenda* (afternoon snack) or as an antipasto on a blazing hot summer day.

BIBITE
DRINKS

Negroni a modo mio

Negroni my way

Preparation time:
5 minutes + 2 hours
of infusion

Makes 1 cocktail

――――

INGREDIENTS

1 to 2 large ice cubes
2 tablespoons gin
2 ½ tablespoons red
  vermouth (e.g. Carpano)
  infused for a few hours
  with 1 sprig rosemary
2 tablespoons Campari
1 slice orange

TIP

Buy a mold for large ice
cubes. Small ice cubes
melt faster and make the
negroni watery.

VARIATIONS

Instead of gin, add
sparkling water for an
Americano.

For a *negroni sbagliato*
(wrong negroni) add
prosecco instead of gin.

Replace the gin with vodka
and you have a negroski.

Finally, for a Campari
spritz (which doesn't
have much to do with a
negroni, except that it also
contains Campari) mix
¼ cup + 2 tablespoons
(90 ml) of prosecco with
¼ cup (60 ml) of Campari
and possibly a splash of
sparkling water. Finish with
a slice of orange.

The negroni is a quintessential Italian cocktail with equal parts Campari, vermouth, and gin. You love it or you hate it. If you are in the latter camp, then you are probably an Aperol lover. I think of the negroni as my drink. It is ultra strong, bittersweet, aromatic, and you are drunk almost immediately after one glass. Cincin! It is a kind of kamikaze version of the Americano (a cocktail with vermouth, Campari, and soda water). Back in 1919, Florentine Count Camillo Negroni felt like something stronger than an Americano, so the bartender replaced the soda with gin and the rest is history. At least that's how the story goes. At the fashionable Caffè Gilli in Florence, you can get the legendary negroni from bartender Luca Picchi, who also wrote a book about it.

When I lived in Florence, I routinely drank two with my friend Pietro during aperitivo, only to invariably arrive late for our dinner dates. Times are changing. Italians these days are on time, and I haven't had two negronis for years. Now when I treat myself to a negroni, I sip it. Over the years I have perfected it by adding just a little more red vermouth to take the edge off of the bitterness. I soak a sprig of rosemary in the vermouth for a few hours ahead of time to make it more flavorful.

Ahead of time, place a high-ball glass, such as a whiskey glass, in the freezer for a while to get cold.

Plop a large ice cube into the chilled glass. Pour in the gin, infused vermouth, and Campari. Squeeze the orange slice above the glass and add. Stir well with a sprig of rosemary, and then comes the very hardest moment: wait a very short time. Just a few minutes, so the orange can release its flavor and the ice can chill the cocktail. Salute.

Polibibita di Lambrusco e Aperol

Cocktail of dry Lambrusco and Aperol

Preparation time:
15 minutes

Makes 1 cocktail

INGREDIENTS

Ice cubes
2 ½ tablespoons Aperol
⅓ cup dry Lambrusco
Squeeze fresh orange
    juice and an orange slice

Cacio e pepe popcorn
¾ cup (100 g) popcorn,
    popped
3 ½ ounces (100 g)
    pecorino cheese, grated
Freshly ground black
    pepper

Polibibita is an old-fashioned Italian word for cocktail, invented by Italian futurists in the 1920s. This radical movement hated tradition and history. *Poli* is Greek for "a lot" and *bibita* means "drink" in Italian. Polibibita thus stands for multiple drinks or a cocktail, in other words. Do you make a good impression in Italy by ordering a polibibita? That's the question. Probably people under seventy won't understand you. But I just wanted to expose my knowledge and hope you're impressed now. What I really want to talk about is dry Lambrusco. No folks, this wine has nothing to do with sweet bubbly wine from the supermarket. In Emilia-Romagna, they serve cold, dry, quality Lambrusco. Delicious with tagliatelle with ragù or in a fresh cocktail. The Italian singer, Ligabue, once released the song "Lambrusco e popcorn," which led me to this combo with *cacio e pepe* (cheese and pepper) popcorn.

Place the ice cubes in a nice glass and pour the Aperol and dry Lambrusco on top. Finish with a squeeze of fresh orange juice. Brown an orange slice with a blowtorch and add as a garnish. I like it best this way. If you add sparkling water to this, you have a Lambrusco spritz.

To make the cacio e pepe popcorn, preheat the oven to 350°F (180°C). Mix the already-popped popcorn with the grated pecorino cheese and a generous amount of freshly ground black pepper. Spread on a baking sheet lined with parchment paper and bake in the preheated oven until the cheese has melted, about 10 minutes. Enjoy your popcorn alongside your polibibita.

BUCA
s. PETRONIO

Bicerìn

Traditional hot chocolate from Turin

Preparation time:
20 minutes

Serves 4

⸻

INGREDIENTS

½ cup (120 ml) heavy
    whipping cream
2 cups (475 ml) whole milk
⅓ cup + 1 teaspoon
    (70 g) cane or granulated
    sugar
4 ¼ ounces (120 g) dark
    chocolate (75% cocoa),
    chopped
½ cup (120 ml)
    hot espresso
Freshly grated nutmeg

TIP

Another method of
making hot chocolate is
with cocoa powder and
cornstarch. The flavor is
a bit less full-bodied but
you still get a thick,
dark chocolate.

To do this, take ½ cup
(50 g) of cocoa powder
and mix it in a saucepan
with ¼ cup (50 g) of
granulated sugar and ¼
cup (35 g) of cornstarch.
Measure out 2 cups
(475 ml) of whole milk.
Pour a splash of the
cold milk into the cocoa
mixture and stir until any
lumps disappear. Pour in
the rest of the milk and
the nutmeg. Keep the
heat on low while stirring
to thicken.

Calorie bomb bicerìn is the emblematic hot drink of Turin with its thick dark chocolate milk, strong coffee, and a layer of whipped cream. Bicerìn comes from the word *bicchierino* (glass) and was already served in the historic Caffè al Bicerìn in 1763. From Cavour to Hemingway to Alexandre Dumas—all were fans. Drink bicerìn like an Irish coffee—through the layers rather than stirring. That way you taste cream first, then the bitterness of coffee and finally the dark chocolate. If you drink bicerìn in a bar and find that you can't stand not to stir, then do it out of the barista's sight, lest he get unnecessarily agitated. I've tried it both ways and can confirm that the layers work best. The proportions of chocolate, coffee, and cream seem to be a local secret, although the barista at Caffè Platti revealed to me that very little coffee goes into it. He also informed me that the drink used to be served deconstructed, with jugs of coffee, chocolate, and cream to put together yourself. I serve bicerìn in glasses that are not too large. It is a divine drink, but too much is sickening. The nutmeg is my own addition.

First, in a bowl, whip the cream until thick but before peaks form, just like Irish coffee; you should still be able to pour it.

In a saucepan, bring the milk to a simmer, add the sugar and chocolate pieces. Keep stirring while the mixture comes back up to a simmer. Whisk energetically for about 5 minutes. At some point the mixture will start to thicken.

Fill four 12-ounce (360-ml) glasses one-third of the way with thick hot chocolate. Then, over the back of a spoon, gently pour the espresso on top so that you get a layer. Finish with a layer of whipped cream. Grate fresh nutmeg on top.

Bombardino con grappa e five spice

Homemade eggnog with grappa, cream, and five-spice powder

Preparation time:
20 minutes

Serves 4

INGREDIENTS

½ cup (120 ml) heavy
   whipping cream
8 egg yolks
Scant ½ cup (90 grams)
   superfine sugar
⅓ cup (80 ml) grappa
Five-spice powder,
   to garnish

TIPS

You can replace the grappa with brandy to make the original recipe or with whiskey for a *bombardino scozzese*. If you add a shot of espresso you have a *calimero*.

You can also use ready-made eggnog but it doesn't compare to making it yourself.

With the remaining egg whites, you can make Jasmine gelato (page 320), Almond cookies (page 371), or an egg white omelet.

In Germany you drink beer on the slopes, in France, vin chaud (warm wine) and in Italy, bombardino—a kind of hot, homemade eggnog made of two-thirds zabaglione and one-third brandy with a dollop of whipped cream. I replace the brandy with grappa and finish my bombardino with five-spice powder. Delicious after a cold winter day.

First whip the cream with a mixer until soft peaks form and set it aside. You can add 1 tablespoon of sugar if you like, but I prefer it without.

Place a heatproof bowl over a saucepan containing a layer of gently boiling water. Keep the heat low. In the bowl, beat the egg yolks with the sugar au bain-marie until light and fluffy.

Pour in the grappa and keep whisking until the mixture begins to rise. Do not let it boil. When the mixture runs off the whisk like a ribbon, it is ready. Divide the warm mixture among four glasses, add a dollop of whipped cream, and sprinkle on a pinch of five-spice powder.

Shottino di cioccolata calda

Thick hot chocolate shot with chili

Preparation time:
10 minutes

Serves 6

INGREDIENTS

2 cups (475 ml) whole milk
⅓ cup (60 g) cane or
  granulated sugar
5 ¼ ounces (150 g) dark
  chocolate (75% cocoa),
  broken into small pieces
½ teaspoon ground
  cinnamon
½ teaspoon ground ginger
2 tablespoons vanilla
  extract
Chili powder

TIP

No chocolate in the
house? Another method
of making cioccolata calda
is with cocoa powder and
cornstarch, which is how
it is usually prepared in
the bar. The flavor then
becomes less full but
you still get a thick, dark
chocolate. To do this, take
⅔ cup (50 g) of cocoa
powder and mix it in a
sauce pan with ¼ cup
(50 g) of granulated
sugar and ½ cup (50 g) of
cornstarch. Measure out
2 cup (475 ml) of whole
milk. Pour a splash of the
cold milk into the cocoa
mixture and stir until any
lumps disappear. Pour in
the rest of the milk, the
cinnamon, ginger, vanilla,
and chili powder. Keep the
heat on low while stirring

When I studied in Florence, I drank a life-changing hot chocolate.
After being served that intensely dark thick liquid for the first
time, it stayed with me for the rest of my life. I drank my first one
at an all-time favorite chocolate shop, Hemingway's. The chocolate
shot was spicy, and it had an aftertaste of chili powder that was so
surprising, it just about got me high. Hemingway's no longer exists,
but luckily, even in the dullest Italian bar, they still make good work
of their hot chocolate. That's why I love that country so much!
With this recipe, you can recreate it at home.

Pour the milk into a saucepan, add the sugar, and heat on low.
Add the chocolate, and melt it in the hot milk mixture. Add the
cinnamon, ginger, and vanilla. Whisk until the mixture thickens.
Remove from the heat when the chocolate milk is the desired
thickness. Taste to see if it is to your taste; you may want it sweeter
than I do. Pour the chocolate milk into small glasses and sprinkle
with a pinch of chili powder.

"EVEN IN A SIMPLE BAR, ITALIANS TURN HOT CHOCOLATE INTO A WORK OF ART. THAT'S WHY I LOVE ITALY SO MUCH."

BASE RECIPES

Brodo vegetale
Vegetable broth

For a full, rich flavor, I start by roasting some of the vegetables. In addition, there are a few ingredients that you may not have in your pantry as standard (yet) that add a lot of flavor, such as *kombu* (seaweed) and dried mushrooms. Once you've tried my version, substitute new ingredients. Broth lends itself perfectly to using up all kinds of leftovers from the fridge.

Preparation time: 50 minutes + 1 hour of infusion

——

INGREDIENTS

1 ¾ ounces (50 g) dashi kombu (dried seaweed)
2 large leeks
2 onions
1 large celery root
1 large carrot
¼ cup (60 ml) olive oil
¾ ounce (20 g) dried porcini
1 garlic bulb
1 fennel tuber, coarsely chopped
4 stalks celery, sliced and leaves set aside
3 to 4 ripe tomatoes, chopped
1 tablespoon coriander seeds
1 tablespoon fennel seeds
1 teaspoon peppercorns
Few sprigs thyme
2 bay leaves
1 tablespoon sea salt

Preheat the oven to 425°F (220°C).

Fill a large pot (capacity at least 6 quarts [5.7L]) with 3 quarts (2.8 L) of water, and soak the kombu dashi in it for 30 minutes.

Cut the whites of the leeks into rings, save the greens. Roughly chop the onions with skin and all. Peel the celery root and cut it into 2-by-2-inch (5-by-5-cm) cubes. Also cut the carrot into small cubes. The smaller the cubes, the more surface area, the more flavor.

Spread the onion and leek rings on a baking sheet lined with parchment paper. Pour 2 tablespoons of the olive oil on top and stir the vegetables with your hands to distribute the oil evenly.

Separately place the celery root and chopped carrot on a baking sheet lined with parchment paper, drizzle on the remaining 2 tablespoons of olive oil and mix to coat the vegetables. Slide both trays into the oven and roast for 25 to 30 minutes until the vegetables are well browned.

Bring the dashi kombu water to a boil. Reduce the temperature and simmer for 15 minutes. Remove the dashi kombu with a slotted spoon or tongs. Add the dried mushrooms and continue to simmer.

Separate the garlic into cloves and crush them in a mortar and add to the dashi kombu water. Add the fennel, celery, tomatoes, roasted vegetables, and leek greens.

Crush the fennel seeds, coriander seeds, and peppercorns in a mortar and add together with the thyme, bay leaf, and a small handful of celery leaves to the pot.

Gently cook the stock uncovered over very low heat for 1 hour. Cool completely. Pour through a sieve and press the vegetables with a masher so that you get all of the flavor and the liquid.

Add the salt gradually at the end. The amount you will want depends upon how much moisture has evaporated. You can also season with soy sauce, a dash of Worcestershire sauce, or fish sauce if desired (but then of course your stock will no longer be 100% vegetarian). You can use it immediately or freeze it in portions. If you freeze it, note what it is, because once frozen you may not remember.

TIPS

If I want a more tomatoey broth, I add a can of tomato purée.

Vary your own seasonings. You can also add leftover wine but make sure the alcohol is cooked off or you will get a bitter taste.

Fondo bruno
Veal Stock

Why is restaurant food always so delicious? The answer, besides butter, is veal stock, also known as the French jus de veau, or fondo bruno in Italian. Veal stock is a boiled broth made with veal bones and the basis for numerous sauces and soups. How far you boil it down depends on the use. For a concentrated stock, boil it down to 4 ¼ cups (1 L). I boil the stock down to 8 ½ cups (2 L) and use it for various purposes, for example, in the risotto on page 164. I pour the stock as a sauce over the risotto so you get a nice contrast between the white risotto and the brown fondo. Making it is certainly not difficult, it just takes some time.

Preparation time: 1 hour + 8 hours of infusion

_____

INGREDIENTS
4 pounds (1.8 kg) veal bones
2 pounds (900 g) beef shank or other meaty bones
3 leeks, whites and greens separated
1 large carrot, diced
½ celery root, diced
2 onions, coarsely chopped
Few sprigs thyme
1 sprig fresh bay leaves or 4 dried leaves
1 bulb garlic

Preheat the oven to 480°F (250°C).

Roast the veal bones for 30 minutes on a baking sheet. Remove the bones from the oven and remove the released fat.

Place the beef shank with the leek whites, carrot, celery root, and onions onto a baking sheet. Sprinkle with salt and roast for 15 minutes or so, until the vegetables have brown spots here and there. Remove from the oven, drain the excess fat, and transfer the bones, shank, and vegetables into a large pot. Add the herbs and enough water to submerge the meat and vegetables. Separate the garlic into cloves, crush them in a mortar, and add them to the pot. Bring the water to a boil then reduce the heat and simmer uncovered for at least 8 hours. Then strain through a very fine sieve (or through a cloth if you want to remove more fat) and boil the stock down to 8 ½ cups (2 L).

Season the stock with salt after reducing to desired consistency. You can use it immediately or freeze it in portions. If you freeze it, note what it is, because once frozen you may not remember.

TIP
You can use this stock to make soup, spoon it over cooked beans, or make another sauce with it.

Fumetto
Fish Stock

At the fish counter, you can ask for the bones and trimmings from whitefish or use the remains of a previously prepared fish. Shrimp peels or heads also add a lot of flavor. Grab the vegetables that you have lying around. If you have a carrot or some dill in the fridge, add that, too.

Preparation time: 15 minutes + 30 to 40 minutes of infusion

_____

INGREDIENTS
2 pounds (900 g) fish bones, heads, and trimmings
2 tablespoons olive oil
1 large onion, coarsely chopped
2 stalks celery, coarsely chopped
1 fennel bulb, coarsely chopped
1 carrot, coarsely chopped
Few parsley stalks, coarsely chopped
1 large leek, cut into rings
½ cup (120 ml) white wine
1 teaspoon fennel seeds
1 teaspoon coriander seeds
3 bay leaves

Rinse the trimmings and bones clean with cold water and drain in a colander.

Heat the olive oil in a large pot and add the onion, celery, fennel, carrot, parsley, and leeks. Sauté them for a few minutes and then add the fish trimmings. Sauté until the fish meat cooks and begins to turn white. Then deglaze with the wine.

Add water to the pot until the vegetables and fish are submerged, briefly bring to a boil, and skim the top after 5 to 7 minutes.

Add the fennel seeds, coriander seeds, and bay leaves. Simmer over low heat for 30 to 40 minutes at most—longer may cause the broth to be bitter. Allow it to cool completely.

Place a clean tea towel or cheesecloth in a large sieve and set it over a large bowl. Pour the broth through the sieve. You can use it immediately or freeze it in portions. If you freeze it, note what it is, because once frozen you may not remember.

TIP
To mix it up a bit, you can add a pinch of saffron or some orange zest while it's cooling down at the end. You can also add some tomato paste at the beginning for a red fish stock.

Brodo di pollo
Chicken Stock

By roasting some of the vegetables and chicken bones beforehand, you will get a deeper flavor. Use bone-rich pieces of chicken such as wings, thighs, and drumsticks. The flavor and the gelatin in the bones makes the broth thick and sticky, which is delicious.

Preparation time: 50 minutes + 1 to 1½ hours of infusion

INGREDIENTS
2 large leeks, whites and greens separated
2 onions
1 large carrot
2 tablespoons vegetable oil
2 stalks celery, coarsely chopped
Couple Italian parsley stalks, coarsely chopped
3 garlic cloves, crushed
½ pounds bone-in chicken pieces*
2 bay leaves, bruised
4 sprigs thyme
  teaspoon black peppercorns
  teaspoon sea salt

*You can also save up bones or use a carcass from a roast chicken and make a broth from that. Or combine chicken meat with bones.

Preheat the oven to 425°F (220°C).

Cut the whites of the leeks into rings, saving the greens. Roughly slice the onions, including the skins. Halve the carrot and cut into slices. Place the vegetables on a baking sheet lined with parchment paper and stir in the vegetable oil, and roast for 25 to 30 minutes until you see brown spots here and there. If you have bones to include in the soup, roast them with the vegetables.

Put the celery, parsley, garlic, chicken pieces, bay leaves, and thyme sprigs in a large pot.

Add the roasted vegetables along with the roasted chicken bones and leek greens. Pour in 3 quarts (2.8 L) of water and bring to a boil. Skim the top after about 10 minutes.

Add the peppercorns. Simmer on very low heat for at least 1 hour, but 2 hours is better. Add the salt gradually at the end. The amount you will want depends upon how much moisture has evaporated. Allow to cool completely then strain the broth and press everything well so that you squeeze out as much flavorful liquid as possible. Use right away or freeze in portions. If you freeze it, note what it is, because once frozen you may not remember.

Pasta fresca all'uovo
Pasta dough with egg

For fresh pasta, I use a mixture of flour and semolina. The proportions are a personal preference, and they depend on the texture you want to achieve. More semolina for a firmer pasta, more egg for a smoother dough. With fazzoletti, I like them to slide across your tongue, so I use little semolina for them. For stuffed pasta, I take a little more. Use the proportions below as a guideline, but experiment to see for yourself what you like best. More information about pasta can be found on page 73.

Preparation time: 20 minutes + 30 minutes to rest
Serves 4

———

INGREDIENTS

Fazzoletti (page 95)
2 cups (250 g) "00" or all-purpose flour
¼ cup + 1 tablespoon (50 g) semolina + extra for dusting
3 eggs
Pinch sea salt

Triangoli (page 86) and Tortelloni (page 88)
1 ⅔ cups (200 g) "00" flour
½ cup + 2 tablespoons (100 g) semolina + extra for dusting
3 eggs
Pinch sea salt

Mix the flour with the semolina. Pour into a pile on your work surface and make a wide dimple in it with your fist. Break the eggs into this and add a pinch of salt.

Using your fingertips or a fork, work in the flour and semolina little by little until you have a coarse dough. Scrape it together with a dough scraper and form it into a ball.

Knead the dough for 10 minutes, until smooth. If necessary, add a little water if the dough feels too dry. It should be firm and elastic, but not sticky. Let the dough rest in plastic wrap for 30 minutes.

You can also make the dough in a food processor using a dough blade. If using a food processor, add the flour, semolina, and salt first, then the eggs, and process until the dough comes together into a ball.

Dust your work surface with semola and knead the pasta dough for another 5 minutes. Divide it into quarters, cover the portions that are not being used with a cloth or plastic wrap to keep them from drying out while you put the other section through the pasta machine.

Press a piece of dough slightly flat and pass it through the pasta machine, starting at the widest setting. Fold in half and repeat two more times. Turn the machine to the next position and continue. If the sheets get too long, cut them in half, so they are more workable.

The thickness of the pasta depends on the type of pasta. For general pasta, you stop after setting 6 or 7, for filled pasta you roll it out thinner because you stick two sheets together (setting 8). I also roll fazzoletti as thinly as filled pasta.

Keep the pasta sheets under a towel so they don't dry out, and work quickly while rolling out the rest of the dough.

TIPS
You'll need a dough scraper and pasta machine for this recipe.

Pasta per culurgiones
Pasta dough for culurgiones

Culurgiones or culurzones are Sardinian dough pillows, traditionally filled with mashed potatoes, pecorino, and sometimes other Sardinian cheeses and mint. The dough is slightly moist, so it sticks together well. Don't roll out the dough too thin, otherwise it will tear.

Culurgiones take some practice, so take your time.

Preparation time: 10 minutes + 30 minutes of resting
Serves 4

_____

INGREDIENTS

1 cup + 1 tablespoon (150 g) "00" flour + extra
1 ¼ cup (50 g) semolina + extra for dusting
½ teaspoon sea salt + extra
½ tablespoon mild olive oil

Mix the flour and semolina with the salt in a bowl. Add the oil, then gradually add ½ cup + 1 tablespoon (135 ml) of lukewarm water. Knead for 10 minutes to form a smooth dough. It may feel slightly wet to the touch, a little more moist than you are used to, although of course, it should not stick. Wrap in plastic wrap and let rest for 30 minutes.

Knead the pasta dough well for another 5 minutes. Divide it into 4 pieces. Pass through the pasta machine, starting at the largest setting. Then fold in half and repeat 2 more times.

Turn the machine to the next setting and repeat the process, cutting long pieces in half. Stop after setting 5 or once the pasta is ⅛ inch (3 mm) thick. The pasta should not be too thin, or it may tear when folded. If you don't have a pasta machine, you can also roll small balls of the dough and use a rolling pin to roll them flat into a disc about 3 inches (7.5 cm) in diameter.

TIP
You'll need a pasta machine for this recipe.
Learn more about making pasta on page 73.

Scialatielli
Amalfi pasta

In the late 1970s, Amalfi chef Enrico Constantino invented this rich pasta. The scialatielli owe their creamy flavor to it, and they are now known throughout Italy. It is a rustic pasta about 5 to 6 inches (13 to 15 cm) long. It is quite thick, and because you use only fine semolina from durum wheat, instead of a combination of durum wheat and "00" flour, the pasta is also nice and chewy. You can make scialatielli using a chitarra, a device used to make four edged spaghetti (spaghetti alla chitarra), but you can also do it by hand. Parsley, lime leaf, or basil are delicious mixed into the dough, but I've also made it with lemon zest. Saffron can also be used. I love to pair scialatielli with seafood (see page 119).

Preparation time: 15 minutes + 30 minutes to rest
Serves 4

———

INGREDIENTS
1 ¾ cups (400 g) semolina + extra for dusting
½ cup + 2 tablespoons (150 ml) whole milk, at room temperature
1 small egg, beaten
1 ½ ounces (40 g) pecorino cheese, finely grated
8 lime leaves, veins removed and very finely chopped
1 tablespoon mild olive oil

Pour the semolina onto your work surface and form it into a mountain. Make a wide crater in it with your fist. Add the milk, egg, grated cheese, and lime leaves. From the edges of the crater, work in the flour with a fork until you have a coarse dough. Add the oil. This whole process can also be done in a bowl, then you make less of a mess.

Scrape it together with a dough scraper or your hands and form it into a ball. Knead it for 10 minutes until it is smooth. Add a little water if it feels too dry. It should be firm and elastic but not sticky. Press into the dough with your finger; if it springs back, it is good. Let the dough rest in plastic wrap for 30 minutes.

You can also make the dough in a food processor with the dough blade. If using a food processor, add the flour, semolina, and salt first, then blend. Next, add the milk, eggs, oil, cheese, and chopped herbs, and process until the dough comes together into a ball. Let the dough rest in plastic wrap for 30 minutes.

After resting, knead the dough well again and divide it into two pieces. Keep one piece under a towel or wrapped in plastic wrap so it doesn't dry out. Using a rolling pin, roll out the other piece of dough to ⅛ to ¼ inch (3 to 6 mm) thick.

Sprinkle with semola and loosely roll again from the sides toward the center. Using a sharp knife, cut into thick strips about ½ inch (13 mm) wide and between 5 and 6 inches (12 and 15 cm) long. Process the remaining piece of dough in the same way.

TIP
You'll need a dough scraper for this recipe.
Learn more about making pasta on page 73.

Pasta integrale
Whole-wheat pasta

You can make whole-wheat pasta in different ways. It can be made with egg or with water. Also, I usually use one part whole-wheat flour and one part semolina, so it won't taste too hearty. Play around with the proportions yourself. For pasta with puttanesca, I use only water, because in southern Italy they usually don't put eggs in pasta dough. But, for example, if I make whole-wheat pasta with mushrooms, I think eggs in the dough works. Choose for yourself. Eggs provide elasticity, which makes the dough a little easier to work with.

Preparation time: 15 minutes + 30 minutes to rest
Serves 4

_____

INGREDIENTS
⅓ cups (150 g) whole-wheat flour + extra
½ cups + 1 tablespoon (250 g) semolina + extra for dusting
¼ teaspoon sea salt
¼ cup + 3 tablespoons (220 ml) water or 4 eggs
tablespoon olive oil

Mix the whole-wheat flour with the semolina and salt. Dump a mound on your work surface and make a wide crater in it with your fist. Pour the water into the crater (or break the eggs into it) and drizzle in the oil. Using your fingertips, work in the flour from the edges of the crater until you have a coarse dough.

Scrape it together with a dough scraper or your hands and form it into a ball. Knead until the dough is smooth, about 10 minutes. Add a little extra water if the dough feels too dry or more flour if it feels sticky. It should be firm and elastic, not too sticky, and spring back when you push your finger in. If not, knead a little longer. Let the dough rest in plastic wrap for 30 minutes.

You can also make pasta dough in a food processor with the dough attachment. If using, put in the whole-wheat flour, semolina, and salt and blend. Next add the water (or eggs) and oil and process until the dough comes together into a kind of ball. Let the dough rest in plastic wrap for 30 minutes.

Knead the pasta dough for another 5 minutes. Dust your work surface with semolina flour. Divide the pasta dough into quarters. Press it a bit flat and pass it through the pasta machine, starting at the widest setting. Fold in half and repeat two more times. Turn the machine to the next position and continue, cutting long strips in half, so it's manageable.

Stop at position 5 and put the attachment for tagliatelle on it. Turn the pasta sheets into tagliatelle and hang to dry over a chair, hanger, or laundry rack. Or place them in heaps on a baking sheet lined with parchment paper or on a clean tea towel dusted with flour. Turn the mounds occasionally so that they dry on all sides.

TIP
You'll need a dough scraper and pasta machine for this recipe.
Learn more about making pasta on page 73.

Pappardelle di segale
Rye pappardelle

Pappardelle is a thick ribbon pasta from Tuscany. The dried variety has a very rough surface, almost like a cat's tongue. The advantage of this is that the sauce sticks well. To get that rough surface, let the pasta sheets dry for a while after you roll them out. The rye flour is my own addition; the traditional variety is usually made with semolina, or a combination with all-purpose flour.

Preparation time: 25 minutes + 30 minutes to rest
Serves 6

———

INGREDIENTS
2 ½ cups (300 g) rye flour
1 ½ cups (200 g) semolina, + extra for dusting
5 eggs

Mix the rye flour and semolina with a pinch of salt. Make a mound on your work surface and make a big, wide crater in it with your fist.

Beat the eggs in a bowl with 1 to 2 tablespoons of water. Rye flour soaks up more moisture, which is why you add some water.

Pour the egg mixture into the crater. Using your fingertips, work in the flour until you have a coarse dough. Scrape it together with a dough scraper or your hands and form it into a ball. Knead for 10 minutes until the dough is smooth. If the dough feels too dry, add a tablespoon of water. If it feels wet, add more rye flour. It should be firm, elastic, and not sticky. Press the dough with your finger; if it springs back, it is good. Let the dough rest in plastic wrap for 30 minutes.

Knead the pasta dough for another 5 minutes. Dust your work surface with semola. Divide the pasta dough into quarters and cover what you don't use with a cloth or plastic wrap to prevent it from drying out until you are ready to use it. Press one piece of dough flat and pass it through the pasta machine, starting at the widest setting. Fold in half and repeat one more time. Turn the machine to the next position and pass through two more times. If the sheets get too long, cut them in half, so they are more workable. Continue until you have sheets about ⅛ inch (3 mm) thick. For pappardelle with a rough surface, let the sheets dry for about 10 minutes on a work surface dusted with semola. Don't let them get too dry or the pasta will break later when rolling up the sheets.

Dust the dough sheets on both sides with some more semola. Roll it up loosely from the top to the center and roll it up loosely from the bottom to the center as well.

With a knife, cut into strands about 1 inch (2 ½ cm) wide. Repeat with the rest of the dough. Hang the pappardelle to dry over a chair, hanger, or laundry rack. Or place them in mounds on a baking sheet lined with parchment paper or on a clean towel dusted with flour. Turn the mounds occasionally so they dry on all sides.

TIPS
You'll need a dough scraper and pasta machine for this recipe.
Learn more about making pasta on page 73.

Gnocchi di patate
Potato gnocchi

Making homemade gnocchi pays off. It takes some time, but it is certainly not difficult, as long as you keep a few things in mind (see page 147 for more information). For gnocchi, I use one part "00" flour and for firmness some semolina. Count on about a one-to-four ratio of flour to the weight of the potatoes—maybe a little more, maybe a little less.

Preparation time: 1 hour

___

INGREDIENTS

1 ½ pounds (700 g) russet potatoes
1 small egg
Sea salt
1 cup (130 g) "00" flour
⅓ cup (45 g) semolina + extra for dusting

Boil the potatoes in their skins until tender. Let cool slightly, remove the skins, and press the potatoes through a food mill. If you don't have a food mill, put it on your wish list immediately—and then press the potatoes through a fine sieve.

Mix the potatos with the egg and a pinch of salt, and add the flour little by little through a sifter to avoid lumps. Knead the mixture into a soft, non-sticky dough.

Sprinkle semola on your work surface and grab a piece of the dough. Roll the dough into a thin, round, even "snake" about ½ inch (13 mm) in diameter. Cut the snake into pieces ½ inch (13 mm) wide.

If you have a gnocchi board (rigagnocchi), you can use it to make ridges in the gnocchi. If not, a fork works well too. If using a fork, cradle a gnocco (gnocchi singular!) on the fork, with the thumb of your other hand gently push it toward the end of the fork's tines so that it forms a roll with ridges. If you push too hard, you will smoosh the gnocco between the tines of the fork, which means you need to push gently. You have to guide the gnocco as it rolls on the fork.

Place the formed gnocchi on a surface dusted with semola or on a clean towel. (I often use a baking sheet; you can fit a lot of gnocchi on that.)

Don't want to cook the gnocchi right away? Store fresh gnocchi in a dry, cool place covered with a cloth. Don't store them in the refrigerator. They will absorb too much moisture.

Cooked gnocchi can be stored in the refrigerator, though, or even frozen. When you are ready to eat them, boil the gnocchi for just a few seconds to heat them and serve them with the sauce of your choice. For example, Gnocchi with creamed leeks, saffron, and hazelnut (page 151) or Gnocchi with zucchini, shrimp, and za'atar (page 148).

TIP
You'll want a food mill to finely process the potatoes. Check out my instructional video on YouTube.

Basic pizza dough

Pizza dough consists of flour, about 60 percent water, salt, and yeast. I add a little more yeast (don't tell the Associazione Verace Pizza Napoletana) to make it easier. You can also add a drizzle of oil to make the dough more pliable, but the Associazione says "No!"

Preparation time: 1 hour + 4 hours to rise + 24 hours to mature in the refrigerator + 30 minutes to rest
Serves 6 (makes 6 dough balls)

——

INGREDIENTS
2 ¼ pounds (1 kg) pizza flour or "00" flour*
1 tablespoon sea salt
2 ¾ cups (650 ml) lukewarm water
1 packet (2¼ teaspoons/7 g) dried yeast
Vegetable oil, to grease the bowl
Semola, for dusting

* If you want a heartier crust, mix in some whole-wheat flour. Say one-to-two ratio whole-wheat flour to "00" flour. Add a little more water (whole-wheat flour is thirsty). This option is delicious with pizzas with flavorful toppings, such as those on pages 269 and 270.

MIX AND KNEAD Mix the flour with the salt and pour onto a clean work surface. Make a well in it. Pour some of the water into the well and mix with the yeast. Make circular movements with your hands and mix the flour through the water. Add more water little by little, and mix into a coarse dough. If necessary, you can add a drop of oil. Bring it all together. Push the dough away from you with your palm, turning it constantly so you don't knead the same place every time. Knead it until the dough is smooth, about 10 minutes. Form it into a ball. You can also make the dough in a food processor using the dough attachment.

RISE Place the ball in a spacious bowl greased with oil and cover with plastic wrap or a damp towel. Let the dough rise for about 2 hours in a warm place until it has doubled in volume. Let it ripen in the refrigerator for another 24 hours. For flavor, texture and digestibility, it is important to give the dough time. After 24 hours, remove the dough from the refrigerator and let it come to room temperature over 30 minutes.

FORM Using a dough scraper, divide the dough into 7- to 9-ounce (200- to 255-g) pieces. Take a piece and form it into a round disk, fold the dough towards each other at the bottom, so that the top becomes smooth and convex and has tension. Make sure all the folds are at the bottom of the ball and press them inward. Place a ball on a clean countertop or large cutting board, place your hand over it, lightly pinch the dough and make circular movements until you have a round tight ball. Repeat with the rest. Place the balls spaced apart on a baking sheet. Cover them with a damp cloth so the balls don't dry out. Let rise for another 2 hours.

STRETCH Take a ball and place it on a surface dusted with semola (see page 73). Flatten the ball from the center, turn it over and repeat. Use your fingertips to push the dough from the center out further, leaving the edge free; this will later become that nice high crust. If necessary, you can lay the dough over your fists and gently stretch it. Pat off the excess semola.

BAKE Place the pizza base on a pizza paddle and top with the fillings of your choice. Slide the pizza into the oven, shaking the paddle if it doesn't come loose. How long you bake depends on the oven you use. Say 5 minutes in a pizza oven and 10 minutes in a regular oven.

TIP
Pizza dough should feel somewhat sticky.

Mostarda di agrumi
Citrus mostarda

Mostarda is a condiment from Lombardy that was originally a method of preserving fruit through the winter. I serve this citrus mostarda with panna cotta. In Italy, people serve mostarda with savory dishes such as stewed meat, chicken, duck, or cheese. To make it, soak fruit with sugar for several days, sometimes without water, sometimes with water. The liquid that is released from the fruit is strained, boiled, and poured back over the fruit. In this way, the fruit remains intact and you get syrupy, whole fruits. You hardly have any work to do, but you should keep in mind that the whole process takes several days.

Preparation time: 5 days

INGREDIENTS
3 oranges
2 lemons
1 ½ cups (300 g) granulated sugar
1 ¼ cups (300 ml) white wine or spumante
1 tablespoon coriander seeds
Sea salt
4 teaspoons mustard powder

Day 1
Bring a pot of water to a boil.

Cut the peel of the oranges and lemons with a peeler or sharp knife. Remove the bitter white pith with a sharp knife and slice the flesh. Lay the slices in layers in a large pan, sprinkle each layer with sugar (use half of the sugar).

Cook the peels in boiling water for 20 minutes. Cut half into gossamer-thin strips, and add them to the sugared citrus slices—the rest of the peels can later be candied. Cover the pan and rest for 6 hours in the refrigerator.

Day 2
In a saucepan, pour the wine, ¾ cup (180 ml) of water, and the remaining ¾ cup (150 g) of sugar. Bring the mixture to a boil then add the coriander seeds and a pinch of salt. Lower the heat and simmer until the liquid reduces slightly. Pour over the lemon and orange slices, cover and let rest for 12 hours.

Days 3 and 4
Strain the syrup and add it to a saucepan. Bring to a boil and reduce it slightly. Pour back over the citrus fruit and let stand for another 12 hours. Repeat this step on day 4.

Day 5
Add the mustard powder into the syrup and mix well. Scoop the fruit into a sterilized jar and pour the syrup on top. Ideally, let the mostarda stand for a day before using it to allow the flavors to meld together.

The mostarda will keep for at least a few weeks in the refrigerator (even months if you vacuum seal it). Just be sure to use a clean spoon every time you scoop some out.

Mostarda di mela cotogna
Quince mustard chutney

I was once in Verona around Christmastime and saw *mostarda* everywhere. It sounds like mustard, but it is a kind of chutney with mustard essence. There are different types. In Mantova they cut quince into pieces like the mostarda in this recipe, in Cremona and Verona, mostarda is a kind of fruit jackpot with whole cherries and small mandarins. Practically whatever fruit comes to mind can be used to make mostarda: figs, tomatoes, pumpkin, apples, pears, citrus fruits. Traditionally, mostarda is eaten with *bollito* (which is a plain boiled meat) together with grated horseradish, yum! Mostarda also goes very well with a cheese board.

——

INGREDIENTS
Juice of 1 lemon
3 cups (500 g) quince, cubed
1 cup (210 g) sugar
4 teaspoons mustard powder

Fill a pan with a little water and squeeze the lemon juice into it.

Peel the quinces, remove the core, cut into cubes and place them in the lemon water, making sure they are submerged. Add the sugar (basically you use half the weight of the fruit in sugar, I don't have a sweet tooth so I use less). Cover and refrigerate for 24 hours.

The next day, remove and reserve the quince pieces and boil the fruit liquid for 10 minutes. Pour the hot liquid over the quince pieces and let them sit for another 24 hours. Repeat this action. By waiting, the natural pectin in the fruit helps it to thicken and gel.

After two 24-hour periods, boil the quince pieces for another 10 minutes, or until you have a thick syrup. Allow to cool and stir in the mustard powder.

Store the mostarda in a sterilized preserving jar.

Serve with the torta with sausage, sage and onion on page 253, or as a condiment for a fancy cheese board, on a slice of porchetta.

If quince is not in season, you can also use apples or pears. The pears should not be too ripe, otherwise the fruit will become mushy during preparation.

You can buy ready-made mostarda in some Italian delis, if you don't want the hassle of making it yourself. I often find it too sweet, though, which is why it's worth making instead. And you make friends if you give it as a gift at a dinner party.

Salsa di prezzemolo e anacardo
Creamy parsley-lime salsa with cashews

This is my interpretation of a salsa with peanuts that I ate and loved at Santo Palato (see page 246). Because of my peanut allergy, I use cashews. I don't know what it is with this combo, but it is addictive. I serve it with oxtail savory pie (see page 251).

Preparation time: 5 minutes

——

INGREDIENTS
1 ½ cups (40 g) Italian parsley leaves, coarsely chopped
¾ cup (105 g) roasted cashews, coarsely chopped
1 ½ teaspoons light soy sauce
Juice from 1 lime

Place the parsley along with 3 tablespoons of water, the cashews, soy sauce, and the lime juice in the measuring cup of a hand blender. Grind to a thick paste. Store in a sealed jar or container in the refrigerator.

Maionese al limone
Lemon mayo

Mayonnaise is often made at home in Italy, with olive oil, which makes it darker in color. I find that taste too intense, and besides, olive oil is very expensive, so I prefer to use a neutral oil, like vegetable oil. This mayo is delicious with everything: grilled vegetables, chicken, a piece of grilled fish, or in a sandwich.

Preparation time: 10 minutes

——

INGREDIENTS
1 egg
1 teaspoon mustard
Juice and zest from 1 lemon
Sea salt
1 cup (240 ml) vegetable oil

Place the egg in the measuring cup of a hand blender. Add the mustard and 3 tablespoons of lemon juice with a pinch of salt. While mixing, pour the oil in a thin stream until you have creamy mayonnaise. Season with lemon zest. Store in a sealed jar or container in the refrigerator.

Maionese di acciughe
Anchovy mayo

This mayonnaise pairs well as a dressing in the salad with breaded chicken (see page 237), but it also goes well on a sandwich or as a dip with artichokes or crudité.

Preparation time: 10 minutes

———

INGREDIENTS
1 egg
1 teaspoon mustard
2 tablespoons lemon juice
1 teaspoon white wine vinegar
Sea salt
10 anchovy fillets, finely chopped
¾ cup + 1 tablespoon (200 ml) vegetable oil

Place the egg in the measuring cup of a hand blender and add the mustard, lemon juice, white wine vinegar, a pinch of salt, and the anchovies. Blend well. Next gradually pour in the oil while continuing to blend until you have a thick mayonnaise. It has a strong flavor, but it pairs well with the salad. Store in a sealed jar or container in the refrigerator.

Pesto piccante con lime
Spicy lime pesto

This fresh spicy lime pesto is delicious with panissa made from chickpea flour (see page 37). But it also makes my mouth water when I think of it with a slice of leftover porchetta on a piece of focaccia. Or with grilled vegetables. Or with a sandwich with buffalo mozzarella.

Preparation time: 10 minutes

———

INGREDIENTS
⅓ cup (40 g) pine nuts or almonds
1½ cups (100 g) basil leaves or a mix of green herbs
2 tablespoons ice water
1 garlic clove
1 small jalapeño pepper
⅔ cup (160 ml) not-too-peppery extra-virgin olive oil + extra
3½ ounces (100 g) Parmesan, grated
Zest and juice from 1 lime
Sea salt

Grind the pine nuts in a food processor.

Add the basil leaves, and while the machine is running, add the ice water, garlic, chili pepper, oil, Parmesan, zest, and 2 tablespoons of lime juice, blending well between each addition. Taste and season with a little salt if necessary. Store leftovers in a sealed jar or container in the refrigerator.

Olio di pomodoro piccante
Spicy tomato oil

This oil is delicious with fish, chicken, in pasta, or in Tuscan soup with gremolata (page 68).

Preparation time: 10 minutes + 1½ hours of cooking + rest for at least 1 hour

———

INGREDIENTS
1 pound (500 g) cherry tomatoes, halved
6 garlic cloves
Sea salt
1 teaspoon chili flakes
½ cup (100 ml) mild olive oil

Preheat the oven to 275°F (135°C).

Place the cherry tomatoes and garlic cloves on a large baking dish. Sprinkle with salt and chili flakes and drizzle 2 tablespoons of olive oil on top. Bake for 1½ hours or until the tomatoes begin to color at the edges. Remove from the oven.

Place the tomato-garlic mixture into a blender, add the rest of the olive oil, and purée.

Let it rest for 1 hour (or preferably overnight), then strain through a fine sieve. Save the remaining tomato purée for tomato bruschetta or flavor soup with it. Store at room temperature in a dark, cool place.

Salsa francese
Green sauce

The French green sauce or sauce gribiche is addictively delicious. They don't acknowledge it in Italian cuisine, but French influences are actually there—and vice versa. Anyway, gribiche sauce goes well with artichokes, asparagus, fish, roasted beets, and braised meat. I serve it with the veal tongue from page 254. Officially, you make it by finely grinding the yolks of hard boiled eggs and mixing them with vinegar and oil to create a sauce. For a quick version, you could work with ready-made mayonnaise.

Preparation time: 10 minutes

INGREDIENTS
3 eggs
1 tablespoon mustard
3 tablespoons + 1 teaspoon vegetable oil
2 to 3 tablespoons white wine vinegar
1 bunch Italian parsley, leaves removed and chopped
½ bunch (¼ oz/7 g) fresh tarragon, chopped
2 tablespoons capers, chopped
2 tablespoons cornichons (small pickles), chopped
Sea salt and freshly ground black pepper

Cook the eggs in boiling water for 10 minutes until hard. Cool, then peel the eggs. Remove the yolks and mash them in a bowl. Add the mustard and then, in a thin stream, add the oil while continuing to stir, until the consistency is like mayonnaise. Add the vinegar.

Now chop the whites of the eggs and add them to the bowl. Add the parsley, tarragon, capers, and cornichons. Season with salt and pepper and store in a sealed jar or container in the refrigerator.

Crispy chili oil

This condiment from Chinese cuisine goes incredibly well with polenta. But also try it with gnocchi with lots of Parmesan.

Preparation time: 10 minutes + 1 hour of cooling

INGREDIENTS
1 cup (240 ml) vegetable oil
3 tablespoons chili flakes
3 tablespoons crushed Aleppo pepper
2 star anise
1 teaspoon ground cinnamon
1 ½-inch (4-cm) piece fresh ginger, grated
2 garlic cloves, crushed
3 tablespoons soy sauce
1 teaspoon palm sugar or brown sugar
Sea salt
Olive oil, for preserving

Heat the vegetable oil to 340°F (170°C) in a saucepan. If you don't have a kitchen thermometer, you can toss a piece of garlic or ginger into the oil—if the oil fizzes, it's hot enough.

Place the chili flakes, Aleppo pepper, star anise, cinnamon, ginger, garlic, soy sauce, and brown sugar in a heatproof bowl, and pour the hot oil over them. Season with a pinch of salt and let cool completely.

You can store the mixture with the vegetable oil in a Mason jar or strain it. Because I like to drizzle it over polenta, I prefer to strain and then store it in mild olive oil.

To do so, pour the mixture through a sieve. Transfer the spices to a sterilized jar. Pour fresh olive oil into the jar until the spices are submerged and store. It does not need to be refrigerated and stays good forever, or at least for several weeks.

Chimichurri
Argentine salsa

This South American salsa goes perfectly with meat, fish, and the crispy mozzarella sandwich (page 42). Prepare the chimichurri an hour in advance of serving so the flavor intensifies. It will keep in the refrigerator for at least a week. It will no longer be a nice fresh green, but the flavor will be even better.

Preparation time: 10 minutes + 30 minutes to 1 hour of infusion

_____

INGREDIENTS
1 teaspoon coarse sea salt
2 garlic cloves
1 small red onion, chopped
½ bunch (¼ oz/7 g) oregano, leaves chopped
4 sprigs mint, leaves chopped
½ bunch (¼ oz/7 g) Italian parsley, chopped
4 sprigs thyme, leaves chopped
1 red bell pepper, seeds removed and chopped
2 tablespoons red wine vinegar
⅓ cup (75 ml) mild olive oil

Heat ¼ cup (60 ml) of water in a saucepan and dissolve the salt in it, then cool.

Mash the garlic cloves into a paste in a mortar. Add the garlic, onion, chopped herbs, pepper, vinegar, and oil to the salted water. Allow to steep, preferably for an 1 hour but at least 30 minutes.

Store leftover chimichurri in a sealable container in the refrigerator; it will keep for at least a week.

Dolcetti di mandorla
Almond Cookies

If you make zabaglione (see pages 221 and 304) or carbonara (see page 101), you are left with unused egg whites, which are perfect for these cookies. These are reminiscent of Tuscan _brutti ma buoni_—irregular, chunky cookies that are ugly, but delicious. I roll the cookies through almond and pistachio slivers, so they get crispy on the outside. Chewy AND crispy. _Delizioso!_

Preparation time: 40 minutes
Makes about 16 cookies

_____

INGREDIENTS
1 ¾ cups (175 g) almond flour
½ cup (90 g) granulated sugar
Zest from 1 lemon
½ teaspoon ground cinnamon
3 egg whites
Sea salt
⅔ cup (75 g) almond slivers or a mixture of pistachio and almond slivers

Preheat the oven to 380°F (190°C).

In a bowl, mix the almond flour with the sugar, lemon zest, and cinnamon.

Beat 2 of the egg whites with a pinch of salt until stiff and glossy then fold it through the almond flour mixture. Beat the last egg white in a small bowl and pour the almond meal on a flat plate.

Form small balls of the almond-lemon mixture, using 2 small spoons. Dip the balls into the beaten egg white using 2 forks and then roll in the almond slivers. They do not have to be nicely round. It's fine if they have irregular shapes. Brutti ma buoni (ugly but delicious), remember?

Place them on a baking sheet lined with parchment paper and bake for about 13 to 15 minutes, until cooked and light brown.

Remove from the oven and let cool. Store in a sealed container at room temperature.

TIPS

If you have more egg whites, you can double the recipe. For variety, replace the lemon zest with orange zest or the almond flour with hazelnut flour and slivers.

Fregolotta
Almond cookie crumbs

Fregolotta, also known as sbrisolona, is a type of crumb cake from the Veneto. I make it into cookie crumbs and also mix in some coconut. I also mix in jasmine tea. These crumbs are delicious with jasmine gelato (page 320), but also sprinkled over custard or sweet rice pudding.

Preparation time: 35 minutes

————

INGREDIENTS
¾ cup + 1 tablespoon (100 g) almond flour
⅔ cup + 1 tablespoon (100 g) all-purpose flour
½ cup (100 g) granulated sugar
Sea salt
½ cup (113 g) cold unsalted butter, diced
1 tablespoon vanilla extract
½ cup (50 g) shredded coconut
3 bags jasmine tea
2 egg yolks, lightly beaten

Preheat the oven to 320°F (160°C).

Place all the ingredients, except the egg yolks, in the food processor. Turn on the processor, and while it mixes, pour in as much egg yolk as needed until it just holds together as chunky crumbs. You may not need all of the egg. If you don't have a food processor, you can mix the ingredients by hand, gradually adding the egg until chunky crumbs form.

Place the crumbs on a baking sheet lined with parchment paper and bake in a single layer for 10 minutes, then stir and return to the oven for an additional 10 minutes, or until the crumbs are light brown and crispy.

Remove from the oven and allow to cool. Store in a sealed container at room temperature.

Torrone di riso e pistacchio con caramello di arancia
Rice pistachio nougat with orange caramel

Torrone (nougat) is made in different places all over Italy and is slightly different everywhere. In the north, torrone is chewy with nuts mixed in, and in Sicily it is crunchy. There, nuts and seeds are rolled in caramel and hardened. For this torrone, I also use puffed rice, because I serve it with saffron rice gelato (page 323), which seemed fitting. If you replace the rice with toasted almonds, you have the classic version.

Preparation time: 15 minutes + 15 minutes cooling

————

INGREDIENTS
1 ½ (150 g) granulated sugar
3 cups (42 g) puffed rice
⅓ cup (45 g) shelled pistachios
¼ cup (35 g) toasted sesame seeds
Zest from 1 orange
Sea salt

Prepare a baking sheet lined with parchment paper.

In a large saucepan, melt the sugar with ¼ cup (60 ml) of water until it begins to bubble and turn darker. Add the puffed rice, pistachios, sesame seeds, orange zest, and a pinch of salt. Remove from the heat and stir until combined, then return to the heat. Continue stirring for several minutes until all the rice grains and nuts are coated and the caramel has darkened. Pour onto the baking sheet, spread the nougat, and allow to harden. Store in a sealable container. It stays crisp for weeks, but will probably be eaten much earlier.

Reginelle
Sicilian sesame cookies

These cookies are a perfect alternative to the long lady fingers in tiramisù, as well as a biscotto delizioso (delicious cookie) for tea or coffee—I eat them with breakfast. By the way, no tahini goes into the original, but I add it to boost the sesame flavor.

Preparation time: 30 minutes + 30 minutes to rest + 20 minutes baking

———

INGREDIENTS
½ cup (113 g) unsalted butter, at room temperature
½ cup (100 g) superfine sugar
Zest from 1 orange
1 teaspoon vanilla extract
3 tablespoons tahini
1 egg, at room temperature
2 cups (250 g) all-purpose flour
1 ½ teapsoon baking powder
Sea salt
½ cup (70 g) sesame seeds

Beat the butter with the sugar, orange zest, vanilla, and tahini until creamy. Beat in the egg, then gradually add the flour, baking powder, and a pinch of salt. Mix until the dough holds together. Scrape it together with a dough scraper and wrap the dough in plastic wrap. Refrigerate for 30 minutes.

Preheat the oven to 360°F (180°C).

Divide the dough into quarters and roll out each piece into a long "snake" about ½ inch (1 ½ cm) in diameter. Cut that again into pieces the length of, say, a long finger. If you're making the cookies for tiramisù, it doesn't matter if they are not uniform in shape; you won't see any of it later anyway. If you are not making them for tiramisù, cut them into pieces about 2 ½ inches (6 cm) long.

Pour the sesame seeds onto a flat plate, then roll the cookies in the sesame seeds, making sure they are well coated on all sides. Bake them on a baking sheet lined with parchment paper for 20 minutes in the preheated oven. Cool on wire racks and enjoy or store in an airtight container.

TIPS
You'll need a dough scraper for this recipe.
To mix up the flavors, you can add saffron or cinnamon to the dough or replace the orange zest with lemon zest.

Croccantino di mandorle
Almond cookie

This almond and coffee cookie is delicious with anything soft and creamy. I serve it with the Apricot gelato (page 315), but it also goes well with mousse or custard.

Preparation time: 5 minutes + 20 minutes in the oven

———

INGREDIENTS
1 egg white
Sea salt
¼ cup (50 g) granulated sugar
1 tablespoon espresso powder
½ cup (55 g) almond meal

Preheat the oven to 350°F (180°C).

In a bowl, whisk the egg white with a pinch of salt, the sugar, and the espresso powder. Mix in the almond meal.

Using a spatula, spread the mixture thinly on a baking sheet lined with parchment paper. Bake for about 20 minutes, until golden brown.

Remove from oven, allow to cool, and break into irregular pieces. Store in an airtight container.

Crema di parmigiano e salsa di pomodoro piccante
Parmesan-mascarpone cream with sweet tomato sambal

I use this cream as a savory filling for the maritozzi (page 290). It is also delicious on a pizza, with roasted vegetables, or on bruschetta.

Preparation time: 40 to 45 minutes + 30 minutes to firm up
Fills 4 to 5 maritozzi

———

INGREDIENTS

Sweet tomato salsa
3 tablespoons vegetable oil
1 onion, chopped
1 large garlic clove, minced
6 medium vine tomatoes, chopped
2 teaspoons chili flakes
1 teaspoon coriander seeds
Sea salt
1½ tablespoons white wine vinegar
¼ cup (30 g) powdered sugar

Parmesan-mascarpone cream
3 ½ ounces (100 g) mascarpone
3 ½ ounces (100 g) Parmesan, grated
Sea salt and freshly ground black pepper
¾ cup + 1 tablespoon (200 ml) heavy whipping cream
Small basil leaves, to garnish

To make the sweet tomato sambal, heat the oil in a skillet, add the onion, and cook over low heat until translucent. Add the garlic and cook for a few more minutes. Add the tomatoes, chili flakes, coriander seeds, a pinch of salt, vinegar, and powdered sugar.

Stir-fry over medium-high heat until most of the liquid has evaporated. Taste and adjust the spices as desired. Remove from the heat and allow to cool.

To make the Parmesan-mascarpone cream, heat the mascarpone in a saucepan over low heat, stir in the Parmesan and allow to melt. Season with a pinch of salt. Remove from the heat and allow to cool.

Meanwhile, beat the whipping cream just until stiff peaks form and fold in the cheese mixture. Allow to set for 30 minutes in the refrigerator.

Cut open the maritozzi and add a tablespoon of sweet tomato sambal in the center. Spoon in the Parmesan-mascarpone cream and smooth with a spatula. Garnish with basil leaves for a tricolor effect and add a twist of freshly ground pepper.

Crema di balsamico e pancetta croccante

Balsamic cream with crispy pancetta

A maritozzo is a Roman roll, traditionally filled with whipped cream. But this book wouldn't be mine if I didn't offer something other than simple cream. This filling is both savory and sweet and very interesting and delicious. It is good for filling 4 to 5 maritozzi. Fill the rest, for example, with ricotta pistachio cream (see recipe on the right). Feel free to experiment. This cream is delicious as a filling for maritozzi, as well as in a tart, doughnut or coffee cake. Or just eat it out of the bowl with a spatula, like recipe tester and editor Niqué.

Preparation time: 15 minutes
Fills 4 to 5 maritozzi

————

INGREDIENTS
1 cup + 2 teaspoons (250 ml) heavy whipping cream
3 tablespoons powdered sugar
4 tablespoons thick, good quality balsamic vinegar (see page 26 about ingredients)
1 ¾ ounces (50 g) diced pancetta

In a bowl, beat the cream until it thickens. Then add the powdered sugar and continue to beat until just stiff. Then add the balsamic vinegar 1 tablespoon at a time, and mix well. Balsamic vinegars can taste quite different depending on the brand, so taste it after each addition and stop when you are happy with the taste.

Fry the pancetta until crispy in a dry skillet, drain the excess fat, and crumble.

Fill the maritozzi with the balsamic cream and sprinkle with pancetta crumbs.

Crema di ricotta e pistacchio

Ricotta-pistachio cream

Preparation time: 10 minutes + 30 minutes to firm up
Fills 3 to 4 maritozzi

————

INGREDIENTS
8 ounces (250 g) ricotta cheese
¼ cup (65 g) pistachio nut butter
1 tablespoon honey (optional)
Zest from 1 lemon
2 tablespoons pistachios, finely chopped
Few dried rosebuds, to garnish (optional)

Drain the ricotta and blend until smooth with the pistachio nut butter. Often the latter is already sweetened, if not, add the honey. Season with the lemon zest and refrigerate for 30 minutes.

Cut open the maritozzi, fill with the cream, smooth with a spatula, and sprinkle with pistachio and rose petals.

Italian Restaurant Recommendations

Needless to say, this is not a complete list because that would be impossible to do. These are either restaurants I have visited or that have been highly recommended to me. Be sure to check to see if they are open before you plan to visit. I would hate for you to travel to one of these destinations only to find it no longer there or simply closed for the day.

FLORENCE

Casalinga, Via dei Michelozzi 9R
In my college days, I could often be found in this traditional trattoria with wood paneling. Recently I visited the place reassured that nothing had changed.

Sostanza il Troia, Via del Porcellana 25R
In this more than 150-year-old trattoria, you'll eat traditional peasant fare while gawking at the family photos on the tiled wall.

Ruggero, Via Senese 89
Out of the range of tourists and my friend Titto's favorite place (see page 30) because of its good menu and low prices.

Il Santo Bevitore, Via di S. Spirito 64R
In my day (early new millennium), this was the place to be. Minne Warmerdam (writer friend who currently lives in Florence) tells me that it is still fun.

Gilda Bistrot, Piazza Lorenzo Ghiberti 40R
Cute bistro with many Art Nouveau elements.

Cibrèo, Via del Verrocchio 5R
Cibrèo has a restaurant (more fancy) trattoria (casual), and caffè (perfect for a coffee or lunch).

Osteria Gucci, Piazza della Signoria 10
This osteria has a fancy-pants menu by celebrity chef, Massimo Bottura. This one is for the enthusiast.

Fuoriporta, Via del Monte alle Croci 10
Florence Restaurant and winebar overlooking the old city walls and the San Niccolò neighbourhood. Famous for its wine from local wine makers and crostini (big crostini)

MILAN

Trippa, Via Giorgio Vasari 1
This modern trattoria by chef Diego Rossi (see page 84) is famous. Rossi also has the osteria Alla Concorrenza, with more emphasis on wines. Make reservations!

Bella Milano, Via Lazzaro Papi 19
Cocktail bar with flavors that will blow your mind. Near Trippa (above).

Altatto, Via Comune Antico 15
A creative vegan and vegetarian restaurant.

Tannico Wine Bar, Via Savona 17
Wine bar with many natural wines and modern dishes.

Erba Brusca, Alzaia Naviglio Pavese 286
Here, the American-French chef cooks non-traditional dishes from his own vegetable garden.

Ratanà, Via Gaetano de Castillia 28
From the same owners as Erba Brusca, this is a place where tradition and innovation come together.

NAPLES

Pizzeria Da Attilio, Via Pignasecca 17
Attilio is famous in Naples. A margherita pizza here costs only €5. Also try the crocchettone (a giant potato croquette with smoked cheese), sausage, and cime di rapa are specials.

Concettina ai Tre Santi,
Via Arena della Sanità 7Bis
Prize-winning gourmet pizzas. Not idyllic (there's a bouncer at the door), but good. There are also "light pizzas." I was skeptical, but they are fantastic. Feather light and smoky.

Pizza fritta Da Gennaro,
Via Giuseppe Simonelli 58
A crispy cloud of happiness. You eat the pizza standing on the street and there are few choices (mozzarella, ricotta, tomato, or prosciutto or a combination) but it's so good you don't need any frills.

Isabella de Champ, Via Arena della Sanità 27
Pizza joint run by Isabella and her sister with pizza from a wood-fired oven and from the fryer with creative fillings and toppings, such as pizza fritta with 'nduja.

Da Michele/Sorbillo, Via Dei Tribunali 32
Can be skipped according to locals, but I mention them anyway because they are the most famous. Therefore, it's mega-touristy, so be warned.

Pizzeria Da Salvo, Riviera di Chiaia 271
I haven't been there myself. Salvatore makes pizza with the legendary Instagram chef from Rome, Max Mariola.

La chitarra, Rampe S. Giovanni Maggiore 1
Trattoria with lots of restaurant rating stickers on the window. You get there through a small street with all kinds of vintage stores. Reservations are a must!

Il miracolo dei pesci, L. go Sermoneta 17
Good seafood restaurant. I haven't been, but it was recommended.

Il garum, Piazza Monteoliveto 2A
Expensive traditional restaurant, but the spaghetti with sea urchin was the best of my life—creamy and salty. The chef is a mantecatura boss. The parmigiana was also addictive. Slightly spicy and super hearty.

Cicciotto a Marechiaro,
Calata Ponticello a Marechiaro 32
I learned about this restaurant as an inside tip from a Neapolitan. Restaurant with nice sea view. You get there by bus.

Mimì alla ferrovia, Via Alfonso D'Aragona 19/21
Famous restaurant near the train station with classics and modern dishes on the menu. An iconic place that will make you feel like you have been there many times.

ROME

Santo Palato,
Piazza Tarquinia Via Gallia 28
Hip neo-trattoria by stalwart Sarah Cicolini (see page 246). She worked in starred establishments and now refines her trattoria food. She also has a wine bar Avanvera. Make reservations!

Piperno, Via Monte dè Cenci 9
Traditional and a tad chic, this trattoria is an absolute must visit in an intimate little square in downtown. Waiters with black bow ties and white coats with tableware, so put on your best clothes.

Rocco Ristorante, Via Giovanni Lanza 93
Laidback trattoria where you meet the occasional celebrity.

Sora Margherita, Piazza delle Cinque Scole 30
Famous for its cacio e pepe and the *carciofi alla giudia* (fried artichoke).

Dino Express, Via Tacito 80
Authentic osteria where you eat like you're in a friend's home.

Dar Filettaro a Santa Barbara,
Largo dei Librari 88
Trattoria with fried baccalà, puntarelle (see page 26) with anchovies, and excellent service.

Barred Roma, Via Cesena 30
Creative Roman food with good local produce and natural wine from two young brothers.

Retrobottega, Via d'Ascanio 26A
Restaurant, wine store, and pasta bar. The chefs forage just outside Rome and let their creativeness and the seasons speak for their non-traditional dishes.

SICILY

La Pescheria, Piazza Alonzo
di Benedetto, Catania
Fish restaurant at the fish market.
Incredibly fresh fish, always good.

Uzeta Bistro Siciliano, Via Penninello 41,
Catania Bar and restaurant with natural wines.
Here they make the best arancino in Catania
according to pastry chef and gelato-maker
Giovanna (page 324).

Me Cumpari Turiddu,
Piazza Turi Ferro 36/38, Catania
Restaurant with unusual interior with draped
lace, chandeliers, and Sicilian classics with
a twist.

Trattoria Bersagliere, Via San Nicolo
All'Albergheria 38, Palermo
One of the city's oldest trattorias with
fluorescent lighting and cheap but excellent
pasta.

Aja Mola, Via dei Cassari 39, Palermo
Modern fish tavern with amazing fish and
unusual desserts.

Pasticceria Costa,
Via G. D'Annunzio 15, Palermo
The place for Sicilian sweets.

Locale, Via Francesco Guardione 88, Palermo
Modern osteria and cocktail bar with piattini
(small plates of snacks).

Trattoria Ai Cascinari,
Via D'Ossuna 43/45, Palermo
Ultra-fashionable trattoria with lots of seafood
and Sicilian classics.

Antico Forno Valenti,
Via Francesco Aguglia 15, Bagheria
Ancient Sicilian bakery in a village near Palermo
with a wood-fired oven where the most divine
sfincione (Sicilian pizza) and breads made with
Sicilian grains are baked.

Cucina costiera by Sjabica,
Piazza del Faro 3/A, Punta Secca
Great fish tavern from chef Joseph Micieli
(see page 139). His more elevated Sjabica is a
few doors down. There is nothing else in Punta
Secca, combine it with a visit to, say, Modica
or Scicli.

Gelateria Musumeci,
Piazza Santa Maria 5, Randazzo
Gelato store and pastry store of
Giovanna Musumeci (see page 324).
The best gelateria according to CNN Travel.
Her cannolo is the tastiest I've eaten, better
than the one at Caffè Sicilia in Noto (sorry).
The granitas are also top notch.

Caffè Sicilia, Corso Vittorio Emanuele 125,
This gelato-maker and pastry chef, Corrado
Assenza, has been doing surprising things
with granitas here for years; he has since
been on Netflix.

Ristorante Crocifisso,
Via Principe Umberto 46, Noto
A slightly fancier joint in Noto with good
reviews that I was recommended by Sicilian
Chiara.

Mulino La Timpa, Via Risorgimento, Ragusa
Antique mill that bakes with ancient grains and
cooks with local produce. They also organize
cooking workshops.

Stazione Vucciria, Spiaggia Torre Conca,
Pollina (municipality of Palermo)
Superbly located seaside restaurant that has
alternating (Michelin) chefs. The first was
Flemish, Kobe Desramaults, the second was
Japanese, Chef Yoji Tokuyoshi.

Strazzantisicilyexperiences.com
Not a restaurant, but the website of chef Emilia
Strazzanti (see page 47). Emilia gives cooking
workshops in Scicli and grew up in London, so
English-speaking, which is helpful if you don't
speak Italian.

TURIN

Consorzio, Via Monte di Pietà 23
Pioneer neo-trattoria cuisine. Consorzio breathes new life into forgotten classics. A must visit if you are in Turin. Make reservations!

Mara dei Boschi, Piazza Carlo Emanuele II 21
Coffee, gelato, and chocolate shop. They work with single-origin coffee and create new, exciting gelato flavors.

Al gatto nero, Corso Filippo Turati 14
An institution brimming with history and iconic 1950s interiors. From President Einaudi to actor Marcello Mastroianni, many celebrities have eaten at this originally Tuscan trattoria. Good wines, too.

Caffè dell'orologio, Via Oddino Morgari 16
This piola (Turin's equivalent of a trattoria) has delicious wines and small bites (no pastas).

Caffè Torino, Piazza San Carlo 204
With its chandeliers and mirrors, waiters in black-and-white attire, and a beautifully decorated bar, you won't want to skip it.

Osteria Antiche Sere, Via Cenischia 9
This is a traditional osteria (wine bar that serves food) outside the city center with lots of tasty regional comfort food.

Scannabue, Largo Saluzzo, 25/h
Vintage style restaurant serving high quality classics with modern techniques.

BOLOGNA

Trattoria Da Me, Via S. Felice 50
Modern trattoria with chef Elisa Rusconi (see page 182) at the helm. The food is very good. Make reservations!

Casa Merlò, Via de' Gombruti 2D
Restaurant in the heart of downtown with lots of good wines, traditional regional dishes, and also new creations. They serve lots of meat.

Antica Osteria Le Mura,
Vicolo del Falcone 13A
Tastefully decorated osteria on the edge of town with a creative and traditional menu.

Osteria Il Rovescio, Via Pietralata 75
Mostly organic food from small regional producers with many vegetarian and vegan dishes.

Oltre, Via Augusto Majani 1B
Traditional dishes prepared with modern tech in a hip setting. From the same guys as Ahimé, a kind of new Nordic Italian restaurant on Via S. Gervasio 6E.

Allegra, Via Galleria 11C, Bologna
Bakery, specialty coffee and natural wine bistrot with non-traditional menu and extremely delicious pastries

Bibliography

Boucher, F. (2013),
Tutto Risotto

Darling-Gansser, M. (2005),
Herst in Piedmont

Grandi, A. (2018),
Denominazione Di Origine Inventata

Kleyn, O. (2019),
Italy, My Stories and Recipes

Lazzaroni, L. (2021),
The New Cucina Italiana

Locatelli, G. (2006),
Made in Italy

Locatelli, G. (2011),
Made in Sicily

Lodi, B. & De Giacomi, L. (1982),
Nonna Genia

Possel, P. (2023),
Anchovies

Roddy, R. (2015),
Five Quarters

Roddy, R. (2021),
An A to Z of Pasta

Thorisson, M. (2020),
Old World Italian

Creating a book is a huge project that you work on with a whole team. It could not have happened without all the special, kind, helpful, sharp, and creative people I mention below.

THE PHOTOGRAPHER Thank you to my husband Remko Kraaijeveld, the best culinary photographer in the Netherlands. Remko, you make my dreams come true.

THE PUBLISHER Thank you dear Miriam Brunsveld for your trust and putting your author's passion first. Thank you bookend and devotee, Wouter Eertink, for your fine production work and so much more. Thank you editor, Sofie Langenberg, for keeping a sharp eye on my recipes and texts. Thank you, Marieke Migchelbrink, for all the PR stunts you came up with and will come up with. Thanks to everyone at Tra Publishing for making this book come out in the United States!

THE CULINARY SOUNDING BOARDS Thank you dear Emma and Yvette for being so thoughtful and sympathetic during this book.

THE RECIPE TESTERS I have a great club of top testers. Thank you Hein Scheffer and Hanneke van Herwerden, Bianca Portis, Nadine Orth, Floris Pronk, Riteke Hoving, Yvette van Boven, Emma de Thouars, Wouter Leeuwenburg, Sarah Sawkat, Lisette Geerligs, and Niqué van den Tillaart.

STYLISTS, CERAMISTS Thank you Marjolein Vonk and Isabelle van der Horst for your style tips. Thank you Marjoke de Heer for your beautiful ceramics and your mother's handkerchiefs. Thanks K'ook Wormerveer for letting me borrow your things. Thank you Corradi & Son for lending us your terrazzo tiles.

RESTAURANT TIPPERS Thanks Minne Warmerdam for sharing your restaurant tips in Rome and Florence.
Thanks Perry the Man for sharing your Palermo tips.
Thank you Rachel Roddy for giving me tips to places and people in Rome and Sicily.

AND MANY OTHER PEOPLE Thank you Mom for that beautiful cuisine in Monteriggione.
Thank you Chiara of Bottega di Chiara in Amsterdam for all your Sicily tips.
Thank you Saskia Balmaekers of website Ciao Tutti for your love and knowledge of Italy.
Thanks Novella Rosi for your spirit and for letting us "borrow" your pizza oven.
Daniela Tasca, thank you for your knowledge and checking my Italian.
Thank you Jasmin Iachella for taking the time to make your grandmother's bonet with me.
Thank you Nicoletta Tavella for sharing your precious culinary knowledge.
Thank you Esther and Sandro Uva of restaurant Mario for photographing me in your restaurant. Thank you make-up artist Bianca Fabrie and Mettina de Jager for making me pretty.
Thank you Vincent and Daffney for pizza baking in Noto with Giuseppe and Enza.
Thank you Baukje Stamm for your design advice.
Thank you Miranda Bruinzeel, my agent, for making my life easier. Grazie Pietro Chelli, *senza di te i miei giochi di parole tornerebbero a metà.*
Thank you Jigal Krant for your outspoken opinion.
Thank you to Daan (Faber) who will always be there for me.

Grazie, GRAZIE.
Grazie infinite, *grazie tante*,
VI RINGRAZIO, ringraziamenti,
grazie dal cuore,
vi sono grata, con immensa
gratitudine, *mille grazie.*

INDEX

Italopunk
145 Recipes to Shock Your Nonna
By Vanja van der Leeden

Photography & Styling
Remko Kraaijeveld

Illustration
Gianluca Cannizzo

Art Direction
Vanja van der Leeden & Wouter Eertink

U.S. Edition Publisher & Creative Director
Ilona Oppenheim

U.S. Edition Publishing Director
Jessica Faroy

U.S. Edition Art Director & Cover Designer
Jefferson Quintana

U.S. Edition Editorial Director
Lisa McGuinness

Typesetting
Leonardo van Schermbeek & Morgane Leoni

Printed and bound in China by Artron Art Co., Ltd.

This edition was first published in 2023 by Nijgh Cuisine,
Amsterdam under the title *Italopop*.

First published in the United States by Tra Publishing, 2025.

ISBN: 978-1962098175

This product is made of FSC ® - certified
and other controlled material.
Tra Publishing is committed to sustainability
in its materials and practices.

Tra Publishing
245 NE 37th Street
Miami, FL 33137
trapublishing.com

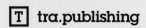